*Overcoming Spiritual Blindness* is a thought provoking and challenging "eye exam" conducted by a skilled cataract surgeon and our good friend, Dr. Jim Gills. Our prayer is that your careful reading of this volume will result in a clearer, more sharply focused vision of the authentic Christian life, and that you will choose to live it for God's glory.

—BILLY GRAHAM AND ANNE GRAHAM LOTZ

Dr. Gills has written an intense and very biblical book on the Christian life as God purposed it. Seen through the eyes of a skillful surgeon and strong student of Scripture, *Overcoming Spiritual Blindness* provides a unique view of what is needed today in every believer. This book will greatly challenge any serious Christian!

—DR. HENRY T. BLACKABY

# OVERCOMING SPIRITUAL BLINDNESS

## James P. Gills, M.D.

CREATION
HOUSE

OVERCOMING SPIRITUAL BLINDNESS by James P. Gills, M.D.
Published by Creation House
A Charisma Media Company
600 Rinehart Road
Lake Mary, Florida 32746
www.charismamedia.com

This book or parts thereof may not be reproduced in any form, stored in a retrieval system, or transmitted in any form by any means—electronic, mechanical, photocopy, recording, or otherwise—without prior written permission of the publisher, except as provided by United States of America copyright law.

Unless otherwise marked, Scripture quotations are from the New King James Version of the Bible. Copyright © 1979, 1980, 1982 by Thomas Nelson, Inc., publishers. Used by permission.

Scripture quotations marked NIV are from the Holy Bible, New International Version. Copyright © 1973, 1978, 1984, International Bible Society. Used by permission.

Scripture quotations marked KJV are from the King James Version of the Bible.

Scripture quotations marked AMP are from the Amplified Bible. Old Testament copyright © 1965, 1987 by the Zondervan Corporation. The Amplified New Testament copyright © 1954, 1958, 1987 by the Lockman Foundation. Used by permission.

Cover design by Terry Clifton

Copyright © 2005 by James P. Gills, M.D.
All rights reserved

Library of Congress Control Number: 2004105940
International Standard Book Number: 978-1-59185-607-8
E-book International Standard Book Number: 978-1-59979-884-4

16 17 18 19 20 — 10 9 8 7 6
Printed in the United States of America

# ACKNOWLEDGMENTS

This book began to take form in my mind as I spent time with my friend, Solomon Mekonnen. His testimony, his life, and his faith inspired the basis for what you will read.

It is clear to me that we do not appreciate the design and gift of life as we should. We do not appreciate enough our Creator, our God and Savior. There is no other way to describe this lack as anything other than *spiritual blindness*. Acknowledgment and appreciation begin as we bow in worship at His feet.

I am grateful to my wife, Heather, to my family, and to all the members of the family of St. Luke's for their support. My thanks also extend to those who helped with this book: Gary Carter, Susan and Ralph McIntosh, Steve Johnson, and Carol Noe, along with the editing and publishing staff at Charisma Media.

# CONTENTS

Foreword by Dr. R. T. Kendall ix

Preface xiii

Introduction 1

**PART I: PROGRESSIONS TO LIVING FAITH** 10

1 Surrender to God—Not Trusting Self 26

2 Internal Relationship—Not External Rituals 31

3 Eternal Priorities—Not Temporal Pursuits 39

4 Living Faith of the Spirit—
Not Rational Faith of the Mind 47

5 God's Security—Not Personal Insecurity 56

6 Christlike Character—Not Sinful Living 61

7 Godly Intimacy—Not Shallow Immaturity 67

8 Insightful Gratitude—Not Blindness of
Ingratitude 73

**PART II: UNDERSTANDING THE NATURE OF
SPIRITUAL BLINDNESS** 77

9 Divided Soul: Darkness vs. Light 82

10 Spiritual Cataracts Obstructing Sight 88

11 Battlefield: Motivations and Imaginations 118

**PART III: BIBLICAL INSIGHT INTO SPIRITUAL BLINDNESS**      130

12   Spiritual Blindness of the Natural Man      134

13   Repentance: Remedy for Spiritual Blindness      139

14   Receiving Spiritual Sight: Abiding in Christ      149

15   Overcoming Blindness Through Life in the Spirit      155

16   Preventing Spiritual Blindness: Growing in Grace      165

17   Divine Defenses Determine Spiritual Victory      172

18   A Divine Paradox: God's Ways vs. Man's Ways      186

**PART IV: UNDERSTANDING THE NATURE OF SPIRITUAL VISION**      193

19   The Value of Suffering      194

20   Reviewing the Grid of Living Faith: T.R.U.S.T.      201

21   Intimate Relationship in Prayer, Praise, and Worship      211

22   The Dynamic of Living Faith: The Unction Function      221

**PART V: YOUR SPIRITUAL SIGHT DETERMINES YOUR ETERNITY**      229

23   We See Through a Glass Darkly      232

24   Living Your Divine Destiny—Forever      239

Conclusion      246

# FOREWORD

A S SOON AS I heard that Dr. James Gills had written a book called *Overcoming Spiritual Blindness* I was intrigued. Who better than a world-famed ophthalmologist with a love for the Bible and theology could write a more interesting and relevant book on such a subject? I could hardly wait to read it. Dr. Gills has performed more cataract operations than any physician on the face of the earth and nobody loves the Word of God more than he does. Of all the books he has written, this one would appear to be his best and most appropriate one yet.

The analogy between the physical and the spiritual realms regarding blindness and sight is a powerful biblical theme, one that is repeated throughout the Scriptures. For example, Isaiah saw a day when God's Messiah would be "a light for the Gentiles, to open eyes that are blind" (Isaiah 42:6–7, NIV). The fulfillment of this prophecy can be alluded to in the event when the resurrected Jesus appeared to Saul, who became the apostle Paul and was sent to the Gentiles "to open their eyes and turn them from darkness to light, and from the power of Satan to God" (Acts

26:18, NIV). Whereas Jesus literally healed blind people, the words of one man healed by Jesus, "I was blind but now I see!" (John 9:25, NIV), became axiomatic for the healing of spiritual blindness as well. One of our most beloved hymns expresses that reality:

> Amazing grace, how sweet the sound
> That saved a wretch like me;
> I once was lost, but now am found;
> Was blind but now I see.
>
> —JOHN NEWTON (1725–1807)

Paul's divine call to give sight to blind Gentiles was not only with regard to the blindness of their preconversion state. Indeed, even after their conversion, he prayed for them, "that the eyes of your heart may be enlightened in order that you may know the hope to which he has called you" (Ephesians 1:18, NIV). Jesus described the horrible condition of spiritual blindness for the one who did not follow through with the light given him: "If then the light within you is darkness, how great is that darkness!" (Matthew 6:23, NIV). Consequently, Christ addressed the lukewarm Laodicean church with a warning, instructing them to acquire "salve to put on your eyes, so you can see" (Revelation 3:18, NIV).

You will especially love this book because of its emphasis on the power and work of the Holy Spirit. What a surgeon does for the cataract hindering sight in the physical eye the Holy Spirit does for the cataracts of our hearts. Dr. Gills thus speaks of various kinds of "spiritual" cataracts: obstructions to our spiritual sight that cloud the lens of the soul. These obstructions include pride, a misguided concept of money, being preoccupied with work, distorted views of sex, and a critical spirit. What he calls "the cataract of bitterness and an unforgiving spirit" gives insight that will enable the reader to gain a perspective of total forgiveness. The list of spiritual cataracts is vast and painfully relevant, designed to give objectivity about ourselves and provide sight to those who did not realize they were blind.

You will profit from this practical message. Dr. Gills' use of acrostics, or grids, enables us to apply certain principles to our daily lives—to see what we had not been able to see because of cataracts that grew slowly and imperceptibly, blinding our souls. The good news is that they can come off instantly. This spiritual surgical work is done by the Holy Spirit who will be released to do His work in us as we choose to cooperate with the timely message of this ophthalmologic preacher.

Do you need spiritual eye surgery? This book is for you. Have you awakened to the fact that you cannot see as you once did, unwittingly blinded by bitterness, unforgiveness, or other cataracts of the heart? You need spiritual cataract surgery and this book is the next step forward on your road to recovery. As we do not know we have been asleep until we wake up, so reading this book may help one to see that he or she was blind when they are given new eyes to see—by the Holy Spirit.

In this book, Dr. Gills in effect leaves the operating room to perform far more important surgery than he does during his normal day. He becomes the instrument of the Spirit of God in this volume, whose divine surgery can have eternal impact in your life. If you submit to the Holy Spirit's spiritual surgery as you might do if you needed an operation for cataracts, you can be healed and the results will be as astonishing and rewarding as what thousands of Dr. Gills' patients have experienced as a result of his surgical expertise. I warmly commend this book to you. May you may never see the same again.

—Dr. R. T. Kendall

# PREFACE

THERE IS A question I like to ask in my books as well as when I meet people personally. Let me ask you, dear reader: "Do you think about your pancreas often?" You may think I am trying to be humorous; perhaps it sounds odd to ask about a "silent" organ, which we normally ignore. The pancreas is not silent, of course. It is a most marvelous, wondrous "machine" engaged in very important work inside your body, day and night. It is made up of billions of individual cells organized and coordinated in multiple, complex tasks that help to keep you alive. It also is integrated into the chemistry and physics of the body as a whole—this includes your heart, brain, kidneys, liver, thumbs, and your ability to love. What weaving that is! *Wow... go you panc!!*  *3 cheers! ✓✓L*

The pancreas is a miracle of biology, one that you continually depend upon, and yet it is merely one piece of the entire tapestry. Have you looked at the stars and wondered about their origins? Probably. Have you also considered the complexity of the earth's atmosphere that protects us even as it builds endlessly unique snowflakes and provides life-sustaining rain? Perhaps. Have you considered your immune system's hunt to destroy a virus lurking in your body in the same light that you admire the lion's determination in stalking its prey? Maybe not.

Have you ever considered how it is that you are capable of reading this page and understanding my words? All these are mysteries, all beautiful and profound, and all exhibiting incomparable design and planning. I am telling you here that all the wonders of life and the universe are testimony of an intelligent Designer. *That Designer is the authentic source of science.* Contrary to the ideas to which we are usually exposed, science is not the basis of understanding, nor is it "sight" in itself; science is but one lens we have been given by the Creator with which to see, and to appreciate *Him.* The truth about science is expressed beautifully in the words:

> …science is far from coldness and calculation, as many people imagine, but is shot through with passion, longing and romance.[1]

Do you experience this passion, longing, and romance? From where do these emotional responses come to us? What is their true origin?

It is a tragic fact of life in our culture, as well as in our personal lives, that we have separated our shared knowledge and our science from their genuine origin. Most individuals learn about their world from television and newspaper reports. Many professionals spend their lives researching and then writing scientific theories. Others apply scientific discoveries to the advantage of us all. However, humanity suffers from a blindness that obscures the truth. Ignoring our true origin, we do not properly experience a wonder of the Creator and His creation.

Modern society—that means you and me—lacks sight and insight through its refusal to see the reality of creation. Our continuing lack of the recognition of, and the appreciation for, the intelligence of the Creator, is spiritual blindness. Yet, the fruits and evidence of His love and wisdom are clearly demonstrated everywhere in our world, and within ourselves.

I am a physician—a member of one scientific group seeking to enhance the well-being of others through the application of science. As I work every day to help restore sight, I marvel more and more at the wonder of the human body. Daily, I am reminded of the truth and wonder of our existence—as well as of the misunderstanding of our privilege, and responsibility, to be grateful for the gift of life. This awareness of the marvel of life began somewhat early for me. As a student of neurophysiology at Duke University, the study of cell physiology and molecular biology intrigued me. While busy inventing a device to measure electrical differences across single cell membranes, I was struck by the gap between what I observed in these living membranes and what "science," as it was offered, was trying to teach me about their origin.

Darwinism—the theory of evolution—has commanded the attention and belief of scientists, and those they convince, for generations. It was apparent to me as a student at Duke, and more so now, how empty the foundations of theories of evolution are. It is significant to me, as an ophthalmologist, that Darwin himself was stumped when he considered the human eye. And what of the human body as a whole? The average human body contains about sixty trillion cells. Each of those cells is an exquisite example of engineering in itself (see diagram).

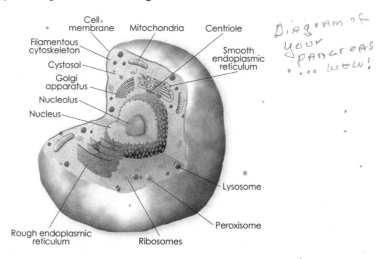

Cell membrane · Mitochondria · Centriole
Filamentous cytoskeleton
Cystosol
Golgi apparatus
Nucleolus
Nucleus
Smooth endoplasmic reticulum
Lysosome
Peroxisome
Rough endoplasmic reticulum · Ribosomes

Diagram of your pancreas wow!

Humanity cannot fully *understand* a human cell, let alone reproduce one. Darwin did not, could not, glimpse the beauty of design in the cell in his time. Now, we have scientific tools in biology and biochemistry that describe and explain structures and systems in terms of mere *nanometers* (a nanometer is a millionth of a meter). Now, more than ever, the truth of God's magnificent intelligence is being exposed to human eyes and minds.

Our greatest sin before God may be our refusal to acknowledge the Lord's hand in our existence, to be grateful for it, and to appreciate it fully. If you and I do not recognize our origin, and the one responsible for our existence, everything else in life is shrouded in darkness and ignorance—*then we are blind.*

# INTRODUCTION

G OD IS THE source of everything; God gives meaning to every-thing. We are spiritually blind unless we sense our hopeless-ness and surrender entirely to the fact of His sovereignty—God is ruler over all. Our friends at International Cooperating Ministries (ICM) express this spiritual reality in a simple "formula." [1]

Jesus Christ + anything = nothing;
Jesus Christ + nothing = everything.

Similarly stated:

Jesus + anything else = spiritual blindness;
Jesus + nothing else = 20/20 spiritual vision.

Until we understand that it is in our hopelessness that we find God and in our weakness that we draw near to Him, and until we refuse to trust ourselves, we will remain spiritually blind. In that blindness we are unable to receive God's divine life, and we are

1

doomed to living outside His sovereign plan for our lives here on earth—and for eternity. Listen to one who expressed this reality in prayer.

> Oh, Divine Majesty, in whose presence the pillars of heaven do quake and tremble, You are more than infinite, and yet in your love the seraphim burn. Give me leave, oh Lord, to lament our *blindness* and ingratitude. We all live deceived, seeking this foolish world and forsaking You who are our God. We all forsake You, the fountain of living water, for the foul mire of the world.
> —MICHAEL MOLINOS, EMPHASIS ADDED[2]

This humble, heartfelt prayer was written by a man who was perhaps the most controversial figure in seventeenth-century Christianity. He *saw* his own weakness as well as the majesty and sovereignty of God. Michael Molinos' only desire was to experience a relationship with God that resulted in complete immersion in the person of his Savior. Anything less than that intimate relationship he lamented as blindness—*spiritual blindness*. Why was Molinos' concept of relationship with God so controversial?

**Opposing paths**

In the church during the seventeenth century, there were two opposite viewpoints, two antagonistic spiritual "pathways" touted as "the way" to finding God. One viewpoint held that *the pathway to God was only through the intense life of prayer and extensive study of the Scriptures*; this pathway Molinos represented. The alternate path, the preferred route of the day, was that which *sought piety through formal displays and external rites.*

Like the showy Pharisees in Jesus' day, most professing Christians in Molinos' time sank their trust and spiritual currency into outward public ceremonies. Jesus Himself condemned the hypocrisy of the Pharisees and modeled a life of prayer and communion with His Father as the correct pathway to God. Molinos' pathway to know God, which still challenges the "status quo" today, reflects the reality of relationship with God as demonstrated in the life of Jesus.

## My friend, Solomon

I have a dear friend named Solomon who speaks candidly and eloquently of his quest for intimacy with God. Born in Ethiopia, orphaned, and then adopted by the Emperor Haile Selassie, he was educated in a mission school. Solomon was steeped in a thorough study of Scripture and immersed in daily devotionals. Physically blinded as a youngster, his study was complicated by this handicap, yet it remained a very serious endeavor. As a boy, Solomon's belief in the message of salvation was sound, but by his own testimony, he had not comprehended the true meaning of a relationship with God. While still in his mid-teens, Solomon precociously focused on a deep question: "Do I believe because I have *been told*, or because I have *experienced*?"

This searching question ultimately led him to a turning point in his life. He realized that, while he had been "practicing" his faith according to what he had been taught, he needed to personally experience a relationship with God. Solomon sought and found a true, personal relationship with God. Then he found himself empowered to live a life of abandon to the sovereign will of God for his life. Embracing that reality, all of life changed for him.

Instead of superficially practicing Christian principles, which he had been taught, Solomon became filled with love and trust for His Savior through progressing in his personal relationship with God. Throughout life, my friend sought to abandon himself to fullness of redemption by practicing a *living faith* in Christ. Though Solomon is physically blind—in the sense that the world understands blindness—the spiritual sight he has experienced empowers him to see life clearly. That is, he *lives* his faith; Solomon appreciates God for who He is.

## Defining spiritual blindness

Perhaps you seek to walk with God, to follow Him, and to experience Him, yet frequently turn your head to other interests. Don't be discouraged. The Lord gives you hope: "My sheep hear

My voice, and I know them, and they follow Me" (John 10:27). He will call you back to Himself again and again. God knows you intimately and knows how to help you!

The Creator's thumbprint is in the color of your eyes, the shape of your hands, and your ability to speak. The beauty and complexity of *all* creation is the mirror of His divinity. Yet, as the apostle Paul declared, "Now we see in a mirror, dimly, but then face to face" (1 Corinthians 13:12). According to the Scriptures, we do not see or appreciate God fully. But the Scriptures also teach that we can progress in our knowledge of Him as we seek Him diligently.

Our goal of reaching the Celestial City is the same as that of John Bunyan's famous pilgrim, Christian; we too often fail to fully abandon ourselves to the journey. Without fully abandoning ourselves to progressing in our life in God, the uncertainty and diversions of this life often obscure and distract our faith. The path God would have us find is not always easily found; it is often not even visible—such is the extent of our blindness. Too often our lives reflect the testimony of the Christians in the Laodicean church.

> …you say, "I am rich, have become wealthy, and have need of nothing"—and do not know that you are wretched, miserable, poor, blind, and naked.
>
> —REVELATION 3:17

To the extent that each of us is prideful, self-sufficient, and unappreciative, we are blind! In our pride and self-sufficiency we cannot reap the spiritual abundance that is associated with the true peace God offers. If we choose to live in complacency, we remain weak and blind. We must begin to progress in a personal relationship with Christ, allowing Him to live in us. We need to allow the Scriptures to be made real to us and learn to live our faith in God. And we must choose to abandon ourselves to the wonderful destiny revealed in God's Word that He has chosen for our lives.

Let us listen to what the Savior said to those who did not choose personal abandonment to God.

I know your deeds, that you are neither cold nor hot. I
wish you were either one or the other! So, because you
are lukewarm—neither hot nor cold—I am about to spit
you out of my mouth.

—REVELATION 3:15–16, NIV

### Finding my way

When I was sixteen-years-old, I was introduced to a man who
was three or four years older than myself. Vibrant and charis-
matic, he spoke to me about a deeper Christian walk. I thought,
*Well, I'm a church member, I memorize Scripture verses—what
more do I need?* He was persistent with me, but could not make
me see what he meant.

Twenty years later, after I had been through the great pain
caused by the daggers of envy and professional rivalry, author/
pastor Jamie Buckingham spoke to me about a deeper Christian
walk, especially regarding how to listen to the voice of the Lord.
Jamie, who is now with the Lord, spoke so passionately about
incorporating God into each moment of the day and encouraged me in living my faith, rather than just practicing Christian
principles.

Embracing God this way required that I learn to forgive, and I
learned to pray for my attackers, being an intercessor rather than
an accuser. Prayer became paramount in my walk with God. As
I progressed in this new *living faith*, I also wrote books on how
one should pray, including the understanding of the importance
of praying with your spouse. Not everyone understood the depth
of intimacy in prayer that I was proposing.

However, I had simply begun to understand what my friends
Solomon and Jamie knew, that everything we do in life requires
turning our trust from ourselves to God—abandoning ourselves
to Him. It means recognizing Him as sovereign Lord, ruler over
all. I have illustrated this relational concept using an acrostic of
the word *trust*. We will progress to a full, living faith that satisfies
our hearts and makes our lives effective if, on every occasion, we
learn to:

Thank God,
Rejoice in Him,
Understand His Word,
Sing out to Him, and exhibit
Thoughtfulness of others.[3]

Truly living our faith means that we continually seek God, believe His promises, and seek the Spirit's strength in order that, as the apostle Paul declared, "Christ may dwell in your hearts through faith" (Ephesians 3:17). Through faith we acknowledge our relationship with God. According to the Scriptures, "Faith is being sure of what we hope for and certain of what we do not see.... By faith we understand that the universe was formed at God's command, so that what is seen was not made out of what was visible" (Hebrews 11:1–3, NIV).

As we have discussed, spiritual blindness is quite simply our refusal to acknowledge God as Lord and Creator, while at the same time choosing foolishly to trust in ourselves. These two choices cause some people to live in unawakened self-alienation from God, while others, like my friend, Solomon, live faith passionately in intimacy with the Lord. In that intimate relationship with God is found the ecstasy of the new believer as well as the satisfaction for those who have long sought to be transparent to God, regardless of the pain that may involve.

Many people teeter between the superficial "practice" of faith, that is, following principles they have been taught, and the satisfying reality of experiencing its fullest flower. We can be so easily diverted in life from our wholehearted pursuit of relationship with God. We must learn to overcome these diversions. The intimacy of living faith in God is a relationship that we must continually strive to attain and to maintain. Yet, it is that divine relationship that every heart yearns to know. Cultivating an intimate relationship with God is filled with promise: "To him who overcomes I will give to eat from the tree of life, which is in the midst of the Paradise of God" (Revelation 2:7).

## A source of gratitude

I have observed in working at my hospital, St. Luke's Cataract and Laser Institute, that the happiest patients often seem to be those who are already blind or perhaps are restricted to wheelchairs. Through what they have lost physically, they experience a more profound gratitude and appreciation for what they still have. Similarly, the paradox of experiencing a broken spirit, makes greater hope and joy possible. The apostle Paul declared this reality.

> But we also glory in tribulations, knowing that tribulation produces perseverance; and perseverance, character; and character, hope. Now hope does not disappoint, because the love of God has been poured out in our hearts by the Holy Spirit who was given to us.
> —ROMANS 5:3–5

To be a true Christian requires a special touch from God by the person of the Holy Spirit. It is in our brokenness and humility, our coming to God and pursuing His way instead of ours, that we begin the progression into a deep, authentic, living faith in God, filled with hope and joy—and gratitude.

My path, and yours, toward a true relationship with God starts with the acknowledgment and appreciation of the miracle and majesty of God's hand within the sixty trillion cells and DNA blueprint that comprise the human body. The design includes the consciousness of God written in our minds. Acknowledging that design, we must rise above our passions, selfishness, and weaknesses. We can only do that by coming to the Savior and finding the cleansing and empowerment He provides through His redemptive work on the cross.

To progress as pilgrims, out of darkness and blindness, to spiritual sight and a living faith will require our embracing the grid of T.R.U.S.T. in our thoughts and actions, as we will discuss. It will require charity and compassion in our hearts, and a brokenness and utter humility before the Lord in our spirits. Choosing to live in that way, we can render ourselves free of impediments from our bodies, our minds, and from just living life in this world, as we climb toward total trust in God, His sovereignty and salvation. A life of full faith is a life filled with peace and hope and joy.

I pray this book will be a source of inspiration and spiritual awakening for you. Your relationship with the Lord is the most important aspect of your life. Though, too often, our spiritual sight is dim and obstructed, it does not have to be. As we will discuss, these obstructions all derive from selfishness—self-dependence. Instead of seeking our own life, we need to abandon ourselves to an earnest search for the living God. *All creatures must respond to their Creator.*

## WHEN THIS PASSING WORLD IS DONE

When this passing world is done,
When has sunk yon glaring sun,
When we stand with Christ in glory,
Looking o'er life's finished story,
Then, Lord, shall I fully know—
Not till then—how much I owe.

When I hear the wicked call,
On the rocks and hills to fall,
When I see them start and shrink
On the fiery deluge brink,
Then, Lord, shall I fully know—
Not till then—how much I owe.

When I stand before the throne,
Dressed in beauty not my own,
When I see Thee as Thou art,
Love Thee with unsinning heart,
Then, Lord, shall I fully know—
Not till then—how much I owe.

When the praise of Heav'n I hear,
Loud as thunders to the ear,
Loud as many waters' noise,
Sweet as harp's melodious voice,
Then, Lord, shall I fully know—
Not till then—how much I owe.

Chosen not for good in me,
Wakened up from wrath to flee,
Hidden in the Savior's side,
By the Spirit sanctified,
Teach me, Lord, on earth to show,
By my love, how much I owe.[4]
——ROBERT MURRAY McCHEYNE, 1837

# PART I:

## PROGRESSIONS TO LIVING FAITH

### THE DYNAMIC

IN THIS FIRST section (Chapters 1–8), I would like to show you a very important reality of faith: the need all have for *progressing* from superficial, external, religious traditions to a satisfying experience of living faith. The new believer first coming to God, the backsliding believer returning to God, as well as the faithful Christian seeking a deeper walk with the Lord, must all move through decisive progressions from a superficial practice of faith toward the true, living faith, which my friend Solomon (See Introduction, page 3), understood. It is not enough to simply follow good, biblical principles for living life; we need to experience a growing, intimate, personal relationship with our God to receive the promises of God for a living faith.

If you have picked up this book as a person who has not yet entered into a personal relationship with Jesus Christ, I invite you to continue reading to see how you can exchange your spiritual blindness for a true vision of life as God intended it to be. If you are a new believer in Christ, or a believer not walking near to God and have a desire to do so, I invite you to continue reading. If you are a believer who still has questions, or you are frustrated with contradictions between what you are living and what you see promised in the Scriptures of abundant life in Christ, I invite you to continue reading also to discover possible answers for your situation.

And for the mature Christian, who may be discouraged or even disappointed in your present relationship with God, or who simply desires more satisfaction in that relationship, I invite you to continue reading as well. As you grasp more fully the spiritual concept of progressing in the practicing of full faith, you will be set free to enjoy new satisfaction and greater spiritual sight.

## A divine tension

As believers, whether recently converted or having walked with God for many years, it is vital to understand that we are on a lifelong journey of progression toward God and are continually being changed into the likeness of Christ. The apostle Paul understood this divine tension.

> But we all, with unveiled face, beholding as in a mirror the glory of the Lord, are being transformed into the same image from glory to glory, just as by the Spirit of the Lord.
> —2 CORINTHIANS 3:18

Without this understanding, we will be overwhelmed when we contemplate the "darkness" that is still within us—the foolish decisions we make that contribute toward our regression from God and the sinful ways that still plague us in our journey. We must take hope in the fact that, by the working of the Holy Spirit in our hearts through conversion, the incorruptible seed of the life of God lives within us (1 Peter 1:23) and we have become new creatures in Christ (2 Corinthians 5:17). No matter how grievous our mistakes, though we may grieve the Holy Spirit because of them, He will continue to work in our lives to chasten us and lead us to repentance.

Sometimes young converts are ignorant of the ways of God and must learn from the Word what pleases and displeases Him. The Holy Spirit is faithful to be our "Teacher" as we respond to His conviction in our hearts, that sense that all is not right in our relationship with God. And every believer who chooses to walk away from the ways of God will find that the Holy Spirit continues His work in his or her life, perhaps chastening them or letting them become filled with their own ways, disillusioned and sick of themselves, longing for the days of their first love with Jesus.

As born-again Christians, we discover a constant tension in our lives between our own personal revival and a tendency to spiritual decline. This dynamic is very important to understand. I ask you: Can you *always* remain entirely, and in every instance, totally forgiving, or free of doubt, or full of love, or enjoying God's presence? This perfection is not possible for anyone. More realistically, the spiritual life of a Christian can be understood as a tension on a continuum between *progression*—moving toward full faith and spiritual sight—and *regression*—moving back to the world, toward selfishness and a superficially practiced faith. The typical Christian life moves back and forth along this line of tension, having the goal of ever moving forward to increased fulfillment as we mature in God.

You are undoubtedly seeking God if you are reading this book, whether to initially find a personal relationship with Christ through accepting His forgiveness for your sin, or to deepen that relationship that you have already begun. Wherever you find yourself on that line of divine tension that represents your *progression* toward full faith, you must know that all Christians are spiritually blind to some degree. In these pages, you will discover some of these obstacles that perhaps remain in your life, keeping you from enjoying 20/20 spiritual sight and receiving the promises of God for all who are His sons and daughters.

Think about how frequently you consider the marvelous functioning of your body—your nerve cells, bones, immune system, and the DNA code that directed their development. They are all an elegant, exquisite testimony to the wisdom and intelligence of our Creator. How often do you thank your Creator for the "miracle" of life? How much do you take for granted? Our degree of ingratitude to God for the gift of life He alone can give reflects our degree of spiritual blindness.

Too easily each of us can be deceived by the empty, fleeting promises of the temporal world to offer us "life." When we get caught up in ourselves, we forget to acknowledge our intelligent Creator, are insensitive to the moving of the Holy Spirit, and lack understanding of the importance of the blood of Christ to our forgiveness. In other words, we are spiritually blind.

Living in full faith, having our spiritual eyes opened, reflects our acceptance and appreciation of God, our belief in His promises, and our ability to rest in His peace as we accept our redemption through the blood of Christ. It also involves casting aside carnal passions and weaknesses as we tell Satan to "get thee behind me." In short, to enjoy fullness of faith means that we choose to rest in God rather than to indulge ourselves.

## THE BEGINNING OF MOVEMENT

Michael Molinos, a devout saint of the seventeenth century, was persecuted because of one fundamental idea about life (see Introduction). His presumed "blasphemy," which shook the church establishment of the day, simply stated, is that all of life is to be one continual act of faith and love to God. Molinos asked everyone to see that he or she could meet God in a personal, rich, and comprehensive way, through faith instead of trusting the external rituals and sacraments of the church unnecessary to a personal, intimate relationship with God.[1]

### Basis for revival

In spite of the controversy this approach to knowing God stirred, it led to a spiritual revival of faith among many. Perhaps we could compare this controversy to the one the apostle Paul stirred when he challenged the Jews regarding the Mosaic law of circumcision. The Jews put all their trust in their following the Law of Moses, especially the external rite of circumcision. They failed to understand the Scriptures that teach the importance of knowing God through relationship. Yet Paul understood, by divine revelation, that "we are the circumcision, who worship God in the Spirit, rejoice in Christ Jesus, and have no confidence in the flesh" (Philippians 3:3). Paul also taught that "circumcision is that of the heart, in the Spirit, not in the letter" (Romans 2:29). God's intent for His creation is that every person experience a heart relationship with Him, enjoying His love and redemption and intimate communion with Him. The "cutting" of our hearts away from worldly attractions and distractions "circumcises" us to a living relationship with God, moving us forward in our progression toward full faith in Him.

Molinos' courageous, though unpopular, intention certainly was to engage the orthodoxy of the medieval church with this spiritual reality of living faith. However, he also sought to challenge each individual to personal relationship with God, encouraging them to seek God through the pathway of prayer. As he viewed it, too many had confused participation in works and external ritual with the fullness of a genuine living faith in the person of Christ. Molinos believed that you and I may unwittingly forsake the ecstasy and joy of a *real* relationship with the Creator for the mere appearance of it, through our confidence in external rites.

In time, Molinos's beliefs began to characterize the theology of the expanding number of European churches emerging from the Catholic Church in the Middle Ages. His insistence on faith in God alone revolutionized entire religious movements, which grew out of that fresh approach to God, renouncing the church rituals that had been added as "requirements" for knowing God. Calvin and the Huguenots in France, Luther in Germany, Knox in Scotland, and later, Wesley and Whitefield in England were all united in their beliefs in the centrality of the Bible and salvation through faith in Christ alone. They taught the truth of the Scriptures that every person must seek personal relationship with the Savior, Jesus Christ, accepting His forgiveness of sin through faith alone.

**Pathway to sight**

In declaring the gospel, the apostle Paul proclaimed exactly what must be believed in order to have a saving faith:

> For I delivered to you first of all that which I also received; that Christ died for our sins according to the Scriptures, and that He was buried, and that He rose again the third day according to the Scriptures.
>
> —1 Corinthians 15:3–4

The apostle Paul stated another wonderful truth:

> For by grace you have been saved through faith, and that not of yourselves; it is the gift of God, not of works, lest anyone should boast.
>
> —Ephesians 2:8–9

This doctrine of justification by faith, and faith alone, is the beginning of movement toward a *personal experience* with God, which Christ Himself indicated to us was the path to light and sight:

> The lamp of the body is the eye. If therefore your eye is good, your whole body will be full of light. But if your eye is bad, your whole body will be full of darkness. If therefore the light that is in you is darkness, how great is that darkness! No one can serve two masters; for either he will hate the one and love the other, or else he will be loyal to the one and despise the other.
>
> —Matthew 6:22-24

Even Old Testament Scriptures teach this reality of finding the pathway to personal relationship with God:

> Trust in the Lord with all your heart and lean not on your own understanding; in all your ways acknowledge him, and he will make your paths straight. Do not be wise in your own eyes; fear the Lord and shun evil.
>
> —Proverbs 3:5-7, niv

hen you first turn your eyes to the Lord and bow to His sovereignty in your life, there is a fundamental transformation of your inner spirit. An essential *completion* is made beginning with the realization that "all have sinned and fall short of the glory of God" (Romans 3:23). It means trusting Christ as one's Savior and finding forgiveness through Him. Though it is impossible to fully describe this new birth of the inner man, accomplished through the work of the Holy Spirit in our lives, we *do* become aware of a new hunger for fellowship with God when it occurs.

The apostle Peter describes the new believer as "having been born again, not of corruptible seed but incorruptible, through the word of God which lives and abides forever" (1 Peter 1:23). He continues, "Therefore, laying aside all malice, all deceit, hypocrisy, envy, and all evil speaking, as newborn babes, desire the pure milk of the word, that you may grow thereby" (1 Peter 2:1–2). The unquenchable thirst of a baby for life-giving milk is the picture the Scriptures use to portray the healthy desire of a new believer for the Word of God.

**Revelation of love**

When we experience the new birth and embrace Christ as our Savior, there is a dedication of our lives to Him at the revelation of God to the soul, and there is the flowering of love. We may be tempted to think of our newly discovered love for God as an act chosen deliberately by us, but it is not.

We don't decide to taste honey for the first time because we know it is sweet; rather, we taste honey and then discover its sweetness to the tongue. In that same way, experiencing God's love is the reflex of a newborn heart called to see the beauty of God in Christ. We surely desire forgiveness and an escape from hell, but salvation is much more than that. It is the beginning of relationship with our blessed Savior, Jesus; without that relationship, heaven would not be heaven. From now on, we learn to desire relationship with Him first of all.

Love is first the advent of a relationship of delight in God and esteem for Him, before it is ever reflected in any kind of *doing* or *acting.* We begin that love relationship by bowing in worship at the feet of Jesus with a faith that embraces Him as our portion and joy alone.

**Embarking on a pilgrimage**

When we are born anew, we become pilgrims in search of the "Celestial City," for which Christian, in John Bunyan's *Pilgrim's Progress*, left all. In this classic allegory, when challenged by a neighbor named *Obstinate* concerning his decision to leave his home in the City of Destruction, where they were born, Christian simply describes the wonders of that Celestial City, as recorded in the "Book"—the Word of God.

> I seek an "inheritance incorruptible, and undefiled, and that fadeth not away" (1 Peter 1:4, KJV), and it is laid up in heaven (Hebrews 11:16), and safe there, to be bestowed, at the time appointed, on them that diligently seek it...there are such things to be had which I spoke of, and many more glories besides; if you believe not me, read here in this book, and for the truth of what is expressed therein, behold, all is confirmed by the blood of Him that made it (Hebrews 13:20, 21; 9:17-21)...
>
> There is an endless kingdom to be inhabited, and everlasting life to be given us, that we may inhabit that kingdom forever (Isaiah 45:17; John 10:27–29). There are crowns of glory to be given us, and garments that will make us shine like the sun in the firmament of Heaven! (2 Timothy 4:8; Revelation 3:4; Matthew 13:43)...There shall be no more crying, nor sorrow; for He that is owner of the place will wipe all tears from our eyes (Isaiah 25:8; Revelation 7:17; 21:4).
>
> There we shall be with seraphims, and Cherubims, creatures that will dazzle your eyes to look on them. There, also, you shall meet with thousands and ten thousands that have gone before us to that Place; none of them are hurtful, but loving and holy, everyone walking in the

sight of God, and standing in His presence with acceptance forever (Isaiah 6:2; 1 Thessalonians 4:16; Revelation 4:4; 7:17)....[2]

To qualify us to enter that Celestial City, as I mentioned, we
must experience a "new birth." In that born-again experience,
the inner man is changed. Before there is any outward demonstration or declaration of that change, when we are born again,
accepting Christ as our Savior, we become a "new creation," as
the apostle Paul confirmed: "Therefore, if anyone is in Christ, he
is a new creation; old things have passed away; behold, all things
have become new" (2 Corinthians 5:17).

Yet, Bunyan's pilgrim, Christian, began to understand, as he
progressed toward the Celestial City, that it is only when we surrender and humbly abandon ourselves to the Lord, that our values, motivations, and imaginations are progressively transformed
to bring honor to Christ, as reflected in our words, actions, activities, and habits. It is this fundamental union with God through
the new birth experience that propels us in our progression to
know Him, making us willing to leave the distractions of life in
this world to become more like Christ.

### Becoming a bride

One of the major themes throughout Old Testament as well as
New Testament Scriptures that describes our relationship with
God is the relationship of a bride to her bridegroom. Jesus used
this intimate metaphor to describe Himself when asked why His
disciples did not fast.

> And Jesus said to them, "Can the friends of the bride-
> groom mourn as long as the bridegroom is with them?
> But the days will come when the bridegroom will be
> taken away from them, and then they will fast."
> —MATTHEW 9:15

Madam Guyon—an acclaimed Christian thinker and writer in
the decadent era of Louis XIV's France—described two types of

union with God. One is the "union of the faculties of the soul"—the will, memory, and understanding. The second and more profound union is the consummation, or "essential union"—spiritual marriage.[3] The true transformation of the inner man is found in the second—the intimate relationship of utter abandon to God's will for our lives. Of course, our life in God should not reflect only one or the other "union" described by Madam Guyon; both are integral to our progression to full faith. But sometimes as we progress toward this deep commitment to God, in our attempt to integrate it with the duties of daily life, we lose the glow of our first love. We depend instead upon the lesser "union of our faculties," becoming caught up in the outward forms of church life, and of serving the needs of others and fulfilling the stewardships of life, leaving aside the reality of intimate relationship with God.

As we stated, Christians seeking authentic spiritual sight *will* be involved in meeting the needs of others practically and in being a diligent steward of their own gifts and talents, rendered to God as a way of honoring Him. It is important to understand that this outward practice of faith and doing God's work is a vital part of our development as believers. Jesus spoke of the importance of putting true faith into practice in His parable in Luke 19:13 (KJV) in which the servants are told: "Occupy till I come."

The problem is that if we *substitute* practical service for intimate relationship with God, we may soon find our heart satisfaction diminishing, peace evaporating, and hunger for God waning. Then we are left only with a desire to conform to external religious patterns and canons of certain spiritual leaders. When this happens, we must acknowledge that we have slipped from the brilliance of God's majesty and need a revival to bring us back to "looking unto Jesus." Stated another way, our *progression* along the continuum toward full faith has become a *regression* toward self-centeredness and self-focus.

## LIVING FAITH

Authentic faith, the faith that my friend Solomon experienced, is really a *process of illumination*, a "coagulation" of our beliefs and thoughts. To achieve such illumination—spiritual sight—requires an essential change in attitude. That alteration involves our *choice* to relinquish our old nature of indifference and independence, and to submit to the authority of our Lord and Creator continually. Only there—in that place of humble submission—will the desirous heart experience *shalom*, the *peace* known only by coming to God entirely, without reservation. Though it begins when we are born again, this process must continue for a lifetime, through our making right choices to progress toward full faith.

The fundamental element of such a living faith is a wholehearted trust in the Lord's promise of salvation. It is not simply a belief in the existence of God and His love. The significance of a living faith is that it opens the door to eternal life. The problem of faith is being able to achieve such a wholehearted immersion into God, by believing what we see revealed in the Word of God. What hinders our wholehearted surrender and trust in God?

**Renewing our minds**

Too frequently, the formal, outward forms of faith as practiced in external religious traditions satisfy minds that have not yet surrendered to God. Living faith requires introspection and personal work, and sometimes involves pain—the pain of change. The major struggle of the pilgrimage you and I are on is to adopt a new way of thinking. It requires a replacement of the *many* complicated, self-centered life principles we have embraced with the *one* principle of Christ-centered, Scripture-based living. That divine principle is simply not a natural way for us to think. The apostle Paul exhorted believers:

> I beseech you therefore, brethren, by the mercies of God, that you present your bodies a living sacrifice, holy, acceptable to God, which is your reasonable service. And do not be conformed to this world, but be transformed

by the renewing of your mind, that you may prove what
is that good and acceptable and perfect will of God.
—ROMANS 12:1–2

True spiritual enlightenment in God—*living faith*—is achieved
by choosing to place Christ in the center of our life as surely as
He is at the center of all creation. *This is spiritual sight.* Many
believers stall themselves in the realm of their outward practice
of Christianity and refuse to enter the complete, glorious frui-
tion of a deeper relationship with Christ. In that transforming
relationship, all attitudes change and we are completely renewed,
desiring to do all things, not merely because we have the ability to
do them, but because we simply want to please Him. We have to
fully realize that we are Christians not only at church on Sunday,
but also when we go to work, to the hospital, a restaurant, or a
department store. *Everything we do must reflect our faith; otherwise it is a dead faith, an empty practice, and we are blind.*

## RECOGNIZING OUR PROGRESS

In the following chapters, I will discuss some of the signs of our
progression toward full faith: our growth, our walk, and the
dynamics of change in our relationship with God between a
*weak faith* and a truly *vibrant faith*. In the following chart, I have
depicted the dynamic of our spirituality, our *progression* from the
event of our "new birth" experience toward full faith, as a continuum from left to right. This illustration represents some aspects
of the believer's movement toward completeness in Christ and
suggests the degrees of separation caused by pride, sin, distraction with worldly things and affairs, fear and concern, and selfishness. Our progress represents our desired emergence from a
state of spiritual blindness, on the left, to the glorious sight of
God and His truth, on the right.

## MOVING TOWARD LIVING FAITH

| FROM | TO |
| --- | --- |
| Spiritual blindness | Spiritual sight/insight |
| Superficial or weak faith | Living, vibrant faith |
| Self-focused faith | Spirit-led faith |

Throughout the book, I will contrast positions along the divine continuum of our progression toward God, as in the above list, to help express the "spiritual provinces" between which we move in our journey. Of course, these lists could never be complete; they are simply representative of some of the common issues we face in our search to get closer to God.

It is important to understand that the "continuum" is not static; it is dynamic, meaning that it is in a constant state of change. For example, the columns of words in the above chart do not indicate a divided, either/or condition of the mind and spirit. I struggle, and so do you, at various points with the tension between proximity to and distance from God, and in different situations of time and place. We find ourselves, regrettably, moving back and forth between these "provinces" to varying degrees as we seek to know God.

Happily, some believers live mostly by the principles of an abiding faith, as shown on the right of the continuum. Yet, no one person is pure enough or mature enough to remain there completely and at all times. The left side of the continuum represents the nagging inclinations of many more of us. Some people practice their faith insincerely, even hypocritically, entrapped in empty acts of "cleaning the outside of the cup" for the sake of appearance like the Pharisees in Jesus' time (Matthew 23:25).

Some professing Christians today are content to believe, for example, that their relationship with God is defined simply by faithful church attendance. Jesus challenged the Pharisees' reliance on *external* righteousness: "Blind Pharisee, first cleanse the inside of the cup and dish, that the outside of them may be clean also…Even so you also outwardly appear righteous to men, but inside you are full of hypocrisy and lawlessness" (Matthew 23:26, 28). The Scriptures teach clearly that though people look at outward appearances, God judges our hearts.

## A NEW BEGINNING

The newly "born-again" believer may find himself or herself wavering between various places of progression along this divine continuum, sometimes enthused and passionate, *moving to the right*, but perhaps also weak in the face of the strong lure of "old ways," pulling them back to the left. Newly converted Christians are likely aware of their shortcomings, but need a greater longing for God's abiding love. Others honestly possess the desire for spiritual sight and have a sincere heart, but find themselves bogged down, motionless, in the muck of the natural world, not knowing how to get free. I encourage you to keep reading if you relate to this description of your walk with God; there is hope for change.

**A prodigal heart**

Along the left side of the continuum, we also recognize the believer who once rested securely in the glow of God's love, but through years of spiritual erosion has regressed from the ecstasy and vision resulting from relationship with God to once again suffer blindness and a heart grieved by its own self-contradictions.

As an ophthalmologist, I frequently treat the eyes of people who suffer from diabetes. In a diabetic eye, the lens will sometimes swell and impede or diminish sight when the body's blood sugar has escalated and health is further compromised. This same lens will experience a shrinking to its normal size and regain its proper role in furnishing sight, once the blood sugar levels have been normalized. In a similar way to the diabetic, our spiritual sight may vary, depending on the state of health of our relationship with God at a given time.

To develop a new appreciation in our hearts for God and His many gifts, there must first be an awakening initiated by the "painful realization" of our prodigal nature. In the parable Jesus told of the "prodigal" son, this younger son left his father's home for no reason and squandered the inheritance his father had provided him. Finally, he came to himself and returned, repentant and broken, to the safety of his father's love. (See Luke 15.) In that same way, we sometimes find ourselves "squandering" our relationship with God, losing sight of Him and His sovereign plan for our lives. To return to the safety of that relationship, we must break through the barriers of alienation and guilt in order to enter the supernatural grace of a full faith in God. That progressive transformation is described by the apostle Paul.

> So then faith comes by hearing, and hearing by the word of God.
>
> —ROMANS 10:17

The safety of our "Father's house" is revealed to us in the Word of God. We find our enlightenment, our spiritual sight, through faithful study, faithful fellowship, faithful prayer, and most importantly, *abandonment to God*. Until we abandon our hearts to God, choosing to obey His Word fully, we have nothing and we have nowhere to go.

The journey on this continuum, the tension creating a seesaw effect in our spiritual lives, is not the same for any two individuals. Your problems and conflicts are different from mine. We all face different obstacles to our spiritual growth.

Debbie Christiansen spoke of the bitterness generated in her heart by the firing of her husband, a former professional football coach for the Tampa Bay Buccaneers, and by the consequent media "feeding frenzy" that maligned her husband's name. This bitterness, a very natural response to her husband's plight, kept Debbie from experiencing deep, abiding peace in Christ, even though she was striving to sincerely practice her faith. The difficulties that she experienced in her Christian walk—the seesaw back and forth on the spiritual continuum—and her determination to overcome them, led her to initiate a women's citywide pursuit of revival. As part of the effort, Anne Graham Lotz was invited to challenge the women of the Tampa Bay area with her message, "Just Give Me Jesus." As God revived her own heart, Debbie emerged from her dry periods and reversals to a new place of peace and rest in her progression toward full faith, strengthened in her relationship with God.

The goals of Christianity are to attain an abiding faith in God for life now and to continue that relationship into eternity. Above all, we must recognize God's sovereignty—His benevolent rule over our lives, even in situations of adversity—and learn to follow His biblical and spiritual direction for our lives. Of course, God's Word is perfect and complete and cannot be represented by any continuum, such as I am using to describe our journey toward completion. However, it is helpful to understand how we move along this continuum, progressing toward spiritual completeness as we develop our intimacy with God and learn to live life at the practical level—how we think and act. As we explore in more detail the concept of *Progressions to Living Faith* in chapters 1 through 8, I encourage you to pray the following prayer for divine illumination that will help you move to the right on the continuum toward a deep, living faith in God.

## OPEN MY EYES, THAT I MAY SEE

Open my eyes, that I may see glimpses of truth Thou
    hast for me;
Place in my hands the wonderful key that shall unclasp
    and set me free.
Silently now I wait for Thee, ready, my God, Thy will to
    see;
Open my eyes, illumine me, Spirit divine![4]
—CLARE H. SCOTT

Chapter 1

# Surrender to God—Not Trusting Self

O NE OF THE largest and most obvious diversions in our progression toward God is our "need" to rely upon ourselves
and our unwillingness to abandon ourselves to Him. It may also
be one of the most difficult obstacles to attaining a *living faith*. This
lack of surrender to God reflects a spirit of independence, which
alienates us from God. *This independence is the very essence of
spiritual blindness.* Unfortunately, it is common to all of humanity, including servants of God whom we admire and respect.

One famous pilgrim who shares the difficulties his independence caused him is William Carey, sometimes referred to as the
"father of modern missions." He was born in England in 1761
and was the first missionary to take God's Word to India. Carey
"trod a path familiar to many before and since: he came under
conviction of sin, sought to please God by his own efforts, and
eventually abandoned such hopes by trusting in Jesus Christ."[1]
After finding peace with God and then entering missionary service, tragedy became a "divine teacher" for Carey. He was faced
with many personal hardships upon arrival in India including

the death of a son, a near-death experience himself, and the mental deterioration of his wife. He also experienced severe poverty and resistance from the British East India Company.

Even as a sincere believer, Carey had to keep renouncing trust and dependence in himself and learn to depend wholly upon God. Only as he renounced his independence and abandoned himself wholly to God was he able to persevere through the many disappointments in his way. By learning to walk on this sometimes painful path of total dependence on God, Carey was able to fulfill God's will to bring the message of salvation to India.

After seven years of hard work, Carey was finally able to welcome the first Indian convert to Christ! William Carey, who never returned to England, went on to establish leper hospitals, produce a Bengali New Testament, inspire forty other translations, build botanical gardens, and set the pattern for later missionary endeavors.[2] He could not have accomplished these things had he not moved from trust in himself to trust and abandoned surrender to God.

## MY INDEPENDENCE

When we cling to the attitude that we belong to ourselves rather than to the Lord, we are seeking an independence from our Creator rather than the dependence upon Him that He wants from us. We are owned by Him through our redemption because we have been bought with a price—the blood of His Son, Jesus Christ. Through salvation, we are freed from our self-ownership that has only served to cause us worry, the fear of loss, envy and covetousness, among other discomforts.

The following chart outlines the contrast between trusting in ourselves and learning to trust wholly in the Lord.

| BELONGING TO OURSELVES | BELONGING TO THE LORD JESUS |
| --- | --- |
| Trust in ourselves | Trust in God |
| Rely on ourselves | Rely on God |

| Owned by self | Owned by God |
|---|---|
| "Floating" on the waters of life | Immersed in God's will |
| Under the bondage of a controlling self | Freedom in abandonment to God |

Our continued trust in ourselves and refusal to release our lives fully into God's hands prevents us from entering His complete freedom from sin and bondage. Only as we abandon ourselves to God can we experience the wonderful freedom the apostle Paul enjoyed, as he declared, "It is no longer I who live, but Christ lives in me" (Galatians 2:20). The beautiful, loving character of Christ will be displayed in all of our thoughts, motives, and actions. Only in that way can we "be filled with all the fullness of God" (Ephesians 3:19), enjoying the promises and blessings for an abundant life that Christ promised (John 10:10).

## MY POWER

Similarly, seeking to live our life and practice our faith by our own power, determination, diligence, and discipline means relying on the "arm of flesh," which also dooms us to failure. Rather, we must learn to rest upon the omnipotent, tireless arm of God, which can enable us, sustain us, and raise us up. As we learn to wait on God and receive direction from Him, we will do those works He shows us to do and in the way He shows us to do them. Then we will know true success in living for God. However, when we rely on our own strengths and self-striving, it will result in limited effectiveness and frustrated failures. The following chart illustrates this dynamic.

| MAN'S POWER | GOD'S POWER |
|---|---|
| Self-power | Power that comes from God (Greek: *dunamis*) |
| Self-striving | Resting in Jesus |

## MY WORKS

Martha, a friend of Jesus, expressed her frustration aloud to the Master. While her sister Mary sat at Jesus' feet in adoration, Martha was left alone to prepare the meal for their guests. Mary cast herself and her eternal destiny upon Jesus and wanted to spend her time in communion with Christ. Martha's faith, like that of so many of us, sought to do God's work through busy-ness and striving rather than through the more effective use of life, resting in Jesus' presence, being "strengthened with might through His Spirit in the inner man" (Ephesians 3:16).

This insightful episode in Jesus' life does not teach us that preparing a meal is wrong. Rather, it speaks to the priority and emphasis of a life that made natural food more important than spiritual "food"—communing with the Master. The Scriptures record that "Martha was distracted with much serving" (Luke 10:40). In the very presence of Jesus, Martha did not enjoy a relationship with Him because of her inordinate concern with her own works. Jesus' loving response to Martha revealed His concern for her: "Martha, Martha, you are worried and troubled about many things. But one thing is needed, and Mary has chosen that good part, which will not be taken away from her" (Luke 10:41–42).

Consider the following contrasting positions (representing the attitude of Martha on the left and the choice of Mary on the right) along the divine continuum and decide where you may need to make some adjustments to assure your progression toward God.

| SERVING OF SELF | SERVING THE LORD JESUS |
|---|---|
| Focus on self | Justified by Jesus |
| Need for personal control | Abandonment to Jesus |
| Self-directed activity | Do all through God's rest |
| Serve God my way | Sit at His feet in worship |

When I focus on myself and my need to direct my own activities, without being directed by the Word of God or by His Spirit,

I am serving only myself. However, in my abandonment to God, I can rest in Him. As I choose to become dependent on God, I am dispossessed of anything of significance other than God alone.

From the beginning of time, after the disobedience of Adam and Eve, mankind has struggled with his independence from God. Though God has continually revealed to mankind His way to return to relationship with Him, people have chosen to follow their own ways. For example, Abel, the second son of Adam and Eve, was able to enter an intimacy with God that his jealous brother, Cain, was not. Abel brought an offering that was pleasing to God. By removing the barrier of his own will between himself and his God at the altar of his relationship to God, Abel lived his faith and worshiped as God commanded him to do.

In contrast, his brother, Cain, chose to bring an offering of his own choosing, which God had not approved. Cain, like so many of us, worshiped according to his own precepts, by what he could get away with, offering to God the work of his own hands in fruits and vegetables rather than the blood sacrifice God required. When Abel received the blessing of God from his worship and Cain did not, Cain raged in jealousy and killed his brother, committing the first murder.

Even our desire to serve God must be submitted to the Lordship of Christ and relinquished to obedience to His ways, which will always result in the blessing of God and our progression toward full faith. A heart that is abandoned to God will learn to "see" the ways of God and will do only those things that please Him. In that way we will truly be followers of Jesus, who declared of Himself, "I must work the works of Him who sent Me while it is day; the night is coming when no one can work" (John 9:4).

Chapter 2

# Internal Relationship—Not External Rituals

B ECAUSE OF THE nature of mankind, it is often far too easy for us to follow prescribed religious ritual, liturgy, and external protocol in the "service of God," rather than cultivating an internal, living faith relationship with Him. External religious service provides a way for many to try to relieve feelings of guilt before their Maker without becoming vulnerable to the risk of offering the gift of themselves to Him. But only as we move toward living faith do we receive the spiritual perspective of life as God intended it.

Have you considered the possibility that your outward performance among your religious community may be your attempt to assuage your guilt before a holy God? If so, you may realize that you are seeking a false comfort in communal participation rather than experiencing true peace in extending yourself personally toward God's arms. Until you commit yourself to a personal relationship with God, being reconciled to Him through receiving Christ as your Savior, you will continue your pathway of legalistic performance and remain blind to true spiritual freedom. And even after entering into such a personal commitment to Christ, it is possible to remain in legalistic bondage rather than learning to cultivate an intimate relationship with God, as we have discussed.

## TRUST IN LEGALISTIC PERFORMANCE

The father of the Methodist Church in England, John Wesley, in his own progression toward a living faith in his Lord, discovered that he was trusting in a legalistic performance of external religion. Initially, the Holy Club under the leadership of Wesley maintained a rigid method of study and a practice of external rules that required strictly regulated lives. This religious code emerged from Wesley's own uncertainty of his salvation and his attempts to secure a place in heaven through his legalistic lifestyle and practice of religion.[1] Later, John Wesley admitted that during those years he lived with a sense of condemnation and dread rather than peace and joy.

Continuing to seek the truth of God's Word, however, Wesley learned that he was full of self-righteousness due to his seeking to please God through his own legalistic works. He saw in the Word that people are saved by faith in Christ alone—receiving the mercy and love He offered for the salvation of mankind, secured through His death on the cross. He began to understand the words of Jesus.

> For God so loved the world that He gave His only begotten Son, that whoever believes in Him should not perish but have everlasting life. For God did not send His Son into the world to condemn the world, but that the world through Him might be saved. He who believes in Him is not condemned; but he who does not believe is condemned already, because he has not believed in the name of the only begotten Son of God. And this is the condemnation, that the light has come into the world, and men loved darkness rather than light, because their deeds were evil.
>
> —JOHN 3:16–19

John Wesley accepted the salvation he saw offered in the Scriptures, entering into a personal relationship with Jesus Christ and receiving the peace and joy they promise. Accepting the light of the Word—Jesus Himself—Wesley was freed from condemnation and guilt, and entered into peace with God. He understood the reality of the apostle Paul's words.

> For by grace you have been saved through faith, and that not of yourselves; it is the gift of God, not of works, lest anyone should boast.
>
> —EPHESIANS 2:8–9

> Therefore, having been justified by faith, we have peace with God through our Lord Jesus Christ, through whom also we have access by faith into this grace in which we stand, and rejoice in hope of the glory of God.
>
> —ROMANS 5:1–2

## PERSONAL ASSURANCE THROUGH FAITH

This personal assurance of salvation through faith in Christ alone eventually became the hallmark of the Methodist Church, which John Wesley founded, but not before its leader himself understood that "unless one is born again, he cannot see the kingdom of God" (John 3:3).

Even today, the institution of the church too often bases its rules of conduct on human effort, which cannot assure eternal salvation, according to the Scriptures. Unfortunately, the church that relies on external ritual is not promoting the true power of faith. Of course, fellowship with God's people in the service of our Savior is a great source of strength and significance in our lives. However, to be effective, it must be a participation that flows from a personal, living, vital relationship with God. Consider the dynamic of the following chart to help evaluate your own progression toward personal relationship with Christ.

| GENERAL RELIGIOUS CODE | PERSONAL IMMERSION IN THE PERSON OF CHRIST |
|---|---|
| Man-made religious formulations | Holy Spirit living in us, directing our lives |
| Cold orthodoxy | Inspiration and anticipation from the Word |
| Rote lessons | Experience and expectation of God's sovereign will |
| Rules written with ink | The Word written on our hearts with the Spirit |

Many Christians content themselves with the formal external duties of their church's teaching. However, many of these rote lessons were written only with ink by man. Some religious rules are mere distraction and hullabaloo, lacking the spiritual inspiration of truly Christ-centered text. Church doctrine based on the Word of God is meant to instruct our lives, and does, but blind obedience to man-made rules can easily guide us away from an authentic relationship to God.

**Deceptive man-made "safety"**

To be sure, there is a deceptive sense of "safety" through following the man-made path of least resistance in remaining within prescribed teachings of the church's hierarchy. In that way, the human mind can convince itself that it is remaining faithful to God while, in fact, the spirit does not take the necessary risk of relinquishing *all* to the Lord. Without that heart relationship with God, we are left empty of the anticipation and expectation of "goodness and mercy" (Psalm 23:6) and are not brought to fully "trust in the Lord…and feed on His faithfulness" (Psalm 37:3). To remain bound by those church doctrines that merely serve a hierarchy, or a building, will prevent our souls from taking flight—finding true faith and meeting the living God.

The Scriptures teach clearly, "The letter kills, but the Spirit gives life" (2 Corinthians 3:6). While the nominal church and

Christian practitioners may tell you what is the "proper" way to live, God asks you to *anticipate*: "Trust in the LORD, and do good; Dwell in the land, and feed on His faithfulness" (Psalm 37:3). Acknowledging God's sovereignty means *seeing* that God's hand is *on* me, *with* me, and *for* me. Only in that personal relationship with God can we experience with the apostle Paul this spiritual reality: "And we know that all things work together for good to those who love God, to those who are the called according to His purpose" (Romans 8:28). That wonderful assurance requires that we move to the right of the following continuum of personal experience with Christ.

| PRACTICE FAITH AS THE PHARISEES | LIVE FAITH ACCORDING TO THE T.R.U.S.T. GRID |
|---|---|
| Relating to church rules | Having a personal relationship with Jesus |
| Formal "rote" prayer | Crying out to Jesus from the heart |
| Legalistic protocol | Inner rest and contentment |
| Circumcision of law | Faith in Christ alone |
| Abiding by duty without love | Abiding in Jesus' love |

In Jesus' day the priests, the Pharisees, lived under the deception of man-made rituals. They led the worship of the people with attention to tiny details they had added to the Law of Moses. Yet, they were not righteous men in their hearts and their system of religion amounted to nothing more than external "fussing." So incensed was Jesus against their hypocrisy that He called these self-righteous and prideful imposters "vipers" (Matthew 12:34). This inclination of the Pharisees toward the formality and external procedure of religion endures today in some Christian churches, both among the leaders and members. People who content themselves with this form of external religion may be constrained by rules and doctrines written by men alone, deceiving themselves that they are "safe" from God's judgment because of their legalistic practices.

The very human tendency to the pride exhibited in the Pharisees, through evaluating one's righteousness by outward displays, also persists in the church today. As a member of a church, you may involve yourself in various attractive activities, membership drives, and organization. You may also seek to distinguish yourself as a "good Christian" by tithing, reading the Bible, and praying in a habitual rather than a heart-felt manner. However, Christ needs us to cry out to Him from our hearts, to relate to Him personally, and to seek the inner rest and contentment He gives through faith in Him alone. In this way we can gain the freedom from lavish public displays of religion, which have little to do with genuine faith. Genuine faith is cultivated through our personal, internal relationship with Him. The following chart illustrates this spiritual reality.

| EXTERNAL ACTIONS | INTERNAL RELATIONSHIP |
| --- | --- |
| Self-centered drive to serve God | Freedom to live in God |
| Good behavior | Jesus alone |
| Martha's work | Mary's peace |
| External pride | Internal wisdom |

## DISTRACTION OF RELIGIOUS WORKS

As we mentioned previously, Martha was distracted with her own work of much serving. And she had a self-pitying attitude toward her sister. She complained, "'Lord, do You not care that my sister has left me to serve alone? Therefore tell her to help me.' And Jesus answered and said to her, 'Martha, Martha, you are worried and troubled about many things. But one thing is needed, and Mary has chosen the good part'" (Luke 10:40–42). Mary sat at the Lord's feet by choice. It was in that place that her love for, and worship of, Jesus were fulfilled. Her priority was personal relationship with the Master.

This is not to say that Martha could not have been similarly immersed in giving to God through her gifts in the kitchen. Her problem was that her hospitality was displaying a focus on her efforts rather than on the Person whom she was serving. She was striving to behave *conventionally*. Mary, on the other hand, was engaged in a tangible, personal relationship with Jesus and had no need to be entangled in what, according to culture, might be viewed as *appropriate*.

A significant part of Mary's beautiful focus stems from her willingness to draw apart, to be quiet with Jesus; anyone who truly progresses toward full faith will do as Mary did. Others, even while perhaps loving their Lord, will not rest from their own works in a manner sufficient to make it their priority to contemplate God. Martha's heart was good, but she was distracted.

Like the Pharisees of Jesus' day, some people find their motivation for doing God's work to be the "superior" external position it affords them in a religious hierarchy. These people may publicly work for their church or community while, at the same time, exhibiting a proud, pompous manner, even accusing their fellow man of being less "religious" than they. In contrast, Christ bids us enter the *shalom* (peace) and satisfaction to be found, quietly and individually, only at His feet. It is only out of this place of personal, humble communion with God that we can and should function, giving ourselves to the wholehearted service of others, as the Scriptures teach:

> Therefore, as we have opportunity, let us do good to all, especially to those who are of the household of faith.
> —GALATIANS 6:10

## TRUE SPIRITUAL WORK

Before gaining true spiritual sight, we spend our energies in futility, basing our duties and actions in the values of the culture around us, our own dreams, and the current social and moral forces. Spiritual sight requires faith in Christ and focus on God rather than on the material climate about us, which speaks to us through the evidence of our senses. In Christ, the moral changes come from inside ourselves through the redemption working in us—the life of Christ resident within. The Scriptures instruct not to be conformed to this world (Romans 12:2), but to "Let your eyes look straight ahead, And your eyelids look right before you" (Proverbs 4:25). In abandoning ourselves to the life of God within, we will find our feet on a straight path toward true righteousness and fullness of faith.

In Jesus' Sermon on the Mount, He began each "beatitude" with the words, "Blessed are…" (Matthew 5:3–11). With spiritual sight, we will see these teachings as the basis for godly *attitudes* that Christ can strengthen in our lives. Jesus said that when that happens, we are blessed, which means, in the original language, *extravagantly happy.* As we become merciful, peacemaking, and pure in heart, our lives will reflect a Christlike character.

George Mueller was a powerful man of faith who lived during the nineteenth century in England. He lived during the extreme poverty of the times that resulted in thousands of children living homeless on the streets. Mueller determined to make a difference for these orphans and began to house, feed, and educate them. His inspiring story reveals the faithfulness of God to a man who placed his faith completely in the love of God to provide for these needy children.[2] In unshakeable, inspired faith, Mueller prayed to God for provision of all the children's needs. They always received everything they required in answer to prayer alone. In this same way, God wants our humility and complete dependence on Him. George Mueller shows us that the path to living faith is in offering ourselves to God in humble devotion. Consider the following chart and evaluate for yourself where your faith is placed.

| FAITH IN MATERIALISM | FAITH IN GOD |
|---|---|
| Giving to worthy causes | Giving like George Mueller |
| May change life under influence | Life changes from inside to outside |

Chapter 3

# ETERNAL PRIORITIES—NOT TEMPORAL PURSUITS

THE BLINDNESS OF the natural man is a result of his complete trust in his five senses: touch, taste, smell, hearing, and sight. We are born, and we die. The natural man thinks only of temporal pursuits and knows nothing about eternal priorities. Without seeking spiritual sight through closeness to God, we are bound to follow our "sense vision" of the *physical present and future* without hope of understanding our *spiritual present and future*. By cultivating an intimate relationship with God, which opens our spiritual eyes, we begin to see and observe the meaninglessness of much that our physical senses "see" at this moment as urgent and necessary. Moving toward full faith in relationship with God completely changes our perspective of life—both temporal and eternal.

## PERSONAL AMBITION: SECULAR OR HOLY?

It is important to determine the motivation of our lives. Is our personal ambition based on secular, worldly values or on a quest for the holy and divine? The great preacher and writer, A. W. Tozer, taught the importance of having a spiritual, eternal perspective of life in his critique of the twentieth-century church and his evaluation of today's Christians. He attacked the superficiality and hypocrisy of the religious system, and taught that "true faith is not only a belief but a moral dynamic."[1]

As Tozer viewed it, the necessary progression to true faith moves us from self-gratification and refusal to humble oneself to cultivating an intimate relationship with God and living in dependence upon Him. For Tozer himself, this progression meant embracing estrangement from "the world of the senses and [entering] into the inner world of communion with God."[2] His journey toward full faith required his receiving a vision of God's majesty, and experiencing wonderment in Him alone, rather than simply looking to God to assist him in meeting his temporal needs.

Do you see the wonder of God in His creation and love Him for who He is? Or do you see God merely as One who will bring satisfaction to your senses and meet your temporal needs? Is your ambition to seek to know Him and the personal destiny He plans for your eternity? Or are you filled with ambition based in worldly values? Evaluate your own spiritual vision as you consider the significance of the following chart, which we will discuss.

| SECULAR AMBITION | HOLY AMBITION |
| --- | --- |
| Appointed king—Saul | Anointed king—David |
| Personal prestige | Spiritual abundance |
| Building temporal structures | Resting in God |

The presiding voice of the temporal world, the overwhelming influence of this brief life, counsels us to try to please and influence people, thereby gaining the personal prestige we seek. We see this faulty motivation for life illustrated in an Old Testament character. King Saul was the first appointed king of Israel, and he demonstrated this tendency to live for the acclaim of the people. In his desire to please the people to gain the personal prestige he craved, Saul blatantly disobeyed the commands of God, and as a result, God tore the kingdom away from him.

King David, on the other hand, the second king anointed to rule Israel, lived his life before God. His life perspective was totally influenced by his living relationship with God. Though he failed miserably at times, David knew the way back to God through deep repentance and lived a victorious life as a result. The Scriptures declare of David, "The LORD has sought for Himself a man after His own heart" (1 Samuel 13:14). It was that intimate relationship with God that kept David moving along the continuum from personal ambition for temporal gain to divine destiny in God. Of course, we know from the New Testament that David fulfilled that destiny; Jesus Christ was born out of the lineage of David.

Kings, pastors, CEOs, or physicians may all try to receive their share of personal power, prestige, and influence in this temporal life. To the natural man, it seems important—at the time. Churches often engage in massive building projects and membership drives for these same reasons. Yet everything of this earth passes away eventually—except the spiritual abundance that we attain through a living faith in God.

Our holy ambition, when we can see it, should be growth—but growth in Christ. Rather than personal prestige, power, and wealth, you and I should seek a personal relationship with our Savior and the spiritual abundance found in Him alone. In a living faith, we are captivated, ravished, and engulfed by Him during our temporal life, and we are prepared to live with Him for eternity.

In contrast, worldly ambition, which focuses the senses on the mere details of this temporal life, withers in comparison to the blessedness of present and future grace in desiring to be with Christ for eternity. When religious works are filled with worldly ambition, the Spirit of God is grieved and withdraws His divine influence. Religious expression through our worship of God is beautiful and uplifting only when it is focused on the Word and faith in Christ. When you are motivated by holy ambition, the Holy Spirit is present, and you find that God inhabits the praises of His people.

## Grasping the Reality of Life and Death

Only the young, and perhaps the very foolish, are not aware that they are on a downhill slide to old age and eventual death. That is the inevitable nature of all physical beings. Existence in a body of flesh and bone is limited to a length of time. Still, we all possess an undying soul that transcends those limitations. It is renewed and quickened, not by food or air, but by a steadfast, unmovable faith.

Only through faith in God's redemption do we grasp the reality of genuine life that lasts forever. The Scriptures teach that "the sting of death is sin" (1 Corinthians 15:56), and relating to our physical body, the apostle Paul declared, "This corruptible must put on incorruption." I will not live forever in my physical body—neither will you—so we must seek redemption through Christ, with eyes on eternity, to grasp the reality of eternal life for our undying soul. Only then can we declare, with the Scriptures, that "death is swallowed up in victory" (1 Corinthians 15:53–54). Consider the dynamic contrast of life and death represented in the following chart.

| Death | Eternal life |
|---|---|
| Natural body of corruption | Incorruptible spiritual body |
| Wages of sin is death | Death is swallowed up in victory |
| Outward man perishes | Inward man is being renewed |

The apostle Paul gave us wonderful insight into the glorious transformation we are promised at death as believers.

> The body is sown in corruption, it is raised in incorruption. It is sown in dishonor, it is raised in glory. It is sown in weakness, it is raised in power. It is sown a natural body, it is raised a spiritual body. There is a natural body, and there is a spiritual body.
>
> —1 Corinthians 15:42–44

If we grasp this spiritual reality of life and death, our behavior will be dramatically impacted. A great many things around us can entice us to live for ourselves in the moment, rather than living for Christ for eternity. The temptation to live independently of God can be all too persuasive: "and the cares of this world, the deceitfulness of riches, and the desires for other things entering in choke the word, and it becomes unfruitful" (Mark 4:19). God's plan cannot be fulfilled in us while we are willingly absorbed by a long list of concerns. Friends, family, schedules, jobs, social involvements—things that we *know* to be temporary—may each interfere at one time or another. Where do you find yourself in the following chart regarding your behavior in this life?

| TEMPORAL BEHAVIOR | ETERNAL BEHAVIOR |
|---|---|
| Living in the world | Living in the bosom of the Trinity |
| Seeking worldly things | Contentment |
| Seeking wisdom of the world | Seeking the Pearl of Great Price |
| Distractions of the world | Focused on faith |
| Lust "love" | True love |

As the above chart indicates, the seduction of our own senses, the lure of experiences, the desire for worldly things, and lust divert us from seeking eternal values. When that happens, we are removed from the intimacy and nearness of a child to the Father, from the grace of the Son, our Savior, and from the peace in the Holy Spirit as Comforter and Sanctifier. If we are fervent in our faith, we can acknowledge the peace and contentment and genuine love found there. We recognize that we are already rich and need none of the world's attractions to add to our abundant life in Christ. The presence of the King in our lives will be obvious to others as well.

If one's faith falls short of the completeness and ecstasy of a vibrant living faith, that individual may seek not only worldly *things* but also fleeting worldly *wisdom*. However, "the kingdom of heaven is like a merchant seeking beautiful pearls, who, when he had found one pearl of great price, went and sold all that he had and bought it" (Matthew 13:45–46). This total abandonment to the true riches of the kingdom is the motivation necessary to attain to full, living faith.

As a new believer, though your search for truth may be earnest, you may find your interests diverted to worldly things, or worldly wisdom, or other distractions of this temporal life. You still seek satisfaction in the very human, world-based ideas that are bounded by space and time. However, as you progress along the continuum toward full faith, you will discover that knowing God is knowing where to look for answers. True love and contentment are found only in the heart that has totally abandoned itself to live in the bosom of the Trinity and to sell all and seek the Pearl of Great Price, which is Christ Himself. There is no real faith without love, and real love exists in a cycle centered on God, for "We love Him because He first loved us" (1 John 4:19).

## AT HOME IN GOD

Jesus told the story of a poor man, covered with sores, who begged crumbs from a rich man's table.

> There was a certain rich man who was clothed in purple and fine linen and fared sumptuously every day. But there was a certain beggar named Lazarus, full of sores, who was laid at his gate, desiring to be fed with the crumbs which fell from the rich man's table.
>
> —LUKE 16:19–21

While Lazarus languished at the gate, the rich man sat wrapped in his finery and blindness to the plight of others. The rich man's complacency originated from his contentment with the moment—*his* moment. He was lost to God by his satisfaction with his possessions. Lazarus, though, expected little from this temporary life. He hoped for mere necessities and received none. Yet, it seems he was sustained by his vision of his future rest in heaven; he was at home in God. Jesus explained that at his death, Lazarus was carried to Abraham's bosom, otherwise known as Paradise.

When the rich man died, he found himself in hell. The rich man was able to look across a great divide and saw the poor man, Lazarus, comforted in Paradise. He first asked that Abraham send Lazarus to him with a drop of water on his finger to cool his tongue from the torment of the flames, but Abraham only reminded him of his comfortable life and of the plight of Lazarus in his life of misery. Then the rich man wanted Lazarus to return to earth and warn the rich man's brothers of the fate awaiting them. Abraham would not allow it, saying, "If they do not listen to Moses and the Prophets, they will not be convinced even if someone rises from the dead" (Luke 16:31, NIV).

This dramatic story is a picture of how the seductiveness of comfort, luxury, and momentary pleasure, apart from an experience with God, will surely doom you or me. The problem was not that the rich man was rich or that Lazarus was destitute; it was that Lazarus was in need and, while the rich man had the means to help, he did not. He was blind to the crushing need of his fellow man, Lazarus. If we content ourselves with material and superficial things in this world instead of seeking our true home in God, we eventually find ourselves facing an eternity in torment as the rich man painfully discovered. Consider your position in the light of the following chart. Are you more at home in the world or in God?

| HOME IN THE WORLD | HOME IN GOD |
| --- | --- |
| The rich man | Lazarus |
| Eternal torment | Eternal comfort and bliss |

## LIVING IN THE PAST

Another possible deception related to living only for this temporal life is getting stuck in the past. It is possible for you to lose yourself in your past because of painful experiences or even very positive ones. Unfortunately, this tendency to living in the past is very natural. Nostalgia, over good or bad experiences, personal "fame" as well as remorse and regret, and an inability to forgive and forget the offenses of others all have a terrible power to tear you from the fullness of a personal immersion in Christ. And resting on past achievements or "fame" will also hinder you from confronting present challenges and addressing the continuing need for change.

To abide at Christ's feet we must be willing to, and learn how to, forgive past hurts without harboring bitterness and grudges. And we must be willing to forget our accomplishments of the past to accept the present challenges. This is difficult to do. True forgiveness requires much more than trying to convince ourselves we have forgiven by saying the right things to those who have hurt us. Total release is found only in knowing the power of God's forgiveness and receiving His emancipation from the pain of uncomfortable memories.

To find this spiritual freedom, the Christian walk requires that you move beyond the social code of expected, accepted norms and set your eyes upon the Lord. He alone can give grace for the cleansing of unforgiveness and bitterness. The seeker can find the strength and love for total forgiveness only by knowing God as the All in All. As you choose to set your affections on things above (Colossians 3:1–2), God will put eternity in your heart and give grace to lay aside the past. The following chart illustrates the difference between having our eyes on God and the deception of living in the past.

| EYES ON PAST | EYES ON GOD |
| --- | --- |
| Forgiving, not forgetting | Total forgiveness |
| Nostalgia over past experiences | Eternity in our hearts |
| Social code passed on | Personal relationship with Christ |

Chapter 4

# LIVING FAITH OF THE SPIRIT— NOT RATIONAL FAITH OF THE MIND

I T IS A sad irony that the apparent gifts of the human mind are also its greatest weaknesses. Darwinists and most modern science advocates demonstrate this reality perfectly, reflecting in their genius a total blindness to the marvel of the Creator's intelligence. We are too easily led to *believe* that our human wisdom is the perfect measurement of life and substance. Because of this innate, though darkened, trust in our own minds, we find it extremely difficult to come to God, acknowledging our need of Him. The apostle Paul understood this spiritual reality: "But the natural man does not receive the things of the Spirit of God, for they are foolishness to him; nor can he know them, because they are spiritually discerned" (1 Corinthians 2:14).

And, even after we have received the wonderful grace of salvation through faith in Christ, it remains difficult for us, as believers, to progress along the continuum toward full faith for the same reason—we tend to trust our own minds. Yet, according to the Scriptures, we remain spiritually impaired to the extent that we do so. Pointing out this fact is not meant to be discouraging but to point to the danger of self-reliance and the need to aggressively abandon ourselves to God to be set free from the spiritual blindness of our natural thinking.

## PROGRESSION OF A PIONEER MISSIONARY

Adoniram Judson was an outstanding pioneer, American missionary who lived a remarkable life, taking the Word of God to the Asian country of Burma (now called Myanmar). His monumental achievements include providing the Burmese people with a grammar, a dictionary, and a Bible in their own language.[1] However, these wonderful achievements would never have happened if Judson had not progressed from his spiritual blindness, characterized by rationalism and his faith in the ideas of man, to an authentic faith in God's supremacy.

Judson was a precocious and gifted child. He was also ambitious. When he went to Brown University, he became enchanted by the academic environment, turning from the traditional religious teachings he received as a child. A fellow student influenced Judson's decision to embrace *deism*, causing him to become skeptical of Christianity. Deism is a system of thought that advocates "natural religion," the seeking of a moral life without recognizing the need for God's gracious redemption. It also denies the hand of the Creator in the laws of the universe. This sounds like the cult of Darwinism, doesn't it? After finishing his studies, Judson went on to New York to work as a playwright.

Content for a time with his career and enamored with the powers of his own mind, Judson experienced a dramatic tragedy that would awaken him to divine truth and turn his life and service to God. One night while he slept at an inn, he heard noises coming from the next room that could only mean that the man therein was dying. By morning the "neighbor" was dead, and Judson wondered if the poor fellow had been a skeptic, like himself, or if he died a Christian. He was shocked and dismayed to discover that the dead man was the same college friend who had influenced Judson's decision to renounce Christianity. From his sound childhood religious upbringing, Judson now realized that unless his friend had changed his philosophy recently, he was lost forever. In that stark moment, Judson also realized that he would be lost as well if he did not change. He promptly returned home, entered seminary, and eventually became a great missionary.[2] Adoniram Judson's spiritual eyes had been opened to the fragile, fallible nature of human intelligence, and to the sin of granting it stature above God's wisdom.

## SECULAR FAITH OR SPIRITUAL FAITH

Psychologist Carl Jung is credited with saying that "religion is a defense against the experience of God."[3] Jung was making the same distinction I have discussed between practicing an external "religious code" and moving toward full faith through a personal relationship with God. Carl Jung used the terms *secular faith* and *spiritual faith*, respectively, to define these two lifestyles. Understanding these terms will help you to determine where you are in your pursuit of faith.

A secular faith is one that, quite rightly, includes God as a part of its focus, but only as He is observed through the lens of human understanding, which is focused on worldly concerns. Such a faith is not necessarily "God-less," but it references God only according to human knowledge. For example, one who embraces a secular faith may recognize God's face in a friend's laughter or a dragonfly's wing, without entering into a relationship with God Himself. You may even pray, do good works befitting a Christian, read the Bible, and still not know how to cry out to God to experience the reality of His presence. We can only cry out to God when we become desperate, having been disillusioned with our own efforts and intellect, casting away all confidence in ourselves.

Conversely, a spiritual faith involves, as we have discussed, becoming born again through the incorruptible seed of God, receiving Christ as our Savior, and embarking on the wonderful faith journey from spiritual blindness to a deeply satisfying personal relationship with God. In cultivating a spiritual faith, we learn to truly abide in Christ through the power of the Holy Spirit, and we are blessed, anointed, and satisfied in fulfilling our divine destiny. We also have comfort and fulfillment as we walk in the light of God's understanding.

Take a moment to consider whether you fall on the side of those embracing secular faith or of those who are cultivating a spiritual faith. Do you properly acknowledge the Creator God, giving Him His rightful place in the universe, or are you more convinced of the power of your mind—your own abilities and ideas, as well as the ideas of others who ignore the truth of the Bible? The following chart shows some contrasting ideas of these two approaches to faith.

| SECULAR FAITH | SPIRITUAL FAITH |
|---|---|
| General knowledge of God | Divine illumination by the Holy Spirit |
| Holy Spirit acknowledged | Holy Spirit gives spiritual light and affection |
| God is about all things | God is in me in every way |
| Focus all over God's kingdom | Focused dead center in God |
| Know light | Walk in light |
| Living for earthly concerns | Fulfilling destiny |

## GEORGE WHITEFIELD'S JOURNEY

George Whitefield, an Oxford graduate and prominent English preacher of the eighteenth century, began his journey toward living faith on the side of secular faith—practicing his religion through his intellect. He sought to learn more and more about his Creator; he read, preached, prayed, and even ministered to prisoners. Yet, when Whitefield read Henry Scougal's *Life of God in the Soul of Man,* he suddenly realized that he must become a new creature; he needed to be born again.[4] He came to understand that true spiritual faith results in the union of the soul with God, allowing the life of Christ to be formed within us.

In his conversion experience, this minister's heart was filled with joy as he felt the weight of sin removed from him. George Whitefield went on to preach an estimated 18,000 sermons in England and New England, becoming a major figure in the Great Awakening. This radical transformation occurred only after he became aware that something was missing within him and sought to know God's salvation, through receiving Christ as Savior.

The same is true for you and me. Progress from practicing a secular faith to living a spiritual faith requires a personal revival by which we are quickened—enlivened and reinvigorated—by the Holy Spirit. This conversion occurs when we enter into a relationship with God, receiving for ourselves God's promises of love and salvation. The chart below contrasts religion of the mind and the relationship of the spirit born again to the true knowledge of God.

| ORGANIZATION OF THE MIND | SPIRIT OCCUPIED WITH JESUS |
|---|---|
| Intellect | Change of heart |
| Interested knowledge | Passion for Christ |
| Man's reasoning | God's reasoning |
| Man's knowledge | God's knowledge |
| Increased understanding | Increased tenderness |
| Prison of the mind | Freedom in Jesus |

## DIVINE DIMENSION OF LIFE

We have seen that one of humanity's most admirable characteristics—our strong intellect—tragically provides one of the greatest barriers to our full faith in God. The natural mind with its senses and the intellect that interprets all of life, imprisons us in a world of spiritual blindness. Stated another way, the mind has a loud voice that can prevent our intimacy and directness with God. Like Thomas, one of Jesus' disciples, who demanded physical proof of his Lord's resurrection before he would believe, we are naturally dependent upon the material data of the senses. We are imprisoned by a man-centered, earth-centered, now-centered lack of vision. We relate to the natural mind speaking loudly in the declaration of Thomas, "Unless I see in His hands the print of the nails, and put my finger into the print of the nails, and put my hand into His side, I will not believe" (John 20:25).

Our openness to Jesus is blocked and distorted by rationalizations, speculations, and human explanations. This scenario does not sound negative to us, however, because we are accustomed to using our natural minds to learn, to read, and to listen, in attempting to grasp more understanding about God. As secular thinkers, we may have genuine interest in spiritual matters. At some stage in our pilgrimage, however, if we are honestly seeking to know God, we must come to see that knowledge is not so much coming to know as it is coming to know our need. That realization is the beginning of a journey to experience the divine dimension of life in God.

We are endowed with spiritual sight when we have been freed of the strictures of a linear intellect and have abandoned ourselves to Christ's love for us and His promise of eternal life. The Scriptures teach clearly our need for this transformation: "'For My thoughts are not your thoughts, Nor are your ways My ways,' says the LORD. 'For as the heavens are higher than the earth, So are My ways higher than your ways, And My thoughts than your thoughts'" (Isaiah 55:8–9).

We naturally depend upon our own minds, but God exists on a far higher dimension of life, which is not attainable by the tiny tools of reasoning. Though we are instinctively attracted to increase our natural understanding, this is not where the essence of life in the Lord lies. Again, the apostle Paul, a highly educated man, understood this dynamic: "Though I speak with the tongues of men and of angels, but have not love, I have become sounding brass or a clanging cymbal. And though I have the gift of prophecy, and understand all mysteries and all knowledge, and though I have all faith, so that I could remove mountains, but have not love, I am nothing" (1 Corinthians 13:1–2). Nothing. Life in God dwarfs all the wonders of the human intellect.

In the quietness and peace of a living, spiritual faith are the seeds of great, Christlike tenderness and compassion. And our compassion for one another along with our love for God are all that He really wants of us. Our tendency toward intellectual complexity obscures what Christ made clear and simple, that "this is eternal life, that they may know You, the only true God, and Jesus Christ whom You have sent" (John 17:3). Rather than following the mind's misdirected quests, we must choose to focus our search for living faith on the "T.R.U.S.T. Grid of Life"—thanksgiving, rejoicing, understanding His Word, singing out to Him in praise, and a commitment to thoughtfulness of our fellow man. Then, in all things, He has preeminence.

## LEARNING STYLES: *LOGOS* AND *RHEMA*

When God speaks to us, He must use the language that can communicate to our heads as well as our hearts. Our experience of God, before we find a full faith and acute spiritual sight, is limited to the things we have learned with our intellect. We have our checklists of thoughts and behaviors passed on to us by the teachers under whom we have studied. And we can, in turn, pass these religious concepts on to others.

In this way, we receive a *logos* from God's Word. *Logos* is a Greek word referring to a concept or idea.[5] We learn by receiving a *logos*, or godly idea, which may teach us a general principle for living a godly life. A person seeking wisdom and faith will try to apply that principle to his own life.

In contrast, when one's heart is entirely open to God and His voice, revelation through *rhema*—a living Word from the Spirit that gives us spiritual understanding—can be detected even above the din of life in the world. A *rhema* gives us instruction in a specific godly principle with a specific application.[6] Once the heart is receptive to the Spirit's *rhema*, God speaks to us personally—our needs, questions, and fears—from His Word. While it is an experience that is individual and therefore difficult to explain or express, it comes as a result of being immersed in God, and growing as new creations in Christ.

As a result of this intimate relationship, where the Word of God becomes a living *rhema* to our spirits, our prayers and discussions and instruction that we share with others transcend mere knowledge and are filled with divine power and passion, as we find ourselves immersed in His redemption. For example, when John Wesley's heart was opened by God's *rhema*, he was transformed from a dispassionate person of religious knowledge to a passionate person, filled with God's Word and Spirit. Wesley was transformed from a person trying to be saved by *working for* God to a person in which the Holy Spirit was *working in him* to do nothing more than God's will.

Consider the difference between *logos* and *rhema* contrasted in the following chart.

| LOGOS | RHEMA |
| --- | --- |
| Religious concepts, principles | Spiritual application of truth and principle |
| Easy to teach others | Individual; difficult to communicate |
| To educate and inform | Passion to change |
| Intellectual relationship | Intimate relationship |

## BELIEVING FACTS OR SEEKING GOD'S FACE

It is possible to believe with a disengaged heart. You may admit to me, "Yes, I believe in God; I believe Jesus was a good man; I believe in heaven and hell; and I believe I have a soul." If I ask if you love and worship God, you may be tempted to say, "I am too busy. My life is difficult right now."

You may be familiar with all the foundations of the Christian faith and believe in their validity and necessity. You may be able to talk the talk and fit in quite nicely with other Christians in your religious community. Even so, this does not mean that you have personally embraced Christ as the Divine Savior. In the province of our minds, authentic, even fervent, belief can appear to be sufficient. However, the Scripture teaches, "But without faith it is impossible to please Him, for he who comes to God must believe that He is, and that He is a rewarder of those who diligently seek Him" (Hebrews 11:6). We must, finally, embrace the self-revelation of God in His promises to us and be renewed by them to diligently seek the Lord. By embracing God as God, you may become fully engaged in His truth for you. Evaluate your personal journey by comparing your relationship to God with the following contrasting ideas.

| I BELIEVE FACTS | I TOUCH GOD |
|---|---|
| Superficial faith | Whole-souled embrace of the Savior |
| Mental assent to truth | Diligent search for God |
| Belief that the promises are true | Embracing the promises as true for me personally |

## Chapter 5

# GOD'S SECURITY—
# NOT PERSONAL INSECURITY

O UR LACK OF security in the world along with the arduous work of "life," taken together, often exact a toll, making it difficult even for believers to see God and partake of His promised *shalom*—His divine peace. As we have discussed, it is *only* in humble abandonment to Him that we will we ever hope to progress from the secular faith of the intellect, at the left of our continuum, to the living faith depicted on the right of it (see page 21). And only as we progress toward living faith will we begin to see the quiet simplicity of ultimate security and contentment that God alone promises to His children.

## AUGUSTINE'S SEARCH FOR SPIRITUAL SIGHT

Before Martin Luther's revolutionary impact on Christendom, no one had influenced the medieval church as much as Augustine. One who studies his life understands that He too had to progress from a secular perspective toward a living faith. He did so from a muddle of insecurity, fear, and disillusionment in empty, broken creeds. Born in Roman North Africa, Augustine had been taught the Word of God by his Christian mother. However, as a young man he became a talented orator and was also enchanted by the philosophies of the world to such an extent that he grew to deny God's teachings and gravitated toward stargazers. Augustine gave himself to sensual pleasures and to his study of philosophy. Yet, pricked in his conscience, he prayed that the Lord would make him holy—at a later time.[1]

Because of Augustine's searching mind, however, he could not ignore his greatest fear—the prospect of dying without ever really knowing God. Would this understanding be found in the philosophies he studied, which contradicted themselves? Or in the teaching of his Christian mother? One day, as he sat in a garden, despairing, he heard a child's voice say, "Take and read." Augustine responded, reaching for the Bible lying there. He opened it randomly and read, "Let us walk properly, as in the day, not in revelry and drunkenness, not in lewdness and lust, not in strife and envy. But put on the Lord Jesus Christ, and make no provision for the flesh, to fulfill its lusts" (Romans 13:13–14).

It was in that moment, Augustine later wrote in his famous *Confessions,* that "as by a clear and constant light infused into my heart, the darkness of all former doubts was driven away."[2] His mother's prayers had finally been answered. Augustine had been set free, had been given the ability to see God's truth, and took his first step toward fulfilling his divine destiny as a preacher of the gospel.

## EVALUATING INSECURITY LEVELS

Perhaps you are familiar with the pain of doubt and insecurity, as well as the confusion of conflicting and competing beliefs. Where will you find your rest? The vision God desires for you comes when you lay your fears at His feet and relinquish yourself to His love. Where do you find yourself in the following continuum? Through genuine faith and repentance, you can move from the left to the right and begin to enjoy the security found only in

God. Consider the following identifiers of "insecurity" and their counterpart of security, found in God alone.

| INSECURITY | SECURITY |
| --- | --- |
| Questioning God's love | Absorbed in God's love |
| Imprisonment | Call to freedom |
| Trials and temptations weakening us | Problems lead to deeper faith and relationship |
| Worry and anxiety | Total peace |
| Lacking assurance of forgiveness | Immersed in God's acceptance |

You may be tempted to question whether you are forgiven, or even *loved* by God. Unless you genuinely cast yourself upon Christ's mercy, you cannot experience the security that comes with unconditional acceptance. You will remain bound by excessive worry and concern. You may testify that you are saved by grace, but still experience a fear of death. Without abandoning ourselves completely to the Savior, our temptations and troubles only present further opportunities for anxiety because "each one is tempted when he is drawn away by his own desires and enticed. Then, when desire has conceived, it gives birth to sin; and sin, when it is full-grown, brings forth death" (James 1:14–15).

You may truly be desirous of meeting God and believing in His salvation, yet find yourself unable to fully touch God because of your own insecurities and doubts. Don't lose heart. As you move closer to God, abandoning yourself to Him and embracing the Son of God by a living faith, you will begin to feel secure in your relationship with Him and experience your sanctification in Him. According to the Scriptures, becoming free of fear and worry requires putting on the "helmet of salvation." In that position, God's presence is constantly before us, filling us with security and confidence.

The psalmist understood this reality when he declared of God, "Your lovingkindness is before my eyes" (Psalm 26:3). Even our trials change in our eyes as we embrace such biblical truth as "tribulation produces perseverance; and perseverance, character; and character, hope" (Romans 5:3–4). And this hope, through the power of the Holy Spirit, also brings peace and joy to us (Romans 15:13).

## THE BLESSING OF ABANDONMENT TO GOD

Receiving the total peace of God's forgiveness and allowing life's problems to lead us into a deeper walk with Him gives us the ability to see life with spiritual eyes and experience greater hope, joy, and understanding. Then we are free to be immersed in His ever-abiding love, which releases us from the bonds that the world generates in our hearts and minds. We become ever more Christ-centered and are satisfied in Him alone. The following chart reflects some of the wonderful benefits of moving from our own confusion to this wonderful relationship of peace with God.

| CONFUSION | PEACE |
| --- | --- |
| Complexity | Contentment |
| Confused walk | Deep in God's Word |
| Martha, troubled in serving | Mary at the feet of Jesus |
| Entanglements of life | Future grace |

Until we hear God's voice revealing Himself and His love to us in His Word, we will not have a living faith. This vital response to God's love is the doorway to true faith and to a deeper faith. Until this reality sinks in and permeates our hearts, we will be hindered by many struggles and complexities in life. We must rest in His faithfulness and not our own commitment!

Walking in a self-dependent spirit can leave us worried, fractured, unsure, and feeling wretched. Where do we find the rest we so desperately need? In the wonderful conclusion offered by Paul, "There is therefore now no condemnation to those who are in Christ Jesus" (Romans 8:1). He knew that the only way to defeat the law of sin working in our flesh was to receive the power of God by faith to walk in the Spirit who gives us spiritual sight through the Word.

Searching for God's truth in our life requires us to live by "every word that proceeds from the mouth of God" (Matthew 4:4). Jesus promises that "if you abide in Me, and My words abide in you, you will ask what you desire, and it shall be done for you. As the Father loved Me, I also have loved you; abide in My love" (John 15:7, 9). Through the Word, we learn to abide in Christ's love and we find our rest and our peace. And we are liberated to worship Him with contentment and assurance. To be content in Him requires our *willingness* to believe Christ's promise that we "are already clean because of the word which I have spoken to you" (John 15:3).

Referencing again the powerful example of Mary and Martha, we realize that Martha was agitated by elements for which she alone was responsible. In other words, *Martha was agitating herself.* You and I are just as adept as she in denying contentment and willfully making our spiritual lives complex and busy. *Spiritual sight requires our attentive repose in God.* There is freedom and rest for all who choose to seek God alone, receiving His Word into our hearts and enjoying the eternal blessings of abandonment to God—now.

Chapter 6

# CHRISTLIKE CHARACTER—NOT SINFUL LIVING

YOU SIN AND I sin. Sin is the primary condition of humanity's fallen nature and *nothing* blinds us and separates us from the Lord as effectively as our sin. The most earnest heart, seeking communion with God, is also desperately human and, therefore, prone to sin. Even as born-again believers in a progression toward God, this inborn tendency to "forget" God through transgression will keep us fluctuating between moments of true ecstatic faith and the pull of our eyes to focus us on the world and its lies. Because of the power of sin to blind us to spiritual reality, when we do sin we are often blind to the fact of our sin.

For that reason, we are truly dependent on the working of the Holy Spirit to bring conviction to our hearts, showing us the true nature of our sin through the Word of God. Only as we choose to recognize and confess our sin can we have our spiritual eyes opened, so that through repentance of our sin we can be cleansed and set free. It is important, as Christians, that we learn to be vigilant against the blinding power of sin by asking some pertinent questions. What are the areas of sin that keep us in darkness? As

Christians, what can we change that will allow us to move forward into a vibrant faith with spiritual sight toward true Christ-like character?

While it is not our intent to categorize sin and would be impossible to list all sin as the Scriptures teach, it may be helpful to consider the following basic sinful motivations that are common to all of humanity, together with the antidote that will make us free from them. As we have stated, sin is the most powerful force that separates us from God. It is also a powerfully divisive force to separate us from each other. As we discuss this terrible aspect of sin, we will consider the following characteristics of its work and the wonderful antidotes that will set us free.

| DIVISIVENESS | UNITY |
|---|---|
| Divisive accuser | One in Christ |
| Bitterness | Forgiving |
| Jealousy | Surrender |
| Colleague Cain | Colleague Abel |

Many of us, even as we progress toward full faith, may discover that we have been embittered through life situations in our dealings with other people. And, closely related to the sin of bitterness, lurks the sin of jealousy that causes us to feel that we deserve more and to desire what others have. The ups and downs of relationships can create stormy emotions, which are most often expressed through divisive accusation of others. We must recognize all of these motivations as sin.

Jesus clearly expressed His desire for His disciples and all who would believe on His name in His high priestly prayer: "And the glory which You gave Me I have given them, that they may be one just as We are one" (John 17:22). In order for us to experience that kind of unity in Christ, we have to be willing to forgive others completely, out of love for God. We cannot harbor bitter resentment or jealous feelings toward others if we are going to live in full faith in Christ.

The tendency to divorce ourselves from other people and to divide people from each other through our backbiting, accusing tongues is not an expression of a mature, living faith. When Jesus prayed to the Father for us, it was out of His concern for us to experience a profound unity and fellowship in mutual love. The mature Christian, walking consistently in a living faith, knows that "truly our fellowship is with the Father and with His Son Jesus Christ" (1 John 1:3). The Scriptures are also very clear, that "If we walk in the light as He is in the light, we have fellowship with one another, and the blood of Jesus Christ His Son cleanses us from all sin" (1 John 1: 7).

## SIN IN THE CHURCH

Jealousy is observed between church congregations and organizations, as well as among individuals. For example, when success is measured by the size of a congregation, there is a desire to grow faster, and build more effectively, than other churches, fostering an unhealthy competition with other gatherings of the Christian body. These jealousies that divide us from one another are sin against God.

To progress directly along the continuum toward full faith, we cannot give in to the desire to exceed others, or other groups, but must instead seek for unity, fellowship, and a sense of community that has its origins and focus based solely on our life in God. Left to ourselves and our own methods, even in a Christian environment, we will not find such a unity of fellowship.

The Scriptures teach that we are the family of God, brothers and sisters in Christ who should esteem others greater than ourselves (Philippians 2:3) and learn to bear one another's burdens to fulfill the law of Christ (Galatians 6:2). An early biblical account of two brothers, Cain and Abel, is significant to us inasmuch as it demonstrates what we can recognize as a relationship between colleagues. We mentioned in chapter one that Abel chose to bring an offering to God that pleased Him, while Cain did not. God's acceptance of Abel's offering made Cain jealous. His jealousy boiled into hatred, resulting in the murder of his brother, Abel.

These two colleagues were ultimately divided by the sin of envy. *All divisiveness is the product of one of two things: envy or the pathological desire for power.* These sins are the opposite of charity, and they are especially evil since their goal is to cause harm to another person. Unity with one another is accomplished by eradicating these two vile tendencies and replacing them with love.

## MORE THAN MINIMUM REQUIREMENTS

We must be willing, both as individuals and collectively, to surrender ourselves and our pride to God. In that place of humble submission, we will find Him—and each other. That wonderful place of fellowship with God and other believers, however, requires that we do more than just meet "minimum requirements." Where do you find yourself in the continuum below?

| MINIMUM REQUIREMENTS | SUBMISSION TO CHRIST |
| --- | --- |
| Observing basic civilities | Receiving divine grace |
| Motivated by guilt | Basking in Jesus |
| Bound by fear | Enjoying freedom |

When we begin our walk with the Lord, we genuinely wish to be godly and to avoid sin. This righteous desire puts us in a frame of mind of wanting to keep all of God's ways. Unfortunately, it is not long before many young Christians default to keeping up the "minimum requirements." That is, we learn to *work at* righteousness. "For we know that the law is spiritual, but I am carnal, sold under sin" (Romans 7:14). We are motivated to action by our feelings of *guilt* more than by our love and faith in God. (See Romans 7:15–24.) When we hide in this manner, it is difficult for us to look up and perceive the absolute beauty of His personal grace.

However, complete submission to God allows for very different attitudes to take root in our hearts. We must genuinely learn to live in the Spirit, as "sons of God," as the Scriptures declare: "For you did not receive the spirit of bondage again to fear, but you received the Spirit of adoption by whom we cry out, 'Abba, Father'" (Romans 8:14–15). As we mature in our faith and progress toward a fuller expression of it, we will grow to desire communion with God more than we desire our sin. Our new freedom creates more hunger for God and counteracts the desire to sin.

When you begin to see life with spiritual eyes, you can truly say that your greatest desire is to love God with all your heart, soul, mind, and strength. Not only are you freed from the bondage of sin and death, you are also freed from the accompanying fear and guilt that prevents you from a more blessed experience of God. Then, "The Spirit Himself bears witness with our spirit that we are children of God" (Romans 8:16).

## RATIONALIZING OUR SIN

Could any position be more desirable than what we have just described? What keeps us from enjoying our spiritual sight in the area of our sin? Consider the following possibilities.

| NOETIC EFFECT OF SIN/ RATIONALIZED SIN | FORGIVENESS |
|---|---|
| Suppression of our sin | Total forgiveness |
| Indulging in sinful nature | Freedom from effect of sin |
| Satan has a corner of life | No corner kept from God |

As creatures who regularly fail, our nature is sinful, and we are in a continual struggle for the integrity of our soul. We look to God for strength in the face of temptation and for forgiveness from our sin. A heart seeking to *live* in God ascends along a narrow and difficult path by foregoing the world with its traps and vices. As we have discussed, this transformation happens by degrees.

However, if we give in to a "rationalizing" faith, we may find ourselves hanging on to sin and losing our progression in one, true direction toward our God. If we rationalize sin in any area of our life, we are trying to "manage" it rather than surrender it to God. For example, we may be capable of recognizing our own sinful nature, as well as admitting that it is hateful to God, while continuing to preserve a proud attitude, hardened to the reality that "the body is dead because of sin" (Romans 8:10). As long as we fail to abandon ourselves completely to God, maintaining some part of ourselves separated from God and free to indulge as we desire, we will remain spiritually blind.

I once knew a beautiful, talented girl from a Christian home. This young lady radiated her inner beauty through her smile. As she began to see more of life and allowed ever larger areas of her soul to serve Satan and the pitfalls of a carnal life, her face changed. Her glow was tarnished, her demeanor was hardened, and her beauty faded. The noetic effect of sin—that intellectual struggle that had contributed to her spiritual demise—literally fleshed itself out in her countenance and body language. In an effort to allow sin its influence while trying to suppress its significance, this girl lost herself and changed into someone else entirely.

Happily, sometime later, in wrenching remorse, this same girl sought the Lord's love and complete forgiveness. In returning wholly to the Lord, she opened all areas of her life to God's light, swept Satan and his shadows out of each corner, and ultimately found the release and relief of God's forgiveness. All of us are given the chance for this same kind of transformation, which occurs through receiving God's forgiveness of our sins in thought and action—totally.

Chapter 7

# GODLY INTIMACY—
# NOT SHALLOW IMMATURITY

THE ONLY WAY to a true faith is through total abandonment to
God, as we have mentioned, which leads us to a *mature faith*.
God does not offer us only a "piece" of Himself or heaven; He offers
us everything. As believers, on the other hand, we are frequently
diverted by life's tasks and temptations and too often offer God less
than our all. Though we may convince ourselves that we "see the
light," our spiritual sight can only become a reality when God is
the sole object of our gaze. In the light of that vision, we will learn
to walk in divine destiny, growing into a mature, intimate relationship and fulfilling the wonderful purposes of God for our lives.

I believe it is possible to practice faith faithlessly. If our search
for God is casual, we can enter into a mere portion of what God
would desire for us in a complete relationship with Him. We may
look for the invisible God with a professed belief in His existence
(as those who practice deism) and still not find His majesty in all
that surrounds us and in all that we are.

For example, when you awaken every morning and, most likely,
look into a mirror, what do you see? Do you observe rumpled

hair and sleepy eyes? Or are you aware of the intricate functioning of your eyes, of your nervous system, or of your heart faithfully beating? Beyond your mental acceptance of God as Creator, do you acknowledge Him gratefully in your construction? Do you observe Him in others around you?

While it is true that a born-again believer has entered into a personal relationship with God and has been reconciled to Him, living in peace under the umbrella of God's sovereignty, this is only a beginning of our journey to know God. We must go beyond that "baby" relationship, into a mature relationship of commitment to the will of God in every area of our lives. We must leave the intellectual acceptance of the truth of God's Word and surrender to its precepts to experience transformation in our thinking. There are those who experience a "theological" peace as they turn to God's Word for nourishment and enlightenment, but their lives do not change significantly.

## PROGRESSING FROM SUPERFICIALITY TO *SHALOM*

The apostle Paul instructs believers: "And do not be conformed to this world, but be transformed by the renewing of your mind, that you may prove what is that good and acceptable and perfect will of God" (Romans 12:2). The Word of God has the power to change attitudes and actions as we surrender to its truth. In that way we will gain spiritual sight and enter into a deeper walk with God, as the following chart indicates.

| SHALLOW IN SPIRIT | DEEP IN SPIRIT |
| --- | --- |
| Deism | God's immanence |
| Mentally "fed" by the Word | Transformed by Word; develop mind of Christ |
| At peace with sovereignty | Personal relationship with our *Shalom* |

In the fullness of a living faith, we seek to go beyond a mental grasp of the Word and receive the mind of Jesus. According to the Scriptures, this is a divine work of grace: "Grace and peace be multiplied to you in the knowledge of God and of Jesus our Lord" (2 Peter 1:2). As we begin our journey into faith, we need to discern and acknowledge that we are sinful and lost without God, and then humbly pray for the Holy Spirit to direct us to Him. As we continue our journey into a living faith, we meet God in a richer, more meaningful way, and we experience a peace that surpasses our initial experience and knowledge of God. We can grow into a mature experience of the spiritual abundance of *shalom*. In the peace of *shalom* we find what Peter describes: "perfect well-being, all necessary good, all spiritual prosperity, and freedom from fears and agitating passions and moral conflicts" (2 Peter 1:2, AMP). It is in the peace of shalom, in nearness to the heart and mind of God, that we live a mature faith.

## PROGRESSING FROM CASUAL PRAYER TO COMMUNION

One characteristic of a mature faith, represented by the chart below, will be learning to enjoy a life of communion with God.

| CASUAL PRAYER | CRYING OUT |
|---|---|
| Intermittent prayer and praise | Continual prayer and praise |

God wants us to *commune* with Him—prayer is the *privilege* granted to every believer. The new Christian often experiences a yearning to talk with the Lord. However, a life full of worldly considerations can dilute that first passion and vigor of prayer. Prayer *can* become as lifeless an activity as brushing teeth. Many who understand the need to communicate with our Creator confess that their actual prayer life declines to an occasional habit and perhaps is even hollow. It is clear that such a habit of prayer is not complete communication.

What is real communication with the Lord? According to the apostle Paul, we should "Rejoice always, pray without ceasing, in everything give thanks; for this is the will of God in Christ Jesus for you" (1 Thessalonians 5:16–18). A faith that is matured to become fully centered in Christ demonstrates the irrepressible need to cry out to God passionately and continuously. And in that depth of relationship, we desire as well to praise Him without reservation. Consider the contrasting positions of the following chart to determine your progress toward a mature faith in God.

| ACQUAINTANCE | INTIMACY |
|---|---|
| Interest in God | Godly compulsion |
| Somewhat occupied with God | Godly obsession |
| Recognize Creator | Creator-Savior has total value |
| Creation has value | Worship Creator, not creation |

## PROGRESSING TOWARD TOTAL SURRENDER

The true believer desires to progress toward God, seeking to know Him more deeply, wishing to move from a mere acquaintance with Him to an intimacy with Him. However, due to the nature of our spiritual blindness, in the midst of our busy lives, it is often much too easy to be content with experiencing God at a superficial, incomplete level.

Certainly, we experience some interest in God and marvel at God's handiwork in the natural world. We may revel in the scientific understanding of the beautiful miracle of life. We may wonder who this Creator is, and even willingly become occupied with His service. We learn of Him in the Word—through the voice of the Holy Spirit. Still, if we seek intimacy with God, we must learn to yield to Him, surrendering ourselves totally. Only in that way does the Creator gain the true value He deserves in our hearts. As the psalmist exclaimed, "The LORD made the heavens. Honor and majesty are before Him; Strength and beauty are in His sanctuary." So, "Give to the LORD the glory due His name"

(Psalm 96:5–6, 8). While we acknowledge God in His creation, God asks that the Creator, not the creation, be of supreme value in our hearts. He is the reference point, the All in All.

While our participation in a community of believers is important, and the church schedule may be part of our practical Christian walk, it is not as vital to our living faith as being obsessed and thoroughly caught up with God. Often, we turn to the Lord only when it is convenient, when we get the impulse, when the conscience pricks us, or when we are stumped by a life situation. However, as we cultivate a living, complete faith, we find ourselves turning to Him because He is God, Creator of all, and we desire to worship Him alone. Where are you in your journey toward total surrender and a complete faith in God? Perhaps the following chart will help to locate you along that continuum.

| JESUS PART OF LIFE | JESUS ALL OF LIFE |
| --- | --- |
| About the Lord Jesus | In the Lord Jesus |
| Jesus has a compartment | Jesus in all of life |
| Faith in self and God | Faith only in God |

When you finally learn to surrender totally to God, Jesus assumes His rightful place in your life. You will see Him in your own experience and in *everything* else: in all of creation and time. The Scriptures are clear that this is the rightful place for our Savior in our lives: "Therefore God also has highly exalted Him and given Him the name which is above every name, that at the name of Jesus every knee should bow, of those in heaven, and of those on earth, and of those under the earth" (Philippians 2:9–10).

You and I need to yearn to give Jesus our whole hearts, not just a compartment or a section of our lives. We find ourselves, when we truly live our faith, brimming over with praise and thanksgiving for the Lord of all. We wish to be fully in the Lord Jesus and experience the power of His love. Jesus is our Protector and

Captain. Jesus is not part of life; Jesus is life. For that reason, the apostle Paul declared, "For to me, to live is Christ, and to die is gain" (Philippians 1:21).

Until we see Christ as foundation, focus, center, and boundary of all of life, our faith wrongly includes our "self" alongside Him. That condition must be recognized as a divided faith. When we practice a divided faith, it falls short of the mystery and majesty of an authentically godly, mature faith. A divided faith reveals a degree of spiritual blindness, and with this lack of vision, we are cut off from the ecstasy, joy, and peace that God offers to those who make Him the center of life.

## Chapter 8

# INSIGHTFUL GRATITUDE—
# NOT BLINDNESS OF
# INGRATITUDE

I N PROPERLY ACKNOWLEDGING the Creator, it is important to understand that you have been preplanned and designed. God meticulously created everything: life, the earth, and the farthest stars. And He planned your life before any of it existed. Every aspect of the beautiful life the Creator has given you—the ability to flourish, your physical preservation, your joy, and the fulfillment of His purpose for you—has been written in the capacity and the code of your marvelous DNA molecules.[1]

That DNA is a vast repository of three billion individual bits of information. Though you have 99 percent in common with every other human being, you also possess your own unique version of humanity. The personal aspect of this reality is overwhelming. God has an anointed purpose for your life, and He articulated the means for its realization within the microscopic DNA "library" found within every single one of the sixty trillion cells that comprise your body.

Why do we so often refuse to acknowledge and appreciate this "miracle?" Ravi Zacharias states that genuine, heartfelt gratitude is the main, and first, component of wonder. How can we live in the blindness of ingratitude and be content with hearts and minds empty of wonder?

## OVERCOMING INGRATITUDE

My life story can be summarized in four words: "I'm not appreciative enough." I have not appreciated my parents enough, my neighbor enough, or my Lord enough. And that lack of appreciation for our great God, the Creator of all, may be one of humankind's worst sins. In that lack of appreciation we discover the root of spiritual blindness.

We always want more than we have. A golfer will look back at the hole he just played and say, "If only I had used a different club..." You and I are always saying, "If only I had this, or, if only I could do that" rather than appreciating God for His provision of life to us.

*Our degree of spiritual sight hinges on the honesty and sincerity with which we appreciate our Lord.* Many people do not appreciate the Lord and His gifts because they are content with the attractions of superficial observations and desires, and they are selfish and proud. It all comes down to answering this question: How can we remain indifferent to the marvelous design of our bodies and the Creator's eternal plans written within them? Having a joyful, thankful spirit is the manner by which we move from a superficial faith to a living faith that authentically has God at its center. Consider the following characteristics to determine your progress toward spiritual sight.

| UNAPPRECIATIVE | APPRECIATIVE |
|---|---|
| Inattentive | Attentive |
| "Use" Jesus | Married to Jesus |
| Thoughtless of others | Thinking of others |
| Slow spiritual growth | Ever-increasing gratitude |
| Apathetic search | Passionate search |

The spiritually conscious person desires to know the Creator. In a godly life of faith, the Creator is acknowledged, adored, and worshiped in gratitude. The honest appreciation of God's creation of humanity, of His blessings in our lives, of the thrill of daily communion with Him, of His love and grace and forgiveness, of the presence of each other, is not a dispassionate exercise of recognition for the godly. Rather, it is a heated, consuming passion. We are His—He the heavenly Bridegroom and we the bride of Christ.

In our spiritual blindness, instead of being married to Jesus, He simply remains a name that identifies us with a religious group. We may remain attentive to details of church and social life while we simmer in self-absorption and ignore our fellow travelers and their needs.

## THE VIRTUE OF GIVING TO OTHERS

We do not naturally, in humble gratitude, see God's hand in our lives, and in our world. And we do not consider others in a thoughtful way, desiring to help. The Scripture clearly teaches that we are to "Bear one another's burdens, and so fulfill the law of Christ" (Galatians 6:2). In the joyful service of others, we can express our voice of appreciation of God.

Carl Jung was once asked what he would do if he felt himself headed for a breakdown. Jung responded that the route to his own well-being would be found in a selfless giving to others. That principle is true for all of us. In our love for, and attentiveness to, our brother and sister, we will find our well-being. Our inattentiveness to, or our refusal to celebrate, God's abundance leaves us blind to His beauty. Cultivating a spirit of gratitude makes it possible for us to move directly toward His presence.

There are so many ways we can cultivate gratitude. For example, contemplate your nervous system, its function, and its integration into the body. Man cannot create *even one* cell to replace the functions of those God created. Perhaps you cannot fully understand the body's cells in order to appreciate them. Then, look to creation for a source of appreciation. The stars above and the autumn leaves speak of His mastery just as clearly.

Until we have reached the point in our journey toward full faith at which we can relinquish our human pride in our attempt to understand and master life, we cannot achieve a pure appreciation for God's mastery and beauty. It is in a spirit of humble appreciation that one *lives* faith and meets God fully. The Lord is our Creator, Provider, Deliverer, Savior, and Friend. The only true way to be close to Him is to love Him and *appreciate* Him. It is there that we can begin to see.

## HERE, O MY LORD, I SEE THEE FACE TO FACE

Here, O my Lord, I see Thee face to face,
Here would I touch and handle things unseen;
Here grasp with firmer hand eternal grace,
And all my weariness upon Thee lean.[2]
—HORATIUS BONAR AND EDWARD DEARLE

# PART II:

# UNDERSTANDING THE NATURE OF SPIRITUAL BLINDNESS

I F YOU CAN read the words on this page, you intuitively understand the principles of light and darkness. Most simply, light allows the possibility of vision, and darkness provides the conditions for blindness. Who has not had a memorable lesson in that distinction by stumbling into a dark room and whacking one's shin? In the articulation of darkness and light lie the defining principles of photography, astronomy, and Michelangelo's masterpieces.

The line between light and dark defines the limits of our world. Look into space: the deep is spattered with dots of light, and all around them and our planet—90 percent of the universe—is the mysterious "dark matter" that escapes our detection in any way other than by its massive gravitational pull.[1] Darkness and light are real, and they are metaphorical. They reach far into all aspects of our life as symbols of our divided nature. It is insightful to remember the Master's words in this regard.

> The lamp of the body is the eye. If therefore your eye is
> good, your whole body will be full of light.
>
> —MATTHEW 6:22

Many of us may think that my friend Solomon, without functioning physical eyes, lives in darkness. Yet, it is obvious that he clearly sees "light." Others of us, blessed with perfectly good physical eyes, live in authentic darkness and yearn for such clarity of spiritual vision as Solomon's. At the very least, we sense its absence. Consider for a moment how the two realms—two modes—of existence really may be conceived.

| DARKNESS | LIGHT |
|----------|-------|
| Death | Life |
| Night | Day |
| Bad | Good |
| Winter | Spring |
| Captivity | Freedom |
| Obscurity | Clarity |
| Sin | Sanctity |

As a metaphor, what does darkness mean to us? Darkness is a curtain, a mantle that cloaks and obscures. It is deep, frequently impenetrable, and apparently solid. In contrast, light is flowing and fluid. It pours into a room or floods a space. It shows itself as pools or beams. It *bathes* us. And light has a *source*. Darkness represents void or lack; light reflects the presence, the existence, of something, as the Scriptures themselves describe.

> The earth was without form, and void; and darkness was
> on the face of the deep. And the Spirit of God was hovering over the face of the waters. Then God said, "Let there
> be light"; and there was light.
>
> —GENESIS 1:2–3

Light, generated by the Spirit of God, initially filled an existential emptiness. The emergence of the light of God at the beginning of time also represents the creation of reason and spiritual sight in man's soul at the time of creation. However, since sin entered into the human race through the disobedience of Adam, as fallen creatures we now need the restoration of spiritual sight. As believers, we become the children of God with true spiritual sight. And we can fulfill the purpose of our creation as instruments of God. Each believer is granted a measure of light to add to the sum of light in the performance of God's grand design and purpose for creation.

## WHAT IS DARKNESS?
## WHAT IS LIGHT?

If we are honest with ourselves, we are frequently aware that our spiritual understanding is dim and hazy. This darkness, which is the natural realm of our minds and senses, is the element of spiritual blindness. It is a state that may make us feel that we are alone and destitute. It is the embodiment of all our negative feelings and desires. And, though we may have glimpses of vision of His peace and perfection, we are prone to again and again sink in the depths of doubt, even while the splendor of God's reality is all around us. This is part of our journey, our existence, our meaning, as human beings on God's earth.

In the beginning, darkness was all there was. God's act in creation was to pierce this vacuum with sun, moon, and stars: light. Into man, He breathed the breath of life and a longing for the Creator. Though humanity is now forever divided between light and darkness, between principalities of good and evil, mankind was brought into existence in wisdom and light.

> He gives wisdom to the wise
> And knowledge to those who
>     have understanding.
> He reveals deep and
>     secret things;

He knows what is in the
darkness,
And light dwells with Him.

—DANIEL 2:21–22

Darkness exists at the level of our own understanding; light exists beyond our ability to describe and most frequently escapes our comprehension. Light cuts through darkness to reveal truth. Jesus told us, "I am the light of the world. Whoever follows me will never walk in darkness, but will have the light of life" (John 8:12, NIV). We begin to really see when we acknowledge Him as the Son of God, our Savior. As humans, we prefer the darkness, the *blindness*; we choose that which separates ourselves from Him. In that darkness, our base and fallen nature is expressed; in light our soul finds flight from all that is sinful.

The Bible provides us with many examples of spiritual darkness. In judgment, God poured out a thick darkness on Egypt's Pharaoh that could literally be seen and felt. (See Exodus 9.) Even more terrible was the darkness poured out on Christ the day of His crucifixion, under an ominous and unnaturally blackened sky. As He endured the penalty that all mankind's sins deserve, He cried in pain and desolation from His cross, "'My God, My God, why have You forsaken Me?'" (Matthew 27:46).

While Christ lay in the silence of His tomb those awful days, the disciples' hearts bled in the emotional darkness of grief and fear and self-recrimination. However, the Scriptures assure us that "Weeping may endure for a night, But joy comes in the morning" (Psalm 30:5). And so it did on the third day when Jesus was resurrected; He illuminated the aching hearts of His friends. All of Scripture confirms that Christ's light is our fortitude. Even the Old Testament psalmist experienced this spiritual reality: "The LORD is my light and my salvation; Whom shall I fear? The LORD is the strength of my life; Of whom shall I be afraid?" (Psalm 27:1).

Darkness is often used as a figure of despair: "When I sit in darkness, The LORD will be a light to me...He will bring me forth to the light; I will see His righteousness" (Micah 7:8–9). The prophet here takes heart from the promise that God will break through his darkness as the only source of light.

Darkness is also a metaphor for our spiritual ignorance of the God of the Bible. Darkness describes our blindness to the redemption that is in Christ. (See Romans 3:24.) The true person of faith trusts in God, even in dark providences, rather than trying to "create" his own light.

> Who among you fears the Lord? Who obeys the voice of His Servant? Who walks in darkness and has no light? Let him trust in the name of the Lord and rely upon his God.
> —ISAIAH 50:10

Spiritual darkness is evil; it is alienation from true, abundant life in God. We experience its manifestation in powerful negative emotions and states of heart and mind. Those who are in spiritual darkness are motivated primarily by anger, resentment, guilt, and despair. In that state, we are bound toward self-destruction and defilement of ourselves and others. We may become filled with a bitter, unforgiving spirit of revenge, with attempts to control and dominate others, with jealousy and lust—all obstructions to our vision of Him.

Spiritual darkness also manifests as ingratitude: "although they knew God, they did not glorify Him as God, nor were thankful, but became futile in their thoughts, and their foolish hearts were darkened" (Romans 1:21). As fallen creatures, we routinely forget to worship God for His intelligent design of ourselves and the universe. The only way to dispel this darkness is to see the light of God by appreciating Him.

How do we experience the division of light and darkness within us? We see it most graphically as a contrast between love and hatred, harmony and conflict, acceptance and ridicule, peace and fear. The victory of light is the victory of God over evil, of the spirit over the body and mind, of understanding and wisdom over confusion and ignorance.

## Chapter 9

# DIVIDED SOUL: DARKNESS VS. LIGHT

HUMANS ARE CREATURES of both the light and the darkness; we are divided souls. The heart of man may seek the truth of the eternal God only to slip back into the shadows of darkness. Christ spoke of this destructive human plight: "And this is the condemnation, that the light has come into the world, and men loved darkness rather than light, because their deeds were evil" (John 3:19). As we have discussed, darkness describes our separation from God. It is tragic to our human nature that we choose this separation over the light of joy in His presence. God has created us with the wings, and the burden, of human choice. God's plan is that we would choose light, live in sanctity, praise Him, and participate in His world of love.

At creation, freedom was God's gift to us. Liberty was the path God planned for us. Unfortunately, because Adam chose disobedience to that freedom that resulted in all of mankind's bondage, we invariably choose bondage over freedom. Through God's great gift of salvation, He has made it possible again to find freedom in Christ: "And you shall know the truth, and the truth shall make you free... Therefore if the Son makes you free, you shall be free indeed" (John 8:32, 36). Only in God's light will the way be clear for us to see light, according to the Scriptures.

> For with You is the fountain of life; In Your light we see light.
>
> —Psalm 36:9

> The path of the righteous is like the first gleam of dawn, shining ever brighter till the full light of day. But the way of the wicked is like deep darkness; they do not know what makes them stumble.
>
> —Proverbs 4:18–19, NIV

Your choice to rest in the light brings death of your old self—a relinquishing of trust in your abilities to navigate in the darkness. We have discussed the fact that God is not apprehended by your intellect. Only in your willingness to submit to the Lordship of Christ, and to love, can you see Him. You may think that humanity was cast into darkness forever when Adam sinned against God and was cast out of the garden, but God revealed His grace and love to this fallen race and offered the opportunity to live eternally in His light.

Jesus often spoke about life and death, light and darkness. He claimed to *be* the Light, the ultimate revelation from God. Yet He was refused, reviled, and executed, even as He sacrificed Himself for His tormentors, murderers, and for you. Even on the cross, Jesus' concern for, and suffering in the place of others, gave proof of God's great divine love and grace. In Jesus' hour of trial, when even the light of the sun seemed to have been snuffed out, the disciples likewise struggled in the blackness of spiritual torment. However, it was out of that terrible darkness, as they came to realize the purpose of the cross, that their spiritual eyes would open, and God's eternal plan become clear to them.

As with anything worthwhile, trust and complete faith do not simply "happen," nor spontaneously fall down around our heads. In order for us to come to the light, God must draw near and speak His powerful Word to us. And we must respond in desire and hunger to see His face, and begin our journey with a living faith.

For example, if you decide to put time and effort into physical fitness, you will enjoy the benefits of a healthier body. If you do the same in business, you may be rewarded with material success. And when you put your trust in God, responding to His light and love, you find the tranquility of a heart that has finally found its resting place in His bosom for eternity.

Those walking in darkness attempt to protect themselves from exposure to the light. (See John 3:20.) But that choice is not without consequence, according to the prophet: "Woe to those who call evil good, and good evil; Who put darkness for light, and light for darkness" (Isaiah 5:20). Light brings us consciousness of God; the darkness prevents us from seeing His positive presence. The darkness of choosing evil over the joy of loving God is a deception and a delusion.

## HOW DOES DARKNESS BECOME LIGHT?

God has not left us to ourselves in our darkness. Rather, He shines His light upon us by the power of His Word. When we turn to God in prayer with a longing in our hearts and ask to be healed and forgiven, the light of God's Word, the light of faith, and, behind it all, the light of God's Spirit, dispel the darkness. We surrender our souls to be flooded with His light, to see clearly, and the darkness melts before Jesus' saving beams of grace.

The darkness of the world, of mortal existence, will leave us isolated and lonely. Somehow, we must become aware of, and be willing to accept, God's light, choosing to trust in the Lord and surrendering ourselves to Him completely. We must see that God's love is deeper and wider than any other, impossible for us to completely fathom. We may imagine ourselves resting in His arms as a trusting child rests in the strong arms of his father.

Next, we need to see that God knows exactly what we are feeling—and cares. He has not abandoned us, and He never will. We must be willing to see that God has the authority and power to do anything, to provide anything. No one else has that power.

God is in control. Learn to see Him in every area of your life: "In all your ways acknowledge Him, And He shall direct your paths" (Proverbs 3:6). He has provided you with life, with a miraculous body, and with a soul that will never find contentment until it chooses Him. He provides food, shelter, and companions. You are secure in God because His love in Christ comes from His free grace—it does not depend upon your actions.

God always provides just what we need, what is ultimately good for us, though we frequently do not see that. Wherever the road leads us, it is God's will that the destination is where we need to be—and this should give us the deepest sense of trust and security.

Jesus challenged the conventional morality when He invited anyone free of sin to cast the first stone at the adulteress. He was introducing life and light rather than condemnation and darkness. Yet, people did not hear Him, and He Himself was attacked as evil rather than good. A blind man was healed by Christ and simultaneously His spiritual sight was activated as his physical sight was restored. He saw Jesus as the Light of the world and worshiped Him. The Pharisees tried to interpret the meaning of Christ inside the restrictions of their darkened intellect and the canons of their religion, and they could not. (See John 9.)

Trust in God is of the heart and, as living faith, is largely beyond our ability to express or explain. Trust in God, which is spiritual sight, begins simply with our awareness of God but grows to pervade every corner of our senses, feeling, and intuition.

You know that most of us, frequently or not, try to find deep meaning in meaningless things. There is a mindlessness at that point that indicates an escape into darkness, an escape from God. In that case, faith, trust, and sight are not in operation in our spirits. As the heart of man surrenders, the light of hope comes to him in the gospel. To open our eyes and hearts is to believe and embrace the Son of God, who is the Light of the world (John 8:12). The Spirit of God powerfully brings the Word of God into our hearts to illumine us and work faith in us.

To the surprise of the brokenhearted sinner, the mercy of Jesus banishes the sadness, despair, and terror he or she has become accustomed to in the darkness of their blindness. Then the path of righteousness and love is found by walking in the Spirit through the quickening power of the Word.

> Your word is a lamp to my feet
> And a light to my path.
>
> —PSALM 119:105

As we walk closer to God, we learn to "Walk as children of light (for the fruit of the Spirit is in all goodness, righteousness, and truth)" (Ephesians 5:8–9). The light of God's countenance is lifted up upon us. (See Numbers 6:24–27.) With this spiritual light we may finally see our own sin, our dependence on the blood of Christ for salvation for eternity, and the life-giving power of His lovingkindness, which is better than life itself (Psalm 63:3).

## Cataracts of My Heart

I'm beginning to understand that I waver in faith,
Because my spiritual vision is in need of correction.
I miss the mark so often because I fail to see,
With the same perspective, O Heavenly Father, as You.

So I repent of both near- and farsightedness today.
There are "cataracts" on the eyes of my heart.
With the skill of a masterful Surgeon, O Lord,
Would You remove them and take them away?

—SUSAN G. MCINTOSH

Chapter 10

# SPIRITUAL CATARACTS OBSTRUCTING SIGHT

W E HAVE ESTABLISHED the truth that faith—a vibrant, living faith—is our spiritual sight. However, each of us, along the path of our personal pilgrimage, passes through the uneven landscape of shadow and light. As we have mentioned, on our journey to full faith, we alternately gravitate toward God's truth and then slip back into the concerns, diversions, pitfalls, and self-preoccupations of carnal man. The Scriptures describe our conflict: "For the flesh lusts against the Spirit, and the Spirit against the flesh; and these are contrary to one another" (Galatians 5:17).

As Christians, we repeatedly experience a sense of distance from God at the center of our soul. Yet, He offers us forgiveness, peace, and rest. Our human nature is fallible and fallen, leading to the recurrent experience of distancing from God. So we must continue to battle against the darkness in our souls to continue to live in the light.

Though we have been born into this existential division, God's voice continually calls us to Himself, to faith, and to spiritual sight. He does this through His Word and the faithful working of the Holy Spirit: "So then faith comes by hearing, and hearing by the word of God" (Romans 10:17). When we attend to His voice and seek Him, light floods our souls and illuminates our paths as surely as the heavens shone when God first decreed, "Let there be light" (Genesis 1:3). God reveals Himself to us as Creator, Redeemer, and Ruler of all life.

When we see life as God does, we *really* see. We begin to see His wisdom, His goodness, and His purpose for the world. We begin to *appreciate* Him and His design, and we begin to trust Him—to *depend* upon Him. Then, we enter a true, heartfelt communion with the Lord Jesus—a person-to-Person relationship that progresses to a vital, impassioned faith. Outside of this enabling light of God, however, we are lost and blind. A great many things can obstruct our spiritual sight and block our vision to a beautiful walk with God.

These obstructions to spiritual sight can be compared to *cataracts*, which obstruct physical sight. A cataract, simply defined, is a clouded lens within the eye. I am an ophthalmologist, concerned with restoring the physical sight of my fellow humans. Cataracts progressively distort and diminish sight. *We all want to see!* It is my privilege as a physician to remove cataracts for those who suffer from them, restoring the precious gift of sight to them.

*Spiritual cataracts*, however, are not so easily removed as physical cataracts. They blind us to God's purpose, making the present dim and the future unclear. The Creator of all is the only Physician who can heal this obstruction to our spiritual sight. Spiritual cataracts are outgrowths of a sinful heart, reflected in our selfishness and self-destructiveness. They are symptoms of sin and divergence from God's will and plan for us.

The desire to be close to God and to worship the Creator is part of every believer's birthright in the Spirit. However, the Scriptures warn that "some have strayed from the faith in their greediness, and pierced themselves through with many sorrows. But you, O man of God, flee these things and pursue righteousness, godliness, faith, love, patience, gentleness" (1 Timothy 6:10–11). The apostle Paul admonishes the young man, Timothy, to pursue the fruit of the Spirit. And to the Corinthians, he declares that the greatest fruit is love: love for God, and love for one's fellow man. (See 1 Corinthians 13:13.) It is when we choose to live a life that lacks love that our eyes are veiled by spiritual cataracts. It is then that we drift from our Lord and from His purposes.

Obstacles to spiritual sight are perhaps numberless, some afflicting certain people and not others. They are individually conditioned by material and temporal forces, often inherited from our family or gathered from experiences, society, and the responses of our own complex personalities. Some of your obstacles to spiritual sight will not be mine, and some of mine will not be yours.

However, several inescapably large areas of life taunt and torment humanity as a whole. For example, there is the spiritual blindness in relationships caused by the cataract of hatred, the blindness in our use of money caused by greed, the blindness of pride that refuses to acknowledge our own faults, and the blindness of prayerlessness, which plagues many believers. These "spiritual" cataracts are particularly persistent self-deceptions. Without their healing by God's grace, we can never see Him. They block our spiritual sight and prevent us from progressing to the full life of faith that God wants us to enjoy. A closer look at these and other spiritual cataracts will be helpful to diagnose our condition and prescribe a cure.

## CATARACT: PRIDE

"'Vanity of vanities,' says the Preacher; 'Vanity of vanities, all is vanity'" (Ecclesiastes 1:2). The word *vanity* means empty, meaningless. I believe that pride is the greatest form of vanity. It is not only considered as one of the seven deadly sins, but the deadliest. Pride is the obstruction from which all others derive.

It was pride that led Lucifer to attempt to usurp God's throne. Pride is our foolish attempt to promote ourselves before our inevitable fall. Pride is an elevated opinion of, and belief in, one's own abilities, merits, accomplishments, and possessions. Within this false belief, the proud seek to rise above other people, nature, and even God.

In reality, what do we have to be proud of in a life that is beyond our control? The sun continues to rise and set, the earth spins, all rivers run to the sea, and generations of people come and go, love and laugh, hurt and die. "I have seen all the works that are done under the sun; and indeed, all is vanity and grasping for the wind" (Ecclesiastes 1:14). No one can grasp the wind—the attempt to do so is empty, valueless, and meaningless. The truth is that our individual lives have true meaning only in relation to the Creator God and our Savior, Jesus Christ. Blindness, caused by pride, keeps us from understanding this basic, eternal truth.

With this particular cataract of pride blinding us, we may be led to boasting, smugness, self-righteousness, and devaluing of others. We demand independence from God and are disobedient and self-willed, trusting in our own imperfect wisdom and judgment. Under the prevailing ideas of our present age, we may even deny His very existence. This is exactly where the false theories of Darwinism lead. The arrogant may declare, "Who needs God? I have a Ferrari."

The sin of our belief in freedom *from* God will never allow us to reach the quiet rest and peace found in His arms. Just as surely, this pride prevents our experiencing fulfilling relationships with others. Through pride, we seek to be seen as superior to our brother, our friends, our spouse. Yet, authentically, pride is mindless human horseplay.

The ministrations of a prideful spirit may whisper to us that our possessions or qualities, objects that we own, or talents we possess, make *us* greater and different from our neighbor. When we receive spiritual sight, God reveals that our possessions are only "treasures on earth, where moth and rust destroy and where thieves break in and steal" (Matthew 6:19).

Our pride is rooted in selfishness at its core. By remaining centered upon ourselves—our activities, methods, thoughts— we do not heed the voice of the Spirit that would counsel, teach, and guide us. God is sovereign, however, and He longs for us to worship Him, and to partake of the abundant, incorruptible treasures of His kingdom.

It is only when we humble ourselves to seek the Lord's authority over us that we can rest in childlike dependence upon Him. Then His love for us and for all creation fills our soul. Then His offer of redemption becomes our experience and we become new creations through Christ Jesus.

Otherwise, this cataract—the sin of pride—leaves us deluded, distant from the Creator, divided from our neighbor, and disappointed and depressed when our measures of worth lose their currency in the minds of others. In pride there can be no rest, no communion, and no joy; only spiritual darkness. In God all of these are found as we rest in His light and peace.

## CATARACT: WRONG VIEW OF MONEY

I have already pointed to the unreal nature of the material things that moths eat, that lose their high-buffed shine, blow a gasket, go out of style, are cut, slashed, or crushed, or become lost. Money is both the provision of those amenities and, often, an end in itself. The problem of this obstacle to our sight lies not with the money, but in our misdirected love of it.

God's Word makes us aware that "we brought nothing into this world, and it is certain we can carry nothing out. And having food and clothing, with these we shall be content. But those who desire to be rich fall into temptation and a snare, and into many foolish and harmful lusts which drown men in destruction and perdition. For the love of money is a root of all kinds of evil" (1 Timothy 6:7–10).

Where is our sight found? "Now godliness with contentment is great gain" (1 Timothy 6:6). Food, clothing—all necessities—are the *natural sources* of our contentment. We may, in fact, possess more than mere necessities, but the vital truth is that our spiritual sufficiency is not derived from such things. With our eyes on heaven we may experience contentment and, through that, godliness. To focus on physical gain is idolatry and results in ceaseless disquiet.

Money and possessions are not intrinsically evil and, surely, God may bless our lives with prosperity. However, our lives are to be lived in proper stewardship, with money serving as a tool, or vehicle, to that end. When we lose sight of God and His vision for us, we allow our need to become greed, and appreciation becomes thankless expectation. Until we are living our faith daily, we are tempted to focus myopically on the tangible, temporary objects that we *believe* are necessary, rather than focusing on the Lord and eternity. We need to consider life in the light of the Scriptures, which ask the question, "What good will it be for a man if he gains the whole world, yet forfeits his soul?" (Matthew 16:26, NIV).

An ungodly preoccupation with the wealth of this world displaces God from His rightful, primary position in our hearts, minds, and souls. We are left with an insatiable vacuum that, according to God's Word, not only can *never* be filled but, rather, increases.

> He who loves silver will not be satisfied with silver;
> Nor he who loves abundance, with increase.
> This also is vanity.
> When goods increase,
> They increase who eat them;
> So what profit have the owners
> Except to see them with their eyes?
> The sleep of a laboring man is sweet,
> Whether he eats little or much;
> But the abundance of the rich will not permit him
> to sleep.
> —ECCLESIASTES 5:10–12

Desire begets desire. Refusal to be content with, and appreciative of, God's blessings in our material life, leaves us without the peace and rest that can only be found in God's sufficiency. This ungodly impulse was observed early in man's history as Adam and Eve's sons, Cain and Seth, each approached their lives very differently. Seth and his descendents lived simple lives, yet they appreciated each blessing from God. Cain and his people, on the other hand, always looked for gain, yet never found satisfaction in all that they had; they were ungrateful. If we allow ourselves to be blinded by the attraction of material riches, we are not free to see the genuine riches of the Spirit that God desires for us.

## CATARACTS: BITTERNESS AND
## AN UNFORGIVING SPIRIT

Our relationships with others are full of potential rapture and potential difficulty, of beauty and injury, equally. The human heart is a fragile instrument of love, too easily fractured and wasted by pain, bitterness, and hatred. The intensity of negative emotions clouds the heart, making them among the densest and most destructive cataracts that cause us to stumble in our Christian walk. The blindness of anger, associated with a refusal to forgive those who have caused us grief, has the power to separate us from God, now and forever. Without the light of a forgiving spirit, we lose sight of our Lord and forfeit our communion with Him. An unforgiving heart also may be evidence that one has never truly experienced *His* forgiveness. Jesus taught, "For if you forgive men their trespasses, your heavenly Father will also forgive you. But if you do not forgive men their trespasses, neither will your Father forgive your trespasses" (Matthew 6:14–15).

It may appear to be humanly impossible to forgive certain transgressions. The truth is that without our eyes focused clearly on the Lord and His will, it is. You have met, or will meet, such a test in life. In Christ, though, you can find the quiet, healing waters for your heart and mind that will free you to forgive. It is our imperative, as God's creation, to do so. Scripture commands it: "Let all bitterness, wrath, anger, clamor, and evil speaking be put away from you, with all malice. And be kind to one another, tenderhearted, forgiving one another, even as God in Christ forgave you" (Ephesians 4:31–32).

Total forgiveness of others, R. T. Kendall indicates, does not require that we blind ourselves to the transgressions of others, but it *does* require that we petition the Father to give us a spirit of graciousness and mercy in our hearts.[1] Joseph was sold into slavery by his own brothers, yet he was able to forgive them entirely, much to their shame. Only with a genuine absence of resentment can this be accomplished, and only in seeking to be like Christ can that absence of resentment be made real. Bitterness eats into the body and the mind, causing illness and unhappiness and, just as surely, blinding us to the leading of the Holy Spirit in our souls. Notwithstanding our desire to live in full faith in the Lord, we must realize that an angry, injured, bitter spirit is unable to rest in God and feel His presence.

"For you were once in darkness, but now you are light in the Lord. Walk as children of light" (Ephesians 5:8). Jesus told us that we must forgive a brother "up to seventy times seven" times (Matthew 18:22). In other words, children of light must continue to forgive without ceasing, and it can only be so with a pure heart liberated from the wrenching grip of bitterness and the desire to blame.

## CATARACT: WORK THAT EXCLUDES GOD

Membership in the community of humanity requires both our willingness to work and our earnest effort in labor. We must produce to survive and to ensure the survival of others. However, it is also true that our toil, occupation, or profession can be an impediment to true spiritual sight. As a wise man asked, "For what has man for all his labor, and for the striving of his heart with which he has toiled under the sun?" (Ecclesiastes 2:22). Work may more readily become a spiritual cataract by virtue of its necessity in a physical world. Without a focus on God, your job can, and does, become a worldly preoccupation that relegates your faith to superficial, secondary actions. Without a true reliance upon God to meet your needs you will be denied the joy of deeper faith.

Some may be consumed by a desire to out-perform and rise above others and to inspire the recognition and admiration of their own name. The meaning of work for many others may be the gain of more and more money. Perhaps work is also an obsession born of the fleeting attractiveness of conquest, challenge, and the accomplishment of difficult tasks. Some of us may, in fact, define our very being by our occupation: "I am a....What are you?" Most frequently, though, the apparent necessity of work leads people into a self-legitimizing busy-ness that detracts from the quantity and quality of time left for God, within the confines of a finite day or week.

Yet the Word of God teaches, "Always give yourselves fully to the work of the Lord, because you know that your labor in the Lord is not in vain" (1 Corinthians 15:58, NIV). The Scriptures also promise: "And whatever you do, do it heartily, as to the Lord and not to men, knowing that from the Lord you will receive the reward of the inheritance; for you serve the Lord Christ" (Colossians 3:23–24). If the extent of your walk with God is to read the Bible a little every day and to attend church on Sunday, the fact is that the bulk of your energies is being poured into labor that is in vain. Priorities must be adjusted.

While we certainly must work—in a formal job or the activities of living—we also must remain mindful of God and of His plan for the direction of our life. We must serve Him in the workplace, and at the same time ensure that our hourly efforts do not rob Him of all the best parts of our time and energies. Living in Christ, we do not wish to separate God from the side of our life that is work. We should seek at all times to do work that honors Him. If you are "lost in your work," "tied to your job," or seek your personal significance in a world-bound task, you are blinded to the true meaning of your existence in this life.

## CATARACTS: INDEPENDENCE AND DEFIANCE

Before willingly submitting to the authority and sovereignty of God, we strive to succeed by our own strengths, and on our own terms. Individuals who have yet to find Christ, or those who practice a faith somewhat distant from a heart fully engaged in His presence, are tempted to be accountable to themselves alone and relieved of their responsibility to God. However, in God's eyes such independence is sin.

Independence is an especially dense cataract that can block spiritual sight. Focusing on oneself, *depending on* oneself, relinquishes no domain to the Lord. Independence, founded in human pride, will keep you isolated from the Lord, in defiance to His sovereignty and Lordship. To defiantly release yourself from responsibility to God leaves you without divine guidance, exposed to mistakes and failure. The Scriptures are clear in this regard: "Poverty and shame will come to him who disdains correction, But he who regards a rebuke will be honored" (Proverbs 13:18).

You and I are God's most prized creation; we are a miracle of design. Were we to see ourselves as such in the mirror every morning, and if we were to give honest attention to the unfathomable mysteries of our cells and their seamless integration in our body, we would immediately understand that the Creator is beautiful and sovereign. We would raise our arms in the joy of life and appreciation for our Lord. We would put under our feet the desire to be independent of Him or to defy Him. We would walk at His side throughout the day.

## CATARACT: HYPOCRISY

Hypocrisy is the act of being—of trying to be—something that we are not. Hypocrisy is a lie, and Jesus has warned us of this obstacle to spiritual sight. When the scribes and Pharisees attacked Him for not engaging in the ritual of washing before dinner, He told His disciples, "Beware of the leaven of the Pharisees, which is hypocrisy" (Luke 12:1). To the Pharisees, He said, "You Pharisees make the outside of the cup and dish clean, but your inward part is full of greed and wickedness" (Luke 11:39).

Hypocrisy is a shell game; it is a wearing of masks; it is an act. It prevents us from being transformed as God requires. Outward hypocrisy, a dishonest face to the world, depends upon our schemes and designs regarding others, and leaves us without peace. In contrast to the hypocrisy of outer displays, Christ offers us the "beatitudes" (Matthew 5:3–12) as the expressions of a genuine heart and person. He declares blessed those who are merciful, peacemakers, and pure in heart, among other sincere characteristics of the genuine person.

Christian psychiatrist, Paul Tournier, distinguishes between the person and the personage.[2] The person is the inner part, and the personage is the outer shell. Many of us go around with manufactured smiles, and manufactured answers to others. Simply agreeing with others, or asking simple, practiced questions are all a function of hypocrisy. Yet one who is inwardly true has a lot more to say and can ask questions of another that demonstrate authentic concern. In these and other ways, they begin to resonate with the inner person of others.

Please understand, however, that Jesus died for the *inner hypocrite,* so that we could surrender ourselves to be something that the natural man is not—namely *saved.* In serving Christ, we may feel insecurity because of our defects. We may at times waver and say, "Oh, I'm not up to this task." Others may point their fingers and claim, "That person is a hypocrite speaking with false modesty." However, that is not the important issue; the important issue is *faithfulness.* God is faithful, and His faithfulness can change the hypocrisy within us into the heart of a faithful servant.

Inward hypocrites who seek the life-changing power of Jesus Christ will find themselves transformed. Learning to be something that has been implanted in us at salvation is learning to love God so much that we change to be nearer to Him. The apostle Paul taught this relationship: "that Christ may dwell in your hearts through faith; that you, being rooted and grounded in love, may be able to comprehend... the love of Christ which passes knowledge" (Ephesians 3:17–19). The inner spirit changes as we come to know God in faith. By seeking to have the nature of Christ inwardly, His Spirit of love then shines through all of our external, world-facing masks.

Let me give a word of reassurance to those who fear their own hypocrisy. There is an important distinction between a hypocrite and the faithful servant who simply feels inadequate, but continues to press on into fullness of faith. That distinction is *faithfulness*, which demonstrates the difference between spiritual blindness and spiritual sight. Faithfulness is not perfection; it is not even maturity. But it is the motivation of love that will determine both perfection and maturity.

## CATARACT: A CRITICAL SPIRIT

Is there any expression of spiritual blindness more blatant than that of a critical spirit? Christ could not have been more plain regarding this sin.

> Judge not, that you be not judged. For with what judgment you judge, you will be judged; and with the measure you use, it will be measured back to you. And why do you look at the speck in your brother's eye, but do not consider the plank in your own eye?
>
> —MATTHEW 7:1–3

A critical and judgmental spirit—nourished by personal pride and fear—makes us focus on the shortcomings of others while remaining *completely* oblivious to our own similar or *greater* weaknesses. Growth in the Lord is not possible under the shadow of such clear contradiction of God's purpose for us. The excessive concern with the faults of others always steals our gaze away from God. The habit of finding fault leaves a mere, tiny space in the heart and mind that excludes love and compassion for our fellow man. It is also too restrictive to allow Christ's healing and sanctifying presence into our spirits. Willfully maintaining a critical spirit will isolate us from both God and humanity.

Focusing your attention on the faults of others is often an attempt to avoid examining yourself, though you may think you know better. Jesus, challenging the sanctimony of scribes, Pharisees, and a restless mob, declared that "He who is without sin" should throw the first stone at an adulteress (John 8:7). Under conviction, their response is noted: "Then those who heard it, being convicted by their conscience, went out one by one" (John 8:9).

We *know* by our conscience that we are as imperfect as the next person is, and that we are sinful before God. A critical spirit masquerades as our "defense" against facing the painful truth of our inner person. However, it also prevents us from supplicating God for forgiveness. This huge blind spot keeps us from progressing into the light of fullness of faith and walking in the forgiveness of our Lord.

The antidote for a critical spirit, as I have mentioned previously, is to become an intercessor for your brother and neighbor, rather than their accuser.

## CATARACT: DISTORTED VIEWS OF SEX

Richard Foster, author of effective books dealing with self-discipline, indicates that one of the trends in Christian society most conspicuous in our day has been the divorce of sexuality from its relationship to our spirituality. He points out that the Bible holds "a high celebrative view of human sexuality."[3] On the other hand, it is obvious to any observer of modern civilization, that sex has *certainly* become divorced from any spiritual or moral basis, to a degree that would have been unimaginable even a generation ago. Sex, in our Western societies, has become iconic, intemperate, primary, all-consuming, degraded, and degrading. It has been immorally unleashed from its rightful place of fulfillment intended by God—the covenant of marriage.

Lust is regarded as one of the seven deadly sins, and with good reason. In lust, unbridled desire excludes all other thoughts and feelings. Real communion with God becomes impossible. "Lust is an untamed, inordinate sexual passion to possess."[4] Within our sexual temptations is the enormous potential to dehumanize others as well as ourselves. Within lust lies the potential for the destruction of couples, families, and innocent lives.

Jamie Buckingham was a spiritual mentor to many in an era when true Christianity was being reborn in the lives of many nominally religious people. At a young age he rose to an elevated position of respect and prominence in his denomination. Still, he was tempted and eventually fell to that temptation with a woman in his congregation.

Naturally, he lost his position in the church. His name and reputation besmirched, he was no longer welcome in those denominational congregations. With one wanton decision, he had destroyed himself, it seemed. Later, however, Jamie found freedom in Christ, and as he rebuilt his Christian life and ministry, he became founder of a new church congregation. He also felt the burden of initiating a special ministry program that reached out to restore people who had lost their way in adultery. Jamie Buckingham experienced the delivering power of Christ in his own life and was able to help others receive that same cleansing power to restore their spiritual sight.

Christ has made it clear to us that sexual righteousness is far deeper than simply avoiding sex outside of marriage: "But I say to you that whoever looks at a woman to lust for her has already committed adultery with her in his heart" (Matthew 5:28). While the adage claims, "love is blind," it can be held without doubt that "lust blinds absolutely." It has the power to carry us past the point of no return and to distract us from God's design for human sexuality, which is within the framework of a positive, uplifting, embracing love, reinforcing and cementing the covenant of marriage. Consider this scriptural injunction:

> And rejoice with the wife of your youth. As a loving deer and a graceful doe, let her breasts satisfy you at all times; And always be enraptured with her love. For why should you, my son, be enraptured by an immoral woman, And be embraced in the arms of a seductress?
> —PROVERBS 5:18–20

Presumably, it is possible to go to church, to read the Bible, to do for others—in other words, to *practice* faith—and yet simultaneously be consumed by sexual fantasy and unholy practice. Such a life denies the Lordship of Christ over common urges. If we seek to truly live our faith within the context of a life of godliness, our sexuality will not exclude the cleansing of the Spirit. Only by seeking holiness in God, and searching for the understanding of His righteous plan for the function of sex in our lives, do we progress toward full faith in this important area. Otherwise, we sell our soul to the temporary, lustful, carnal world. In a healthy, godly sexuality we experience unity with our spouse and deep appreciation for the Creator and the mystery and joy of His creation.

## CATARACT: NEGATIVE IMAGINATIONS

Motivating the darkened heart and mind are a variety of negative imaginations that create a cataract of spiritual blindness. Deep within the human mind and heart are corners of darkness and self-inflicted suffering that we know as *fear*, *worry*, and *self-pity*. We fear—that is conclusive. We fear death, each other, failure, solitude, old age, lack of acceptance, and pain. Humanity fears much and fears mightily. The Scriptures affirm this reality: "Oh how they are brought to desolation, as in a moment! They are utterly consumed with terrors" (Psalm 73:19). "Trouble and anguish make him afraid; They overpower him, like a king ready for battle" (Job 15:24). This biblical metaphor of a battle-ready king is apt. It indicates the powerful nature of fear.

### Dispelling fear

Fear involves anticipation. It can be described as a negative imagination. We are utterly consumed, in a moment, with dread of things that do not yet exist or have not yet occurred. In this darkness, we move far from the Lord, blind to the guiding, soothing hand that reaches out to comfort us. In contrast, listen to the confidence of the psalmist: "The LORD is my light and my salvation; Whom shall I fear? The LORD is the strength of my life; Of whom shall I be afraid?" (Psalm 27:1). Before we learn to completely surrender to the Lord, we seem to prefer a state of suspension. Even having found God, we may frequently lapse back into fear and its dedicated partner—worry.

**Defeating worry**

There are situations in life that cause me to worry. Perhaps it is the same for you. However, worry has become a habitual companion for some people. Continuous worry diminishes our experience of life and of God. Habitual worry and anxiety can cause illness, physical and mental. It can disrupt relationships and leave us simply "going through the motions" in our spiritual life. Worry will always leave us in agitation, preventing God's peace and tranquility from entering our hearts and minds. Many sins, such as unbelief, selfishness, covetousness, and disobedience, express themselves in worry.

I want to live in faith, trusting that the Lord will provide and care for me. Christ consoles and encourages me to seek this trust: "'Are not two sparrows sold for a copper coin? And not one of them falls to the ground apart from your Father's will. But the very hairs of your head are all numbered. Do not fear therefore; you are of more value than many sparrows'" (Matthew 10:29–31).

God's wisdom teaches us the consequences of not coming to God.

> When your terror comes like a storm,
> And your destruction comes like a whirlwind,
> When distress and anguish come upon you.
> Then they will call on me, but I will not answer;
> They will seek me diligently, but they will not find me.
> Because they hated knowledge
> And did not choose the fear of the LORD.
> —PROVERBS 1:27–29

It is important to live life in the fear of the Lord, learning to know Him, so that when storms approach us, as they often do in life, we will be able to receive His promise: "But whoever listens to me will dwell safely" (Proverbs 1:33). That sounds pretty simple. However, it takes daily devotion to God's Word and submission to His will, as well as touching Him in prayer, to nurture the faith required to surrender our fears and worries to Him absolutely.

Until then we will live with the grim facts of insecurity, stress, and suffering.

**Discovering self-pity**

With an inappropriate focus on yourself, you will begin to feel sorry for yourself. Self-pity is *self*-centeredness rather than *God*-centeredness. And this is a stubborn cause of blindness simply because it is so easy to fall into unaware, and we all do from time to time. If we think selfishly, we will be selfish. Rather than putting our minds on Christ and our relationship with Him, we are bound and diminished by the cataract of self-pity. If we are pitying ourselves, it is because we do not believe that there is Someone willing to assist us personally in all we need for life. It means, simply, that we *do not trust* God's promises to us. The Scriptures declare: "Blessed is the man who trusts in the LORD, and whose hope is in the LORD" (Jeremiah 17:7–8).

How can mere mortals grapple with these blinding cataracts of fear, worry, and self-pity? In our progression from spiritual blindness to spiritual sight, God asks that we "seek first the kingdom of God and His righteousness, and all these things shall be added to you. Therefore do not worry about tomorrow..." (Matthew 6:33–34). As I wrote in my book, *Rx for Worry*,[5] the way out of the thicket of anxiety and worry is to come before God with thanksgiving: "Be anxious for nothing, but in everything by prayer and supplication, with thanksgiving, let your requests be known to God" (Philippians 4:6). With a thankful heart, you will be engulfed in the Lord's presence for now and eternity. In thanksgiving you come to God and begin to see Him and His love for you more clearly. Before God, you have eternal hope and provision, and the cares of the world have no dominion.

## CATARACT: LAZINESS

Sloth, indolence, idleness, disengagement, indifference, negligence—God speaks directly about this cataract of laziness: "One who is slack in his work is brother to one who destroys"

(Proverbs 18:9, NIV). Laziness only leads to decline in physical life: "If anyone will not work, neither shall he eat" (2 Thessalonians 3:10). Laziness leads also to blindness in spiritual life: "The soul of a lazy man desires, and has nothing; But the soul of the diligent shall be made rich" (Proverbs 13:4).

As faithful stewards, God expects us to provide for ourselves and for one another: "But if anyone does not provide for his own, and especially for those of his household, he has denied the faith and is worse than an unbeliever" (1 Timothy 5:8). Additionally, prayer, worship, and thanksgiving are not passive acts. In a life that tends toward the mere practice of faith, our time with God, our prayer life, may sometimes be performed mechanically or perhaps not at all. Laziness exerts a powerful force upon the soul that increases as each moment passes. To learn to live one's faith, to seek out God and desire to reach up to Him—in short, to *see*—requires effort, self-sacrifice, and *demonstration*.

God wants us to be enthusiastic. Life is a miracle and a gift. Laziness and apathy—all the paths of least resistance—are at direct odds with the jubilance in the Creator's intelligence. Joy and wonder are integral to true faith.

To multiply your spiritual treasure you need to be good and faithful servants. A lazy person—physically or spiritually—will not reap any crops from seeds he or she has not sown. A living, growing faith in God is a relationship that requires fervent desire and earnest effort to see it through: "not lagging in diligence, fervent in spirit, serving the Lord" (Romans 12:11). By laziness and laxness, you shut God out and remain in darkness: "The sluggard is wiser in his own eyes than seven men who answer discreetly" (Proverbs 26:16, NIV). You need to receive the life found in His promises to energize you. You need to expect His presence in your life, in your soul, the way a sprout strives to break the surface of the dark loam to touch the sky.

## Cataracts: Elitism and Exclusivity

Clans, cliques, castes—it may be an unfortunate, inherent attribute of our fallen human nature that we seek not only to distinguish ourselves from others, but to separate ourselves from them. Pride, as we have discussed, causes people to elevate themselves above their neighbors and to exclude them from their own experience of life. Many gravitate toward, and cling to, those who *appear* to be the same and can confirm that their blindness is justified. We learn to identify with false differences and to reinforce them in a group. Kings are not commoners, and farmers are not doctors. One is better than another; at least, so we think. But our evaluations are not of God.

Blindness from the cataracts of elitism and exclusivity causes the refusal of the compassion and unity that characterized the thrust of Christ's ministry on earth. Unfortunately, this cataract develops in the church as much as anywhere. Certain denominations feel more socially significant than other denominations. Some denominations believe their Bible focus to be superior. Others feel superior in their focus on expressions of worship. And each darkened divisiveness represents a little fear, a little pride, and a little *lie*.

It has been said that the ground is level at the foot of the cross, that is, when we kneel humbly to acknowledge our need of a Savior, we recognize that we are all sinners in need of grace. Unfortunately, some believers leave that place of humility and begin to exalt themselves within their view of church government, as though true believers elsewhere were inferior. Some feel that their rituals and liturgy are more precisely biblical and view other groups as second-class. Some believers try to elevate themselves through pride in the beauty of their church buildings.

Some constantly need to ask themselves the question: "Who's on top?" We should instead be asking, "Whose supremacy do we recognize, God's or our own?" Where can we find the essence of our humility, and by extension, our humanity? Proper acknowledgement of God is the basis of humility and respect for our fellow man.

When we think about the human creation—the pancreas, immune system, and brain—we *must* recognize the Creator. Through that recognition alone some of us will be led to find a posture of submission and complete surrender and, lying face down, arms outspread, pray earnestly. This very private act must be done with a humble heart that understands one great truth: "I am but a simple, plain person; I am a sinner; I am saved by grace." Nothing else matters. The only exclusivity we can rightfully claim is to be exclusively dead to all we are, and allow Christ to have full control continually, as we position ourselves humbly at the foot of His cross.

The school at which I studied medicine is perhaps the best in the country. The work I have done in life has attracted considerable acclaim; I have written bestselling books and have been the recipient of accolades and honors from many diverse people and groups. I have been associated with famous and powerful individuals. However, this personal résumé does not impress me. The important thing, for me, is not found in those achievements—too easily they mislead and leave one stumbling blindly. What is important to me is to acknowledge God's majesty and mastery in my life, to put Him "on top" of *everything*, to recognize my sinful nature, and rejoice in the grace by which the Lord has saved me. Here is the common ground that I share within the family of God's children: I am a sinner saved by grace. That understanding helps one to see with the light of inclusivity.

If you struggle with the cataract of elitism and exclusivity, you are still alive to self rather than "hidden with Christ in God" (Colossians 3:3). See God's love, comprehend and accept His gift of salvation, never stop thanking Him, and be healed of the cataract of exclusivity and, thereby, be open to God's desires in your service to others.

## Cataract: Impatience

While it may not be immediately apparent how a lack of patience can darken our spiritual vision, the fact is that impatience is as much a hindrance to a living faith as any other "cataract." It is important to note that the Bible instructs us concerning patience: "But let patience have its perfect work, that you may be perfect and complete, lacking nothing" (James 1:4). What do we lack without patience? We lack trust in the Lord. The walk of faith gives us a rest in God for the next step—even when unseen by us.

The psalmist understood this aspect of relationship with God: "'You are my God.' My times are in Your hand" (Psalm 31:14–15). Impatience causes us to seek inadequate human solutions rather than waiting on the Lord for His wisdom to resolve life situations. Impatience implies diminishing faith in God, often because He is not answering within a timetable we understand. According to the Scriptures, God's timing is not ours. God does answer prayers, but how impertinent of us to tell Him how and when to do it.

God dwells in eternity, beyond the realm of time. One of the reasons He has given us the gift of time is to test our hearts. The Scriptures declare: "And let us not grow weary while doing good, for in due season we shall reap if we do not lose heart" (Galatians 6:9). We must maintain our confidence that God will provide for us as we use our time to do good.

Any failure on our part to wait on God's timing hinders our relationship with Him. There is a season for everything, and waiting on God shows trust in Him and leads us to His promise: "Eternal life to those who by patient continuance in doing good seek for glory, honor, and immortality" (Romans 2:7). Patience shows our willingness to submit our lives to God.

Likewise, our relationships with God's children suffer when impatience clouds the heart. The Bible is very clear concerning how we are to relate to others: "Therefore, as the elect of God, holy and beloved, put on tender mercies, kindness, humility, meekness, longsuffering" (Colossians 3:12). God's work on earth requires us to love others as we would ourselves, and that means giving time—patience, really—as much as giving anything else.

## CATARACT: DAILY DISTRACTIONS

You may know this routine: Sunday morning at 11 a.m. you go to church, after which you thank the pastor for his message, and head home to eat dinner and spend time with the family. Then Monday morning is the beginning of a busy workweek that unfortunately may include too few thoughts of the Lord and His love until the following Sunday morning.

Consider the following radical statement made by the apostle Paul:

> I press toward the goal for the prize of the upward call of God in Christ Jesus.
>
> —PHILIPPIANS 3:14

Are my eyes, like Paul's, on the goal? Are *yours*? In the hurly-burly of modern life it is far too common to give only certain hours of certain days to God and to devote the overwhelming majority of our time and energy to our own worldly interests.

Imagine saying to your spouse, "I can think about you, love you, and spend time with you for one hour at eight o'clock every Tuesday night. Outside of that, I am pretty busy. Sorry. I promise to pay attention during that hour though. Maybe." Does that sound like passion? Or genuine love? If you were progressing toward full faith, rather than merely practicing an intellectual faith, if you truly loved God, would you ever want to be anywhere else than in His presence?

What could powerfully divert our minds and interests so completely from progressing toward full faith in God? Almost anything, as it turns out. Consider this biblical warning:

> Do not love the world or anything in the world. If anyone loves the world, the love of the Father is not in him. For everything in the world—the craving of sinful man,

> the lust of his eyes and the boasting of what he has and
> does—comes not from the Father but from the world.
> The world and its desires pass away, but the man who
> does the will of God lives forever.
>
> —1 JOHN 2:15–17, NIV

The new jet-ski, concerns for one's family, a vacation in the Alps, shopping—with these in mind, the question should be "What *doesn't* divert us from God?" There are many misleading attractions of the flesh, and there are also "noble pursuits" such as education, career, and family—that can tear our gaze from the Lord just as effectively. Yet, it is a fact that we cannot serve two masters. God wants us to cherish Him. Cultivating this relationship requires both discipline and vigilance. As long as we define ourselves by what we *have* and what we *do*, we will be blind and lost to God's higher purposes of intimacy and divine destiny.

## CATARACT: LEGALISM

> Therefore if the Son makes you free, you shall be free
> indeed.
>
> —JOHN 8:36

God wishes us to be free—free to worship Him fully. The history of the church, unfortunately, includes codes, rules, and man-made doctrines that stifle the spirit of spontaneity, joy, and release that a fully-lived faith enjoys. Even in the days of the primitive church, legalists were trying to enforce their views.

> And certain men came down from Judea and taught the
> brethren, "Unless you are circumcised according to the
> custom of Moses, you cannot be saved."
>
> —ACTS 15:1

The ritual of circumcision, as important as any other to the Hebrews, had become redundant under the new covenant with

Christ, as the Scriptures clearly explain: "For we are the circumcision, who worship God in the Spirit, rejoice in Christ Jesus, and have no confidence in the flesh" (Philippians 3:3). Jesus moved among us with a message of our redemption through God's grace and love alone.

The outward observance of rites and forms too often serves to quench the Spirit. We may become bound by external religious guidelines and thereby forfeit our freedom in God. In that framework you and I will never be liberated and exercise our real faith in the power of the Spirit. Legalism and formality can become bigger than God, in our minds, and blind us to His beauty. Those who draw closest to the Lord, in the past as now, seem to lose interest in the ceremonies, traditions, trappings, and buildings that are a part of Christendom, which most people erroneously identify as the Christian walk itself. A Christian's duty is not to himself or others first, but to Jesus Christ. All else flows from that relationship.

The attraction of legalism—or cookie-cutter Christianity—for many, is precisely the external engagement in detail and outward forms of "religiousness." We may believe that it looks like devotion to God, but it is actually serving to insulate us from meeting the Lord face to face. Pride can keep us from facing the complete abandonment to Jesus that His love deserves. Attempting to show love for God through the public adherence to man-made rules is a reflection of pride. It is also in such a manner that church hierarchies are built and maintained, and worldly power within the Christian body wrongly becomes an aspect of "spiritual life."

We must learn not just to attend church services, but also to *be* the church. To cultivate relationship with God and other believers in Christ is to be a part of the living organism that is the church. That is what it means to live in full faith, to see beyond the religious restrictions—perhaps even tyranny—of legalism. We must seek the Lord in simplicity, humility, and freedom from the distraction of spiritually hollow exercise. John Piper says that our greatest joy is found in God alone, and He is most glorified when we are satisfied in Him—only Him![6] In that intimate relationship with God, we become a temple, a vessel for communion with the living God, rather than a practitioner of static, earthbound law.

### Called to liberty

Jesus died to set you free! Your refusal to look for Him alone, laying aside the tangle of religious habits, is to remain in darkness and to miss breaking out into His brilliant illumination of freedom. Without illumination, no one can see. Freedom is the power or condition of acting without compulsion within, or coercion without. In the light of freedom, you are free to love and serve God with all of your heart and to walk in His will for your life.

The apostle Paul warned the Galatians: "Stand fast therefore in the liberty by which Christ has made us free, and do not be entangled again with a yoke of bondage" (Galatians 5:1). Our yokes of bondage are many: sin, guilt, and errant thoughts and emotions. The bondage of legalism, or the conformity to a religious code, is no less heavy for the heart that needs to fly heavenward. Under legalistic codes, we feel the *necessity* of an action or behavior as one's application of specific rules, which sanction certain behaviors and prohibit others. Often these "rules," established by religious leaders, go beyond what is written in the Bible for our obedience. The dress code that many congregations implicitly maintain on Sunday mornings is a good example of a legal requirement, the breaking of which may cause people to show their disapproval, resulting in a sense of guilt. There may be many things one can say in favor of a dress code, but its power to bring us closer to the throne of God is not one of them.

Legalism may also be understood in the terms of conscience. Conscience, wrongly instructed, aimed, or focused, is as condemning as law, if not more so in some cases. Everyone has experienced both the subtlety and paralyzing power of the expectations and opinions of others pressed upon our conscience. False guilt, especially as projected by others, is also a paralyzing factor for some of us.

David delighted in going to the house of God because he met God there and he enjoyed the fellowship of spiritually-minded people. (See Psalm 122:1.) Let us seek the same joys! In fulfilling Christ's commandment to love, I find my sight, and in that sight I find freedom from worries, from the effect of sin, from unhappiness, dissatisfaction, and endless searching. I also taste the freedom that comes from giving and caring.

**Loving what God loves**

It is also important, as we seek to avoid the cataract of legalism, to guard against developing a negative attitude toward God's law or His church, which He loves. True spiritual vision embraces the truth of all that God provided for our redemption. God's moral law, rightly viewed, is His loving direction for our good. Moses told the children of Israel to love the Lord and "to serve the LORD your God with all your heart and with all your soul and to keep the commandments of the LORD and His statutes which I command you today for your good" (Deuteronomy 10:12–13). The psalmist loved and meditated on the law of God all the day (Psalm 119:97) and the apostle John said, "His commandments are not burdensome" (1 John 5:3). Many teachers that God has raised up for His people have taught correctly that the Ten Commandments are ultimately promises of what the grace of God is going to accomplish in His redeemed! When God's true authority is embraced with a delight to honor Him above all, we are experiencing true spiritual vision.

Also, God has given us His church as one of the great helps that we so desperately need to walk in victory in the Christian life. The church is ordained to be the family of God, lovingly bearing one another's burdens and so fulfilling the law of Christ (Galatians 6:2). A true local church that is spiritually minded embraces God's calling for them so that its members genuinely "love one another" (Galatians 5:13).

What a joy it is to fellowship, worship, and serve the Lord together with God's own children! They delight to hear God teach them through the preaching of His Word, and they pour out their hearts together at the throne of grace through prayer. We bless God for every godly church throughout the world, for each one is part of the "church of the living God, the pillar and ground of the truth" (1 Timothy 3:15).

Avoiding legalism and embracing all that God's Word teaches is the way to progress to the mature faith that loves what God loves and sees as God sees.

## CATARACT: ENVY

The Pharisees, out of envy, belittled Jesus and eventually set out to destroy Him. So blind were they in their formal social stature that any love or devotion given to Jesus by the people was a political insult to them. No doubt, the spiritual attributes they saw in Him, which their hearts intuitively recognized to be of pure beauty and grace, also goaded their prideful self-perceptions. In unspoken shame, which they would never admit in their own minds, they must have seen in Jesus the beauty of character they knew they lacked. They hated Him for that; they envied Him for that. You and I are like the Pharisees.

Envy is one of the greatest forms of selfishness, and it is most markedly seen among people who are in the same social group or profession. Preachers may be envious of other preachers who make more money, have larger churches, or receive greater recognition; even spiritual leaders are not above this sinful cataract. The same is true of career professionals, like ophthalmologists. An orthopedic surgeon will not feel or express the same envy toward an eye doctor that another eye doctor might be tempted to do. Two eighteen-year-old girls are quite likely to be envious of one another for a myriad of reasons, but why should they worry about the thirty-six-year-old woman beside them? You can frequently see this same dynamic working inside any group you wish to dissect.

Envy only leads to pain. Consumed by its acrid, insatiable flame, people set out to build themselves up by running others down. It may be that all our sin and psychological problems find their initial basis in selfishness, along with pride. Envy blinds us to the beautiful creation of the one who is envied. In that same way, it blinds us as well to the realities of compassion and humility in Christ.

Envy consumes the body as surely as it does the spirit. All the "bile" of its powerful negativity makes envy a potent cause of stress disorders, sleeplessness, disinterest in exercise and nutrition, and perhaps far more serious illnesses also. The peace of God brings healing to the soul as we determine to be reconciled to God and to people as well. Learning to esteem others and to love them with God's love can heal more ills than doctors can heal.

Envy often leads to one particularly terrible effect: an impulse to control another—a control so complete that any sense of personal reality is lost along the way. That need to control is in itself a blinding cataract, which we will discuss.

## CATARACT: THE "NEED" FOR POWER AND CONTROL

The need to control is potentially the most desperate and dangerous wedge between any two individuals or groups; it is a cataract that is set against the light of God entering the heart. It is all-consuming. Based in insecurity and founded upon hatred, it destroys its object by denying it freedom. This inordinate "need to control" can bloat to such extremes that it compromises the controller's view of reality, and at that point it is considered pathological.

Lust for power, position, eminence, and recognition is a blinding cataract in itself. It tears one's mind and efforts from God's glorious purpose as it seeks fulfillment in self-importance. However, a greater danger of this inordinate desire for power is the expression of that desire to control others.

This sinful cataract of control may easily be observed within families, between lovers, friends, coworkers, members of clubs and groups, between organizations, collectives, and associations—it is *everywhere*. It can also be observed as the motor of politics. Frequently in the political realm, actions and reactions are seen in the terms of "zero-sum dyads." This term simply means that for one person or group to observe a benefit, another must endure a loss or deficit. The problem with such thinking is that cooperation, altruism, and mutually beneficial options are rarely considered, or even *perceived.*

For example, in Florida we have the optometrists seeking certain considerations from the government for their political and economic agenda. They make annual contributions to the political party that seems to promise help. Likewise, ophthalmologists have their list of desires and also make contributions in the hope of affecting the government sufficiently for their ends. Back and forth it goes with no one seeking potential common ground—and so the division, based on the envy of each other's position or power, is destined to continue until the sun burns out. Many people blindly seek to rule other people to satisfy their need for control. They wish to see these others do things their way.

Jesus gave us an exquisite example of the antidote for seeking power and control over others. It happened after the eating of the Passover for the last time with His disciples, as the Scriptures record: "Jesus, knowing that the Father had given all things into His hands, and that He had come from God and was going to God, rose... and began to wash the disciples' feet" (John 13:3–5). With full knowledge of His preeminent position in the universe, Jesus humbly knelt before mere men and washed their feet, just as a servant would. In this way, Jesus demonstrated *pure spiritual sight* knowing that serving did not diminish His own value.

You will be blinded by this cataract if you are seeking to overpower and control. You will only be illumined by God's glory when you seek to love and serve without regard to yourself. I must, and you must, humbly serve as Jesus did in order to be free from this devastating cataract.

## FATHER I KNOW THAT ALL MY LIFE

Father I know that all my life is portioned out for me
The changes that are sure to come I do not fear to see
I ask Thee for a present mind intent on pleasing Thee.

I would not have the restless will that hurries to and fro
Seeking for some great thing to do or secret thing to know
I would be treated as a child and guided where I go.

I ask Thee for the daily strength to none that ask denied
A mind to blend with outward life while keeping at
    Thy side
Content to fill a little space if Thou be glorified.

In service which Thy will appoints there are no bonds
    for me
My secret heart is taught the truth that makes Thy
    children free
A life of self-renouncing love is one of liberty.[7]
—ANNA L. WARING, 1850

Chapter 11

# BATTLEFIELD: MOTIVATIONS AND IMAGINATIONS

M Y USE OF the term *battlefield* is not accidental; it reflects the reality of the relentless struggle, even within believers, for supremacy of the natural mind over the godly desires of the spirit. The motivations and imaginations of the "self" that are not surrendered in abandonment to the Savior constantly challenge the godly desires for submission to God and walking in divine destiny. Thus, we have evidenced the validity of the continuum we have referenced throughout, as it either charts our progress toward full faith or our regression to sinful bondage.

Jesus' parable of the sower and the seed in Mark chapter 4 illustrates one of the essential truths in this book. That is, to progress toward full faith and intimate relationship with God, we must make sure that we keep the weeds of our lives plucked up so they will not hinder a fruitful life: thirty, sixty, or a hundred fold increase.

My book, *Imaginations: More Than You Think*,[1] discusses the impact of dark, negative thoughts and emotions on that continuum. You may earnestly intend to live for the Lord, yet life itself seems to be always intruding and tearing you from the task. Your main occupation ought to be Christ, but you are often preoccupied and concerned with other issues.

The Shepherd, however, keeps faithfully bringing us back into the fold. That is Christianity in a nutshell: we are constantly failing, straying, and stumbling in the dark, and then being led back into the fold of Christ by the light He shines into our darkened hearts. Within that dynamic lie the issues of our values, attitudes, motivations, intentions, and energies, along with the battlefield they represent.

## THE BATTLEFIELD OF THE MIND

Joyce Meyer has entitled one of her books *Battlefield of the Mind*.[2] She discusses the biblical dynamic of the renewing process of our minds necessary to walking with God. The struggle of the carnal mind against our spirit for faith is not only relentless, it can also be disorienting and is frequently savage in its destructive designs. The believer desires a relationship of love, illumination, and peaceful, joyful rest with his or her Creator. Yet, as Michael Molinos wrote many years ago, "Your self is the greatest devil of all."[3] Have you considered the destructive power of your "natural" thoughts? What is the cause of many of your troubles and disquiet? "Self love... stands as your greatest hindrance in obtaining precious peace."[4]

I cannot stress enough to you that the reality of living faith, walking with God in this world unhampered by spiritual blindness, is found in your willingness to let go of your "self." The degree to which you abandon yourself to be led by God's Spirit determines the degree of movement from the left of the continuum, representing your natural life, to the right of the continuum, representing your spiritual life.

We must adopt an attitude of humility that rejects the blindness of our ego to regain spiritual sight and have our minds illuminated by the truth of God. The Bible declares: "For if anyone thinks himself to be something, when he is nothing, he deceives himself" (Galatians 6:3). Living apart from God's purposes, we are tempted to think we are "someone" based on our worldly achievements. The Bible calls this deception.

It is our core values that distinguish us as individuals. They shape our attitudes and perspectives. Our dreams and imaginations determine our motivations, which are the forces of the heart and mind and are reflected by our words and actions. After salvation, our most essential core values necessarily change. No longer are we motivated by our ego needs, but by our love for God. Yet, to progress in that relationship toward complete abandonment to God, we will have to encounter the battlefield of the mind, which wants to maintain control.

Your mind-set at any given point in this process is a full expression of the state of your faith in the pursuit of life. Furthermore, the mind-set you choose now is the mind-set that you will have for eternity, according to the Scriptures: "Do not be deceived, God is not mocked; for whatever a man sows, that he will also reap. For he who sows to his flesh will of the flesh reap corruption, but he who sows to the Spirit will of the Spirit reap everlasting life" (Galatians 6:7–8). We are stewards of our souls and responsible agents in the process of our spiritual development. It is imperative that our mind-set and motivations be controlled by the Holy Spirit in order to win the battle for our minds.

### Biblical strategy for victory

The apostle Peter strongly urged believers to avoid spiritual blindness by winning the battle of the mind and seeking God to change motivations to develop in them the character of Christ.

> Grace and peace be multiplied to you in the knowledge of God and of Jesus our Lord, as His divine power has given to us all things that pertain to life and godliness, through the knowledge of Him who called us by glory and virtue, by which have been given to us exceedingly great and precious promises, that through these you may be partakers of the divine nature, having escaped the corruption that is in the world through lust.

> But also for this very reason, giving all diligence, add to your faith virtue, to virtue knowledge, to knowledge self-control, to self-control perseverance, to perseverance godliness, to godliness brotherly kindness, and to brotherly kindness love.
>
> For if these things are yours and abound, you will be neither barren nor unfruitful in the knowledge of our Lord Jesus Christ. For he who lacks these things is shortsighted, even to blindness, and has forgotten that he was cleansed from his old sins.
>
> —2 PETER 1:2–9

Peter states plainly that fruitfulness is assured if we receive the divine power that gives us all we need to develop the character of Christ. And he declares that those who lack these virtues are "shortsighted, even to blindness," forgetting the source of our salvation. To find "still waters" (Psalm 23:2), we must hold our relationship with God above all other things we perceive. To redeem our values, attitudes, imaginations, and finally, our motivations requires that we submit to God and diligently seek love, justice, and righteousness. This is the strategy for victory in the "battlefield" that will determine our fulfillment of divine destiny as we progress toward full faith.

## POSITIVE AND NEGATIVE MOTIVATIONS

As we have discussed, there are many types of blinding, spiritual cataracts that interfere with our faith and move us in directions away from God. Our pride, selfishness, unbridled passions, moods, fears, distorted perceptions, and desire to control, to name a few, can hinder our relationship with the Lord and negatively affect our behavior within the body of Christ and with unbelievers. These cataracts involve negative motivations for our life and must be confronted in order to be removed.

### Negative motivations

Actions always affect other people—they are meant to do so. Our actions are often part of a personal agenda that is a plan or principle, which organizes our thoughts in preparation of action. The problem is that these agendas are too commonly based upon selfish imaginations that look for personal gain. Selfish, dark feelings of greed, distrust, cynicism, and negativity form motivations that produce complaints, criticism, control, and even worse. Such motivations are entirely outside of the T.R.U.S.T. grid as a basis and means for finding our vision in God. Any agenda for action that arises out of negative attitudes and motivations is destined to injure others and alienate one further from God.

True religion, social norms, ideals, tastes, and learning are necessary elements for mankind's prosperity. The theories of mathematician and philosopher, Fourier, concluded that strong differences among people created *too much* spice, and that we seem to naturally reject the things that we do not understand or that challenge us. We judge and criticize those who are unlike us or who hold different propositions for life. This intolerant attitude can only lead to dissension, disagreement, disharmony, and destructive agendas of action. Godly motivations and imaginations, which act as an antidote to these negatives, can only be developed in an intimate relationship with the Creator by those who seek Him and seek to serve Him completely.

We often need to untrain the impulses that have been taught to us or simply absorbed into our mentality. We might refer to these impulses as a *"dynamic collage."* That is to say, self-preservation and self-protection, as well as self-consciousness and self-esteem, are natural and normal. But they are continually in dynamic flux, or change, in response to others around us. This influence of people in our lives greatly determines our self-image that supports our thoughts, motives, and actions, both wholesome and otherwise.

And, we are kept in the dark by these enigmatic motivations, which lead to words and actions that can easily become lies. Often—and you know this—the dark motivations underneath our actions can be neatly covered and misrepresented by beautiful, sedate, flesh and blood exteriors. In fact, very few of us consistently behave genuinely in the company of others. We are more concerned with presenting an "image" for people to approve our worth.

If we choose to take the path of humility, we can expect others to misunderstand and think less of us. For example, I know a man who holds world records in sailing and ballooning. Yet, choosing to live in genuine humility, he appears to others as an ordinary fellow. Predictably, in the social "shell-game," people typically treat him condescendingly. Not knowing of his great ability and achievements, the negative is always *assumed*.

Living in a genuine transparency in dealing with others requires a work of divine grace in our lives. We must receive that grace as a gift, according to the Scriptures: "For by grace you have been saved through faith, and that not of yourselves; it is the gift of God, not of works, lest anyone should boast" (Ephesians 2:8–9). The Christian dynamic is simple and peaceful only when we are truly living our faith. Negative thoughts and motivations will destroy us on the "battlefield" and divide us from others. Only by focusing on Christ and engaging with Him in continuous prayer, praise, and worship are we able to surrender fully our sinful, selfish selves to Him.

**Positive motivations**

> To those who have obtained like precious faith with us by the righteousness of our God and Savior Jesus Christ: Grace and peace be multiplied to you in the knowledge of God and of Jesus our Lord.
>
> —2 PETER 1:1–2

God's Word promises grace and peace to be multiplied to our lives in the knowledge of God. The word *peace* in the Amplified Bible is described as "perfect well-being, all necessary good, all spiritual prosperity, and freedom from fears and agitating passions and moral conflicts" (2 Peter 1:1–2, AMP). Whether we are anxious and fearful due to our tenacious desire to be independent, or bitter over hurts, or restless due to envy and a desire to control others, we are not abiding in the freedom and *shalom* that

God wants to give us. God offers freedom and *shalom* to those who live lives that are completely surrendered to Him.

According to the Scriptures, as we have seen, we must seek these graces: diligence, virtue, knowledge, self-control, perseverance, godliness, brotherly kindness, and love. (See 2 Peter 1:4–7.) If we lack these, we are "shortsighted, even to blindness" (2 Peter 1:9). In His divine power, by grace, God gives us everything for life and godliness. You will only experience tranquility and true joy when you have surrendered all to God. The Scriptures teach clearly what our motivation should be.

> Keep your heart with all diligence,
> For out of it spring the issues of life.
>
> —PROVERBS 4:23

> Set your mind on things above, not on things on the earth.
>
> —COLOSSIANS 3:2

It is important to note that the Bible urges great caution in the area of our thoughts and it warns against their corruption. The apostle Paul tells us that if we ponder the flesh, we will walk in the flesh; if we ponder the Spirit, we will walk in the Spirit. (See Romans 8.) The challenge for us is to ensure that we start with a proper mind-set, which will lead to proper behavior. It must not be forgotten that we are responsible for our mind-set in daily life as well as for eternity! We will reap what we sow; the eternal harvest is equal to the planting in our mental activity (Galatians 6:7–10).

But, we cannot depend on ourselves for change, but on God's power within us. What refuels our inner motivations is taking to heart the outpouring of God's love to us. We need the infilling of the Holy Spirit for Him to work in our hearts. We must renounce all self-help and attempts to work out our problems ourselves. God has spoken and promised to show Himself strong. We must be like little children relying on our heavenly Father's mighty arm. Like Paul, we say that we have no confidence in the flesh but rejoice in Jesus Christ! (Philippians 3:2–3). God must quicken us, enabling us to change our motivation. It is our part to see our weakness, in earnest desire and longing, convinced of the fact that we cannot help ourselves; we must trust God for divine enablement. No one can rest until resting in Him.

We need to acknowledge and appreciate the Lord's holiness. Our mind-set must be aligned with God and the Holy Spirit. We know that any godliness we might display derives from our relationship with God, rather than anything we do to try to create an "image." In this relationship, humility is still the most important orientation of the creation to the Creator. Such humility must be expressed in every stage of spiritual growth. It becomes more prominent as we mature spiritually.

Children seek to place themselves at the center of attention, while mature individuals understand their place and accept responsibility for themselves, their conduct, and their views. The apostle Paul expressed this mature mind-set: "For we can do nothing against the truth, but for the truth. For we are glad when we are weak and you are strong" (2 Corinthians 13:8–9).

Spiritual maturity comes from walking in God's peace. A mature person, motivated by godly desire, is willing to accept blame and ceases to blame others. The spiritually mature believer also demonstrates perseverance, which leads him or her on with trust in the Lord, even in the face of adversity. And the mature believer is strengthened against the temptations of the world due to self-control, which leads to temperance and balance in the daily conduct of life.

How does maturity alter you outwardly when you see with the spiritual sight God desires? When you have surrendered to God, you cease your struggle with Him and find peace within your own soul. *Anticipation* becomes an energizing, motivating force in a life of faith—anticipation of God's inestimable love for us, of His forgiveness of us, of His faithfulness to us at all times, including moments of adversity, as well as in eternity and our place there.

The sport of skiing provides a good illustration for the concept of *anticipation*. As a skier's body heads down the hill and into a turn, the descent is caused by the natural law of gravity, and mediated by the side of the hill, its white surface, and the skier's own body. If the skier tries to turn the skis at every turn with his legs, he will soon wear himself out. Rather, in the transition from one turn to the next, the skier sets a platform in the snow and plants a pole. His knees assume the role of a coiled spring waiting to release the potential energy in exuberant motion. The weight on the skis now headed downward can easily be turned because of the springboard effect of the leg muscles recoiling without effort. The resulting bounce elevates the skier and his skis as he shifts from the downhill ski to the other and heads down.

Heading into the next turn, the skier once more rests his weight into the platform of the snow, and uses no strength except the weight of the skis to find a line into the side of the hill. This platform allows the skier again to coil somewhat, which facilitates the spring action of the leg muscles that shoot the skier on to the opposite ski once more and down the hill. The trip to the bottom of the hill becomes smooth and enjoyable when he can rest in the anticipation of the action of the skis under the effortless coiling and recoiling of the leg muscles in line on the hill.

It is with similar anticipation that we must learn to rest in our redemption in Christ. We can learn to relax in our ever-consistent God and, as a result, end our personal—and futile—struggle to "tame" the mountain. Rather than angst and agitation, we can enjoy a cooling wind on our faces, a sense of exhilaration and shalom—the spiritual prosperity that comes from resting in His arms, having laid aside dark passions, moral conflicts, bitterness, and agitations. *Shalom* is the peace of God that we can anticipate and by which we have the means to live, move, respond to others, interpret life, and worship.

## RESPONSE TO ADVERSITY

Trial and adversity are powerful forces in life, similar to the inevitable pull of gravity. Satan's work surely is to lure and tempt us with the things of the world and the flesh. His greatest deception might be that of blinding us to God's light and truth with negativity and attitudes of hopelessness and defeat. Perhaps the place of deepest darkness is a sense of isolation and abandonment in adversity. When filled with such feelings you may feel you cannot lift your eyes from your feet to move toward every pilgrim's wonderful destination—the Celestial City. Yet it is only when we are brought to feel this extreme of hopelessness that we can see the greatest spiritual light God gives.

One of the biggest aspects in the believer's walk is the difference in how we respond to pain and adversity. Author Dr. Henry Brandt has pointed out that it is not circumstances that dictate our responses but that which lies within us. What is within us? Two influences will be found in every believer's heart: God's grace *and* remaining sin.

To which influence will you choose to yield? How you think, feel, and react to adversity are within your control; it is your responsibility to determine your thoughts, actions, and reactions. You decide whether to act out of anger, jealousy, or self-pity, or to live as Christ taught. There is much truth in the adage that it's the sails, not the gales, that determine where we shall go. We set our sails and choose our path in faith, using the winds of adversity to our advantage. If we choose otherwise, the Scriptures admonish that "whatever is not from faith is sin" (Romans 14:23). And the Scriptures are filled with promises for help in adversity: "And He said to me, 'My grace is sufficient for you, for My strength is made perfect in weakness'" (2 Corinthians 12:9).

Many people are not effective in ministry *until* they have been tested or hurt. I remember meeting my friend and colleague, Dr. Jim Rowsey, at a time when his wife was dying of cancer. As he talked to me about the prospect of losing her, tears streamed down his face. Yet he continued to smile. I thought at the time how he must have drawn many people to the Lord with that smile—the graceful smile of joy in the Lord in the midst of tribulation. Especially in times of adversity, we must think about how we think. Victory becomes a question of our focus and our choice to orient ourselves appropriately to the elements of the T.R.U.S.T. grid.

## FOCUS

The biblical deliverer, Joseph, demonstrated eternal focus when he expressed forgiveness of his brothers' wickedness against him: "But as for you, you meant evil against me; but God meant it for good" (Genesis 50:20). Following Joseph's example of his total forgiveness of his brothers, we need to exercise forgiveness as deliberately as we might exercise our bodies. Such forgiveness is only possible as we choose to focus on our eternal destiny and take responsibility for own faults and shortcomings, rather than focusing on those of our neighbor.

Such powerful spiritual sight is accomplished by yielding to the Holy Spirit working within us. Submitting to His divine work in our lives is an important link in our spiritual development that allows us to become encouragers of, and intercessors for, others—rather than being their critics and accusers, as we have mentioned. Are you an encourager? When you have been abused or hurt by others, it is easy to become critical, point a finger, and judge them. However, it is important to keep in mind that you are just as fallible as the next person.

I know that I must let the beauty of God's life overflow in me. I may have been bitten, but I cannot choose to become bitter. Instead of criticizing and accusing others, I must engage in constant prayer on their behalf, forgiving them and blessing them. Strengthening my faith in this regard depends on whether I possess a self-righteous spirit or am yielded to the Holy Spirit. God's forgiveness alone can free me from cynicism and negativity regarding others.

Barnabas came from Cyprus and was a great peacemaker and encourager of those around him. (See Acts 4:36; 9:27.) That leaves us with the outstanding question: can we similarly find it within ourselves to be encouragers and peacemakers regardless of our circumstances or situations? To do so reflects the essence of Christianity.

The beloved hymn, "At the Cross," declares: "And there by faith, I received my sight, and now I am happy all the day." When we are freed from selfishness and criticism by the Holy Spirit through the cross of Christ and can live in the joy and thanksgiving of God's grace and love, we are *happy*. To live any other way means living in the darkness of blindness and incomplete faith. Our hope and prayer for each other and ourselves—in a real, living faith—should be that of Paul to the Corinthians: "Become complete. Be of good comfort, be of one mind, live in peace; and the God of love and peace be with you" (2 Corinthians 13:11). This is what it means to have spiritual sight in our relationships with others.

# PART III:

# BIBLICAL INSIGHT
# INTO SPIRITUAL BLINDNESS

I N PARTS I and II, we have concluded that we are blind under the dark wrap of sin and selfishness when we are left to our own ways and "wisdom." Yet, we have the wonderful hope, as believers, that the Spirit of God can empower each of us to escape this darkness and to gain spiritual sight by simply seeking Him. What is the most effective way to do that? Where do we find the antidote for our cataracts, blindness, and shortsightedness? The Word of God—His revealed wisdom—provides the answers we need, giving us true direction to guide our hearts into His glorious light. His Word declares:

> Where there is no vision, the people perish.
> —PROVERBS 29:18, KJV

God's redemptive desire is to remove our spiritual cataracts and correct our myopia (near-sightedness). Without His vision, I perish, you perish, we all perish. There are many full and rich chapters in Scripture that address this problem of our need for new sight; they offer to illuminate our path out of darkness into the light of God's love. In fact, the Bible as a whole reveals a unified message that extensively deals with our spiritual sight.

## SCRIPTURAL TRUTHS OF SPIRITUAL SIGHT

Once you begin to understand the pervasiveness of spiritual blindness, you can comprehend the Great Physician's diagnostic and prescriptive wisdom for sight revealed in His Word. The Bible's wealth of beautiful passages addressing our spiritual blindness is too extensive for the pages of this book. However, I would particularly like to discuss the helpful themes of seven of them with you in the following chapters. Let me summarize their themes.

### Blindness of natural man

First, we will look at some biblical passages that reveal the differences in blindness and vision or understanding between the Christian walking with the Lord and the man of the world whose life is filled with temporal concerns and a clouded view of what is really meaningful. Scripture clearly teaches God's perspective on the folly of humanity, blind to Him and full of itself: "But the natural man does not receive the things of the Spirit of God, for they are foolishness to him; nor can he know them, because they are spiritually discerned" (1 Corinthians 2:14).

### The pathway of repentance

Then we will review passages that describe the pathway toward spiritual sight, marked by repentance, as described in Psalm 51. Without repentance we are inevitably living for ourselves and are blind to God. The consequence of such selfishness is a profound grief. It is the sorrow of having spurned God's goodness. Honestly coming in touch with this pain often represents the first ray of light that leads us out of spiritual blindness through repentance. The grief, however, must be transformed into action by personally seeking God's help. We must turn to a new center of life—God, not ourselves. God delights in receiving us when we come to Him through the cross, accepting the pardon of the risen Lord Jesus.

### Abiding in Christ

Following repentance, union with Christ is pictured and set forth in the principles of the allegory of the vine and the branches in John 15. This beautiful metaphor, taught by Jesus, shows us how to abide in the living Son of God daily—even hourly.

### Life in the Holy Spirit

Then, the work of the Spirit in the lives of believers is opened up to us in Romans 7 and 8, some of the most masterful passages of the Bible. The Spirit Himself enables us to grasp the reality of how He prevails in our lives when we abide in Christ and engage in a heartfelt trust in Him.

### Growing in grace

The call for real, and radical, practical change in our lives is laid out for us in 2 Peter 1. This chapter reflects the Spirit's work that the apostle Paul taught in Romans 8, though it is presented through Peter's practical outlook. May you and I, by God's grace, be enabled to make the real changes of character and habit as they are mapped out in this chapter.

### Victorious in spiritual warfare

We also must continually live with the "thunder" in our ears of spiritual warfare while we serve the Savior. It is an incessant battle to remain fervent, faithful, and focused. In Ephesians 6 we read of the armor of God that equips us to stand firm, press forward, and fight the good fight of faith.

### Ecstasy of worship

Finally, a refreshing, rejuvenating fountain flows from the message of Ephesians 3:14–21, drawing us into the ecstasy of being filled with the Spirit's power, the Son's love, and the fullness of the Father. The inward worship of the soul described in this chapter can blossom in our lives. Through it we experience the ecstasy of intimacy with God and the crowning victory of an overcoming warrior, never losing sight of the glory and the worthiness of our God.

I invite you to explore these seven realms of potential vision-filled victory in the next chapters and to be filled with anticipation for them to be realized in your walk toward progressive faith.

## EMBRACING PARADOX

Finally, to conclude Part III, we will discuss the necessity of embracing the divine paradoxes that God presents to us. Only as our faith grows and matures, through submission to His sovereignty, can we enjoy the divine intimacy of our relationship with God and receive the blessings of a living faith.

Chapter 12

# SPIRITUAL BLINDNESS OF THE NATURAL MAN

ACCORDING TO SCRIPTURE, the natural man (or woman) remains rooted and tied to this world. He has not experienced the realities of God's spiritual realm, nor is he aware of the significance and greatness of those realities. The things of God are foolishness to him because, without having his spirit made alive to God, he pays attention only to his sense perceptions.

> ...the natural man does not receive the things of the Spirit of God for they are foolishness to him; nor can he know them, because they are spiritually discerned.
> —1 CORINTHIANS 2:14

The natural man does not view life from God's perspective; he only perceives life by his five outward-facing senses. In this way, he remains unawakened to God and lives by his own wisdom and sight. But the Bible calls us to walk by faith—spiritual sight—and not by the sight of our fallible, human senses. (See 2 Corinthians 5.)

Modern human science teaches the natural man that the world—life and the amazingly complex cell—evolved from nothingness rather than from the intelligence of the glorious Creator. You may also believe this because you believe that science is *man's* knowledge. In reality, science is *God's* knowledge revealed to man.

The natural man thinks he is a good person; he sees no overarching authority or accountability. Until the natural man has *the anointing of recognizing God's ultimate sovereignty*, he is bound by his own imperfection and cannot see the spiritual design of the human soul, Satan's evil schemes, and the greater, transcendent power of the Holy Spirit. The natural man is unaware that his own inner spirit is a battleground for dark spiritual powers and principalities—things far above his head.

## AWAKENED TO THE SUPERNATURAL

Unless you hear God's voice speaking to you from the Scriptures, you will remain in that natural, darkened state of being. Jesus said, "The words that I speak to you are spirit, and they are life" (John 6:63). Jesus told Nicodemus, a religious teacher of the Jews, that his education would not save him. He explained that unless he became born again by the Spirit he would never see the kingdom of God. (See John 3.)

Only in that supernatural experience of accepting Christ as Savior and being born again will you receive a supernatural change of your desires and motivations. Coming to know the wonderful forgiveness and life of Christ within you births desires to please God and to live in devotion to Jesus. Until that happens, the Bible will not make sense to you. The Bible calls you to love the Savior as your first affection and your portion in life. But you will not serve God and sacrifice yourself to honor Him without first being given a new heart by accepting Christ as your personal Savior.

The natural man who views the universe as a clutch of impersonal forces also views Jesus as merely a historical figure. The natural man has no conception of the present and living Christ walking beside the believer, as He did with the disciples on the road to Emmaus. The Bible says, "Taste and see that the LORD is good" (Psalm 34:8), but the unbeliever does not taste and he cannot *see*. His completely natural state leaves him focused on the immediate and apparent rather than on the eternal.

For us to depart from such blindness and to enter into a living faith in Christ, we must believe He is risen and waiting in heaven to welcome us. This hope must stir us to live our lives here in the light of eternity. To have true peace we must believe that we are forgiven and delivered from the judgment of hell. Our total redemption is accomplished by the blood of Jesus shed for us at Calvary. We can look into the face of death and know that we are "more than conquerors through Him who loved us" (Romans 8:37).

The unbeliever often tries to put aside considerations of mortality. He or she does not take to heart what the prophet said: "Prepare to meet your God" (Amos 4:12). Believers know that Jesus offered Himself to pay for our sins; we understand God's great offer of mercy to us in Jesus. Living as a natural man, one cannot understand the purpose for the cross as the doorway to forgiveness, heaven, and the heart of God.

You must believe that God calls you to come to Him in repentance and He will receive you. Repentance is the great reality of true Christian conversion. There is a sorrow you experience because you realize, as David did, that any commission of sin is actually against God Himself. The Bible declares, "For godly sorrow produces repentance leading to salvation, not to be regretted; but the sorrow of the world produces death" (2 Corinthians 7:10).

Through repentance you are grieved that you have been so unthankful to the God who created you, and that you have ignored Him and gone your own way. To know that His love is offered to you, in spite of all of this, brings remorse and hope combined in each repentant tear. However, the natural man continues to be hardened to this wonderful reality.

Once you receive forgiveness for your sin and are born again, your spirit is alive to God, and you become a spiritual being. Of course, the sin principle within us still competes for pre-eminence. But the new creation, the spirit man within, begins to take control of your life as he progresses toward a mature relationship with God, choosing His peace and light over the conflict and darkness of the natural man without God.

### Receiving the promises of God

A spiritual man also believes that God answers prayer because God has promised to do so, and He is ever faithful. Believers know that when we worship we are being heard by God in heaven and that He takes pleasure in our praise. We know that God is sovereign and works all things together for our good. (See Romans 8:28.)

I believe that when I give a cup of cold water to another in need, in Jesus' name, that Jesus has promised to reward me for it. (See Matthew 10:42.) I believe that the Holy Spirit indwells my life and that He will continue to revive my faith. I believe that the emotions of love toward Christ, delight in prayer and praise, and gratitude for God's love and our creation, are all affections that arise from the Holy Spirit's supernatural actions upon my soul. These are the fruit of the Spirit-filled life. In sad contrast, the natural man has not felt the love of God poured into his heart, and so does not see the vastness of his own emptiness.

### Strength in adversity

Believers are sure that anything that comes between God and us is the same as an idol that displeases God, for which we must repent and cast aside. This awareness is an essential part of life for those who are serious about relating one-on-one with God as a Person, as the King and Joy of life. It is the way to spiritual sight. The world is full of its icons and idols for the unbeliever. The believer, on the other hand, experiences unspeakable joy, love that surpasses knowledge, and peace that passes all understanding in relationship with the Creator and Savior. To the unbeliever, the natural man, these wonderful characteristics can only ever be unknown realities of God's kingdom.

When weak, disappointed, and facing sorrow, the believer can truly say, "Thy will be done" (looking to God in faith). In submission to God's sovereignty, you will experience strength and know fellowship with Christ in His sufferings. Then you will learn to exchange your weakness, as you wait on God for His strength and "mount up with wings like eagles" (Isaiah 40:31).

When we choose to resist temptation and to pursue purity, we experience the reality of the happiness and joy promised in Christ's benediction:

> Blessed are the pure in heart, for they shall see God.
> —MATTHEW 5:8

When we forgive others who wrong us we become channels of God's grace and conductors of the same love that God has shown to us. God is at work in us when we forgive; without that divine work, we would become bitter and self-destructive. These spiritual blessings seem as foolishness to the unbeliever.

The natural man is missing the best part of life, which is the reality and ecstasy of experiencing the gracious presence of God. Believers know what it means to dwell in the secret place of the Most High and to abide under the shadow of the Almighty (Psalm 91:1). We know what it means for God to draw near to us, to manifest Himself to us, and pour out His Spirit upon us as anointing oil from heaven. We may then say:

> The LORD make His face shine upon you, and be gracious to you; the LORD lift up His countenance upon you, and give you peace.
> —NUMBERS 6:25–26

The person blind in spiritual darkness has never seen heaven opened as John did, and heard the voice of God in Scripture say, "Come up here" (Revelation 4:1).

Chapter 13

# Repentance: Remedy for Spiritual Blindness

G OD IS THE light of our lives and our guiding star. Yet, until we have an authentic, personal encounter with the Lord, we do not see the marked difference between His holiness and our unclean, sinful nature. In the gloom of our sin that we seemingly prefer to Him, most of us remain disoriented, blind, and lost. In that state, we are unable to see His beautiful face, His helpful hand, or the road that He prepares for us.

In the last chapter, we introduced the need for personal repentance in order to receive spiritual sight. We will now explore that truth through the Scriptures to see how we can be delivered from our spiritual blindness through the power of repentance. When our eyes are opened to His grace, we can sing the beloved hymn:

> Amazing grace, how sweet the sound that saved a wretch like me!
>
> —John Newton[1]

## A NEW PERSPECTIVE ON LIFE

Deliverance from our spiritual blindness to sight in the light of God, demands a *metanoia* within us. Metanoia means a total change of perspective, a complete transformation of mind. Our whole perspective of life changes when we meet God in His glorious sinlessness—when we see Him in His majestic holiness. This change is brought about first by repentance of sin, and then by coming to a place of humility and brokenness before the Lord. This humble repentance is essential to a real change in the inner person. The prophet, Isaiah, experienced this metanoia.

> In the year that King Uzziah died I saw also the Lord sitting upon a throne, high and lifted up, and His train filled the temple... Then said I, Woe is me! for I am undone; because I am a man of unclean lips, and I dwell in the midst of a people of unclean lips: for mine eyes have seen the King, the LORD of hosts.
>
> —ISAIAH 6:1–6, KJV

In the new perspective of a life recast by repentance, you will see God as He really is and not as you may have imagined Him. Recognition of the Savior and His redemption is your only hope. Without repentance all external change is mere pretense.

There is no greater chapter in the Bible on repentance than Psalm 51. It represents the cry of a broken, contrite, and humbled heart that longs to see and to be close to his Lord and Creator again. This cry of repentance was inspired by the historical background of King David's fall into sin. (See 2 Samuel 11–12.) David understood that his sin had separated him from His God, and that thought broke his heart.

## THE SHOCKING REALITY OF DAVID'S SIN

Reading this story may remind you of a dark Shakespearean drama. The narrative recorded in 2 Samuel is full of lust, covetousness, adultery, deceit, and murder. David, the king, first found himself in the wrong place at the wrong time when he willfully neglected his regal responsibilities of accompanying his armies to war. As he lounged around the palace with little to do, he spied his neighbor's wife bathing on her rooftop. Bathsheba was instantly desirable to David, prompting him to soon abuse his authority and have her brought before him. David then seduced Bathsheba while her husband, Uriah, was bravely fighting at the war front—where David ought to have been himself.

Bathsheba became pregnant, and the king compounded his transgressions with deceit. For a convenient coverup, David brought Uriah home from the battlefield and encouraged him to sleep with his wife. However, Uriah possessed an upright spirit and he did not think it was proper to enjoy his wife's company while his colleagues struggled in war. David's final trick, an attempt to corrupt Uriah's noble resolve with alcohol, also failed. So David redeployed Uriah to the front while secretly instructing the commander, Joab, to ensure that Uriah would die in battle. After the predictable death, David took Bathsheba as his own wife. David's conspicuous blindness is apparent in his greed and reckless disregard for human life. It was all so unnecessary. David had all that he needed in his life, but he was unable to see clearly. He had forgotten the God who had done so much for him—the God he had known so well when He wrote Psalm 23. David was blind to his own sin, and his heart was hardened to God's will.

## Spiritual Blindness Exposed

The prophet Nathan came to David after these events and told him a story about a wealthy man who had many sheep but took his poor neighbor's only lamb in order to feed a visiting guest. David's reaction was immediate. He thought that this wealthy man surely deserved death. With his eyes clouded by sin, David could not recognize himself in the story. Nathan admonished, "Thou art the man!" Instantly, David's vision was restored in that moment of truth, and he exclaimed, "I have sinned."

David had certainly sinned against God. He had rejected and mocked God's commandments. He had been ungrateful for all the good that God had extended to him. In this instance, David had forgotten the goodness God had shown to him, ever since the days he had been a shepherd boy, to be seated upon the throne representing God's rule over His people. David had counted God's wisdom as foolishness and did not heed His commands. The earthly king cast aside God's friendship to please himself. David dragged God's glory into the muck in which he had plunged himself. He neither feared nor honored God at that point. For a time, he willfully cast aside all the sweetness of God's beautiful holiness while he embraced his own greedy pleasure.

## SINCERE REPENTANCE

I acknowledge my transgressions,
And my sin is always before me.
Against You, You only, have I sinned,
And done this evil in Your sight.

—PSALM 51:3–4

You cannot cause a man with a full stomach to cry out in the way that a hungry man does. Likewise, you cannot make a man with a good opinion of himself cry out for mercy like one who feels—*sees*—his vileness. Psalm 51 shows us that David, with his heart freshly stung and aware, was now humiliated and spiritually crushed. He was *overwhelmed* with sorrow. In Psalm 51, David is finally open, honest, and transparent with God. David had finished lying to himself and excusing himself—he finally took full responsibility for his actions and then sought God's forgiveness.

David had seen that the evil he had committed in God's sight had defiled others, had wronged them, and had brought them down to his own degraded level. He had at one time esteemed God's lovingkindness as better than life itself. By repenting, David came to see again that his life meant nothing without the warmth of God's smile upon him. His sense of separation from God and his sense of God's displeasure were more painful to him than having his bones broken. Knowing that the dark night of his soul would be banished by finding God's reassuring love once again, David prayed fervently:

> Make me hear joy and gladness,
> That the bones You have broken may rejoice.
> Hide Your face from my sins,
> And blot out all my iniquities.
>
> —PSALM 51:8–9

In his past, David had known such joy as the strength of his life, but it had been a long time since his soul could say, as it once had, "my cup runneth over." Seeing his sin with his restored vision, he could not continue with his life unless God gave him this joy again. "Restore to me the joy of Your salvation, And uphold me by Your generous Spirit" (Psalm 51:12).

David's cry, "Do not take your Holy Spirit from me" (Psalm 51:11), tells us that David knew he could not live for God without the help of the Holy Spirit. In his repentance of *dependence on self*, he cast himself on the everlasting arms of God. David saw that he needed God's hand upon his soul to keep him from evil. He needed the river of God to flow through his soul again so that he might find his refreshment in the pleasures of God. When God answered this heartfelt, humble prayer, David looked forward to being able to say once more, "My soul follows close behind You; Your right hand upholds me" (Psalm 63:8).

## HOW CAN THERE BE FORGIVENESS FOR ME?

David came to see that God could cleanse him and make him "whiter than snow" (Psalm 51:7). It became clear that God could remove the sense of defilement and guilt. David sought the relief that only God could give.

You might reasonably ask, "How could David ever believe that he could be forgiven?" You might also observe that when his eyes were finally opened, it would be easy for him to see himself as a hopeless case. Yet, there was one thing that David knew that helped him in his despair. God had promised this king of Israel that He would be a Father to him: "I will be his Father, and he shall be My son" (2 Samuel 7:14; see also Psalm 2:6–7). What David desired most was to be restored in his relationship with God. God was his Father, his first love, his joy and portion in life. This relationship is what David had cast aside, and it was to this he desired to return.

David would one day understand intimately how a father's heart feels toward a rebellious child. When his proud, self-serving son, Absalom, was killed, David displayed great love and pity crying, "O my son Absalom—my son, my son Absalom—if only I had died in your place!" (2 Samuel 18:33). To plead God's grace, David knew that he was pleading the grace and mercy in the heart of God *as His Father*.

David could faithfully believe that he would be forgiven, in spite of the greatness of his sin. To know the Father-heart of God is to be saved from desperation and despair, which follows when we harden our hearts, pursue our sin, and are then awakened to see the horror of our ugly, ungodly selves.

## AM I AS BAD AS DAVID?

Does Psalm 51 apply to all of us or only to those who have fallen as far as David had? You might say, "I'm a good person. I have not committed any act like David did. Am I as bad as David?" Yet the Bible declares that there is none righteous (see Romans 3:10), and if I think I am righteous, I am profoundly deceived. Isaiah 65:5 describes such a person as one who says to God, "Keep to yourself, do not come near me, for I am holier than thou." God replies that such spiritual blindness is "Smoke in my nostrils, a fire that burns all day." God is great, glorious, majestic, almighty, and infinitely holy.

It has been said: "If we cannot be awakened to see our danger, we cannot be saved." That is because we will blindly continue in sin "as an ox goes to the slaughter" (Proverbs 7:22). Each of us falls into the category of "the greatest sinner" because we have broken the greatest commandment: "You shall love the LORD your God with all your heart" (Deuteronomy 6:5). Before we are born again, we all have put our "self" above God. We have forgotten God and have not lived in thankfulness toward Him. We have all rejected God's appointed King over our lives—King Jesus.

We could also ask the question, "Am I better than the apostle Paul?" Paul painted himself as chief among sinners (1 Timothy 1:15). The Scriptures are clear in declaring that all have sinned and come short of the glory of God (Romans 3:23). If we take God's Word to heart, we will realize that we can only be reconciled to God by coming in repentant faith to the welcoming arms of Jesus who declared, "Come to Me...and I will give you rest" (Matthew 11:28). To begin living a life that is pleasing to God, we must receive salvation through the blood of Christ alone, who paid for our sin through His death on the cross. Accepting that foundation based on the Savior's life and death, we will experience a new birth: "no other foundation can anyone lay than that which is laid, which is Jesus Christ" (1 Corinthians 3:11).

To answer the question, "Am I as bad as David in God's sight?" we must respond, "Surely I am!" And then, in humble repentance, we can know the wonderful cleansing that David experienced.

## THE ONLY HOPE

From beginning to end, the Bible gives great encouragement to sinners who come to God in repentance and faith. David displayed wonderful insight into the ways of God with our souls. He based his human plea for mercy on the mercy He knew was in the heart of God. David believed in the grace, mercy, and pity of God toward His fallen creation. Whenever we stop believing in those redemptive attributes of God, we have no light, and nowhere to run.

Jesus told of a Pharisee and a tax collector who went up to pray. The Pharisee commended himself, but the tax collector lifted his eyes, beat his breast and cried, "God, be merciful to me a sinner!" (Luke 18: 9–13). Then Jesus declared, "I tell you, this man went down to his house justified rather than the other [the Pharisee]; for everyone who exalts himself will be humbled, and he who humbles himself will be exalted" (Luke 18:14). There is hope for all of us who, like David or the tax collector, approach God humbly in repentance and cry out earnestly, "Have mercy upon me, O God, according to Your lovingkindness; According to the multitude of Your tender mercies, Blot out my transgressions. Wash me thoroughly from my iniquity, And cleanse me from my sin" (Psalm 51:1–2).

You may feel that there is no forgiveness for one as guilty, defiled, rebellious, ungrateful, and wicked as you when you sin against God's goodness. That is because you do not know the depth of God's love for you. Let your repentance include David's prayer, "Create in me a clean heart, O God, And renew a steadfast spirit within me" (Psalm 51:10). The transformed David not only wanted to have his guilt removed and communion with God restored, *he did not want to fall, and be blinded, again.* He wanted his joy to be found in pleasing God by walking in His light and truth.

## A GOLDEN VERSE

One of the special verses of Psalm 51 is verse 17: "A broken and a contrite heart—These, O God, You will not despise." David had been broken in spirit; he had recognized himself as arrogant and loathed it. God saw David's repentant heart and delighted in it. He welcomed David back into His presence and restored David's joy by making His face to shine again upon his renewed servant.

The prodigal son, returning home from a wasteful life, expected the worst even as he turned to face it. However, his father, upon seeing from a distance his lost son returning, "had compassion, and ran and fell on his neck and kissed him" (Luke 15:20). This loving, forgiving, restoring heart of our heavenly Father is as available for you as it was for King David, the prodigal son, and it is true for all who come to God humbly and in repentance.

From the place of repentance, I know that I will rejoice as I hear the Father say, "'Bring out the best robe and put it on him, and put a ring on his hand and sandals on his feet. And bring the fatted calf here and kill it, and let us eat and be merry; for this my son was dead and is alive again; he was lost and is found.' And they began to be merry" (Luke 15:22–24). This is a beautiful picture of the great deliverance from a life of blindness into a life of spiritual vision and communion with God, our Father.

## In Evil Long I Took Delight (I Saw One Hanging on a Tree)

In evil long I took delight,
Unawed by shame or fear,
Till a new object struck my sight,
And stopp'd my wild career:

I saw One hanging on a Tree
In agonies and blood,
Who fix'd His languid eyes on me.
As near His Cross I stood.

Sure never till my latest breath,
Can I forget that look:
It seem'd to charge me with His death,
Though not a word He spoke:

My conscience felt and own'd the guilt,
And plunged me in despair:
I saw my sins His Blood had spilt,
And help'd to nail Him there.
Alas! I knew not what I did!
But now my tears are vain:
Where shall my trembling soul be hid?
For I the Lord have slain!

A second look He gave, which said,
"I freely all forgive;
This blood is for thy ransom paid;
I die that thou may'st live."
Thus, while His death my sin displays
In all its blackest hue,
Such is the mystery of grace,
It seals my pardon too.

With pleasing grief, and mournful joy,
My spirit now is fill'd,
That I should such a life destroy,
Yet live by Him I kill'd!

—JOHN NEWTON, 1779[2]

Chapter 14

# RECEIVING SPIRITUAL SIGHT: ABIDING IN CHRIST

THE SAVIOR TELLS us that the essence of spiritual sight is simple: we understand that without Him we can do nothing (John 15:5). It is in our spiritual blindness that we convince ourselves that we can live life by our own strength and understanding. As true believers, we realize that we can only live by the power of His life within us. All that we experience comes our way through God's providential purpose for our lives.

## SPIRITUAL BLINDNESS—SPIRITUAL SIGHT

Jesus' words in John 15 illustrate the spiritual reality of abiding in Christ using the allegory of a grapevine. Christ is the vine and believers are the branches abiding in that vine. God the Father is the vinedresser who constantly attends to the condition of each branch.

The spiritual lesson learned is that the strength of the believer's inner life is derived only from union with Christ. This union, the connection between the vine and the branches, is supernatural, invisible, and inexplicable. A Seeing Eye dog is useless to the blind owner unless the two are in union. However, once trust is established, the blind person moves about by the sight of the dog alone. When you get to the point at which you are ready to live in union with the Lord, dependent on His sight and insight, you can accomplish great things. Without Him, any one of us will certainly stumble and fall. A parallel passage found in Colossians 3:3 beautifully describes the believer's life in these words: "Your life is hidden with Christ in God."

## "I AM THE TRUE VINE, AND MY FATHER IS THE VINEDRESSER" (JOHN 15:1)

The Father has a purpose for your life: to enjoy communion with Him, to bear the fruit of Christlike character, the fruit of obedience, and the fruit of usefulness. It is a spiritual reality that you need godly motivation to grow and to avoid the spiritual decline of indifference in the Christian life.

Referring to the analogy at hand, either to prevent or to bring us out of spiritual backsliding, the Father continually prunes our branch. The vinedresser sometimes cuts a branch vigorously in order to encourage fruitfulness. This pruning means that God brings painful experiences into our lives to make us seek Him more earnestly. And those who are already bearing fruit are pruned so they may bear even more fruit. In times of suffering you often have nothing else to hold to other than this reality. Through the pruning, you will come to a new awareness, as the prodigal son did, and seek greater communion with Christ. He "grafts" us into Him so that we can draw life from Him. This fellowship with Christ gives us the strength to persevere and grow, and to rejoice in the midst of our trials.

It is not unusual to initially feel distanced from God when we are surprised by some disappointment or discouragement—a pruning. To forestall this, the Savior tells us in advance, "You are already clean because of the word which I have spoken to you" (John 15:3). Here, Jesus assures us that we are the forgiven children of God and that our trials are a call to draw nearer to Him, rather than a break in communion with Him. The principle of maintaining your assurance in your trials, by remembering Christ's words, will keep your faith focused on the open heart of God. God *entrusts* you with your trials or "prunings." As George Mueller, who provided for thousands of orphans, asked one ambitious young man, "Do you want great faith? Are you willing to endure great trials to develop great faith?" [1]

## Abiding in Christ—Dependence, Communion, Abandonment

As we have mentioned, to grow in the Christian life we must learn to live in dependence on the Son of God as the branches of a vine depend on the vine for nourishment and vitality. To live in dependence on the Savior we have to learn repeatedly the futility of living by our own means, our own intellect and strength. I know that I must learn again and again, in greater measure each time, the truth that "without Me you can do nothing" (John 15:5).

To be dependent on Christ means, in part, to learn to live in the Word and in prayer. The Savior said, "Man shall not live by bread alone, but by every word that proceeds from the mouth of God" (Matthew 4:4). If we do not depend on the Word of God revealed to us by the work of the Holy Spirit, we are merely trying to nourish our souls with the world's thoughts, which is blindness. When our eyes are opened to the true condition of our spiritual life, that verse rings with power in our hearts: "Without Me you can do nothing." And it follows, that a life of communion through prayer must accompany our devotion to His Word in order to be dependent upon Him.

Cultivating a life of dependence on Christ's life within you is called "abiding." Abiding involves, first of all, a conviction that we cannot live the Christian life successfully in any other way. Then, it produces a quickened communion with Christ, a walk with God, and a life of abandonment to Him. This life of dependence is deepened by growth in prayer and saturation with the Word of God.

The Savior Himself lays down this vital principle of growth: "If you abide in me, and My words abide in you..." (John 15:7). His words stir up faith, prayer, hunger, and a desire for God. He summons and we are drawn to Him. If only we would implement the reality of that old spiritual song—"Every time I feel the Spirit moving in my heart, I will pray!"—then we truly would bear spiritual fruit.

## ABIDE IN MY LOVE

A crucial part of abiding in the Lord Jesus is spelled out in John 15:9: "As the Father loved Me, I also have loved you; abide in My love." The command is "Abide in My love." He tells us to never forget and always to keep before our hearts this great truth—His love for us! This was the secret of Paul's daring and courageous faith—it was rooted in the Savior's love. He declared, "I live by faith in the Son of God, who loved me and gave Himself for me" (Galatians 2:20). Believing and receiving His love is the only way to experience His joy abiding in our hearts. His divinely personal love, known and felt, cannot but cause joy to flow forth from our hearts, motivating us to abide even more deeply in Him. Here is the true picture of the blessed inner life of abiding in Christ.

Why do we not realize that when we are disheartened and full of self-pity, we are spiritually blind, have lost sight of Him, and have our eyes fixated on ourselves? He has told us that only in keeping our eyes on Him would we know the peace and joy that the world cannot give. (See John 14:27.)

To keep our understanding of Christ's love at its highest potential, He reminds us that His love is Calvary love. We see the reality of this divine love so frequently in Scripture, yet in the living of our lives, we forget it too often: "Greater love has no one than this, than to lay down one's life for his friends" (John 15:13). No one loves us like the Lord Jesus does. And His love does not change or fail. If He was willing to be nailed to the cross for us, we should know that in our darkest moments there is no obstacle that He cannot help us avoid or climb over. There is nothing He won't do for us—if we seek Him.

## LOVE ONE ANOTHER

No believer can truly walk this close to the Savior and not love other believers who do the same. Obviously, the greater challenge is to love those in the family of God who are careless with their attitudes and make life difficult for others around them. This was too often true of the disciples themselves, but Christ loved them still, and He is our pattern. The King calls us to "love one another" (John 15:12, 17). This does not mean to love only the "loveable," it means love everyone.

The divine love—the fruit of the vine—flourishes through our "branches" as a result of our sacred union with Jesus. The Savior opens up to us His secrets and says, in effect, "Would a master confide in his slave? No. So don't you see that you are My friends?" He also says, "You did not choose Me, but I chose you" (John 15:16). In our more humble, sane moments we may acknowledge, "I would surely not have chosen someone like me!"

For example, the apostle Paul considered himself to be the chief of sinners (1 Timothy 1:15). We may want to argue that such a title more aptly refers to ourselves. However, no matter the degree of our sinfulness, the Scriptures are clear that God set His love on us before we cast our eyes on Him: "while we were still sinners, Christ died for us" (Romans 5:8). And our love for Him is always in response to His love for us: "We love Him because He first loved us" (1 John 4:19).

This hopefully causes you to ask, "Why would He take such interest in me? Why would He call me His friend? Why would He choose me? Why would He die for me?" For me, these are the questions that proceed from a spirit of humility, gratitude, and wonder. We honor the Son of God when we say, "I don't know the answer, but, Lord Jesus, I believe You! I love You! I adore You!

I give my life to You!" This devoted worship is some of the richest fruit of the true Vine.

The world, dying in its spiritual blindness, may hate us without a cause, as they did the Savior (John 15:18–27). Yet, it is also a wonderful reality that the Holy Spirit is able to open others' eyes, as He does ours. To that end, we need to boldly share with others the spiritual sight God has given to us. In that way we will be truly fruitful, allowing the divine love of God to touch hurting lives, bringing the possibility of spiritual sight to them as well.

## OPEN OUR EYES, LORD

Open our eyes, Lord, we want to see Jesus,
To reach out and touch Him,
And say that we love Him.
Lord, we want to see Jesus.[2]

Chapter 15

# OVERCOMING BLINDNESS THROUGH LIFE IN THE SPIRIT

A S WE DISCUSSED the necessity of repentance to bring us into a personal relationship with God, and the accompanying "broken and contrite heart" (Psalm 51:17) to which He responds, we come to understand that our brokenness is a vital part of our progression toward mature faith. Yet, it seems to be a paradox to the exultant, victorious faith the Scriptures promise to the believer. Are we to grovel in sorrow for sin, or rejoice in the hope of spiritual sight through faith in God alone? As we shall see, in a later chapter, life in God is filled with paradox, which cannot be resolved by the "either/or" solutions of the intellect.

## THE AGONY AND THE ECSTASY

In Romans 7 through 8, the apostle Paul expresses the two fundamental states of Christian consciousness. The first state is expressed in the exclamation, "O wretched man that I am!" (Romans 7:24). It is the essential posture of repentance that believers must not only experience at the beginning of their walk with God, but must maintain throughout their lives.

The second state of a believer's awareness is expressed in the prayer, "Abba, Father" (Romans 8:15). This utterance describes childlike faith that has found God as a loving Father through the redemption of Christ and the power of the Holy Spirit. It reveals a loving relationship in which, as believers, we desire to please our heavenly Father.

Yet, Paul found that what he wanted to do, he often failed to accomplish. Although he found delight in the law of God according to the inner man, the principle of self-will and evil desires kept springing up in his heart, even in the midst of doing something good. (See Romans 7:19–22.) By experience, Paul learned the painful reality that, even with good intentions, the principle of indwelling sin was a great, enduring burden, and in his sinful flesh there dwelt no good thing (Romans 7:18). Paul spent his life, as all true believers do, learning and relearning what Jesus said: "without Me you can do nothing" (John 15:5). This continual process is represented by our movement back and forth on the continuum, as we have discussed, moving us forward in our progression to mature faith.

However daunting and distressing your battle with sin may be, you can find some encouragement in Paul's discussion. At least Paul knew there was a battle in his soul. To be engaged in this battle at all shows you have been born again and do not desire to sin. The unbeliever delights in his sin or simply rationalizes it when it is convenient. Paul felt disappointment in his sin and longed for God's help to grow. This attitude toward sin is *the beginning of spiritual sight!*

We might ask why Paul, as a mature believer, still could speak of this battle with sin in the present tense: "I am doing"; but "I hate it." The answer lies in the realization that we are never completely free from sin and that the closer we get to God the more sensitive we become to what displeases Him. If we have tender hearts toward God, we will always be ashamed of our sins, which are fundamentally based in "the lust of the flesh, the lust of the eyes, and the pride of life" (1 John 2:16). This spiritual battle with temptations and failures is our human lot as long as we remain in this world.

It is true, if we are vigilant, that we are sometimes stronger than the temptation we face and gain a victory over it. However, at times we simply do not resist the devil, the flesh, and the world in the moment of temptation. As believers, we will finally come to our senses and cry out in despair within ourselves, as Paul did, to receive the divine deliverance offered us.

The believer in Jesus does not ultimately despair; he thanks God, as Paul did, for the victory he has in Jesus his Savior (Romans 7:25). He learns to go again to the cleansing blood of Christ and receive forgiveness, with no condemnation. (See Romans 8:1.) Instead of despair, he rejoices that once again his faith in the power of Christ's redemption has rescued him again, and he thanks God for not abandoning him in his sin. He is assured that one day this battle against sin will be over. Until then, he has found the pathway to progressing toward full faith.

## THE DELIVERANCE OF THE SPIRIT

Paul continues in Romans 8 with a triumphant note that shows us there is much more victory for every believer: "There is therefore now no condemnation to those who are in Christ Jesus" (Romans 8:1). The repentant believer has much to rejoice in as a sinner saved by grace; he has much to draw strength from; he finds that God will enable him by the work of the Spirit in his life.

As a believer, I have the blessed work of the Holy Spirit in my life to comfort me in my trials and discouragements. What man cannot do, God did by sending the Savior to offer Himself up in our place. Now the risen Lord sends the Spirit of God to deliver us from the law of sin and death. Just as the aerodynamic lift under the wings of a twenty-ton plane cheats gravity and raises the craft up into the clouds, a more powerful principle than sin is imparted to us: this is the Spirit's purpose in the child of God as we set our mind on the things of God rather than on the things of the flesh. (See Romans 8:5.)

Spiritual strength against sin is imparted to us by the Spirit of God, and He teaches us to accept this divine enablement through prayer. It is by the Spirit that we cry out, "Abba, Father" (Romans 8:15). In the Aramaic language of the first century, "Abba" is a toddler's first attempt to say, "Father." It is similar to our affectionate expression, "Daddy." When we call God "Abba" in our struggles against sin, we are saying, "O God, You are my Father. I am Your child, helpless and needy." In a downward spiral into some temptation, we can learn to cry out earnestly, "Abba, Father, pity me, deliver me, and strengthen me to resist and fight this temptation and honor You." God shows Himself to be a Father indeed and delights in answering this filial prayer. We owe the desire to seek His face in prayer to the blessed outpouring of His Spirit in our lives. As Paul declared, "You did not receive the spirit of bondage again to fear, but you received the Spirit of adoption by whom we cry out, 'Abba, Father'" (Romans 8:15).

## THE ASSURANCE OF THE SPIRIT

That Spirit-wrought prayer, calling God our Father, is the heavenly confirmation that you have been adopted into God's family. You are His beloved child, and He wants you to know it! The Holy Spirit also convinces you that God indeed has embraced you as His own: "The Spirit Himself bears witness with our spirit that we are children of God" (Romans 8:16). Remember that this heavenly embrace of God is given to those who, with a broken and penitent heart signifying the beginning of clear vision, cry out, "O wretched man that I am! Who will deliver me?" (Romans 7:24). In response, the Father pours the heavenly anointing oil on your wounds and pours out His love in your heart. (See Romans 5:5.) And you are made to "taste and see" the goodness of the Lord in His divine love by this comforting assurance of the Holy Spirit. (See Psalm 34:8.)

## ADORATION AND WORSHIP
## THROUGH THE SPIRIT

We also cry, "Abba, Father," in appreciation, gratitude, wonder, and joy at knowing God and enjoying His presence. As His creation, we have the privilege of saying, "O Father, how blessed I am to have You, to rest in Christ's redemption, to have the Divine Comforter as my Advocate and heavenly Helper. O Father, I love You, adore You, and I bow down before You!" What a wonder it is to step into the throne room of heaven and behold the King and heavenly Bridegroom, the Lord Jesus, on the throne! How indescribable is His gaze of delight upon me. Why does He love me so? Humbled, yet believing, I embrace His love and say, "I believe You, Lord. I believe that You love me with an everlasting love. May I keep this ever before me and abide in Your love. May this always be the crown I wear each day that I am crowned with Your lovingkindness." (See Psalm 103:4.)

## THE SPIRIT'S HELP IN PRAYER IN
## THE MIDST OF TRIALS

Paul continues his discourse in Romans 8, explaining that in a spirit of prayer we "groan" with all of creation at the trials and heartaches and difficult surprises of life. (See Romans 8:23.) The Spirit is given to us as the first fruits of the heavenly harvest that is yet to come in life. We live in hope and confidence of what He will do in our lives. He enables us to be fruitful in prayer though we may feel confused, bewildered, and perplexed at the painful circumstances staring us in the face. As the apostle says, "The Spirit also helps in our weaknesses. For we do not know what we should pray for as we ought, but the Spirit Himself makes intercession for us with groanings which cannot be uttered" (Romans 8:26).

In our experience of the Spirit's help, we may truly pray:

> *Lord, You know that at times I can hardly pray. I groan
> in my trials, heartbreaks, and disappointments. But there
> is given to me from the Spirit of God, deeper desires than*

159

*what I can express. Lord, You know what I desire. Hear the prayer of the Spirit of God through these groanings. Heavenly Father, You know that my prayer is that of Moses: "Please, show me Your glory" (Exodus 33:18).*

*In this trial I long to be like Job and say, "Though He slay me, yet will I trust Him" (Job 13:15). You know that my longing is to stay near to You in the midst of my disappointments. Help me not to be diverted by the temporary vision provided by time and my senses. May I maintain my joyful gaze upon my Redeemer and my focus on eternity. Father, thank You that You see and hear and understand my Spirit-wrought groans.*

You will begin to see with spiritual eyes even when you are only capable of saying, "O God, help me. You hear my deepest desire to know Christ in the power of His resurrection." Though you may begin prayer stumbling and groping in your own darkness toward the throne of grace, by the help of the Spirit of God, you can mount up with wings as eagles and can shout in victory, like the bride in the Song of Solomon: "I am my beloved's, And my beloved is mine" (Song of Solomon 6:3).

## RESTING IN GOD'S PROMISES

The Spirit of God continues to work in wonderful ways in the lives of those seeking greater spiritual sight. He teaches us to trust God's promises so that we can say from the heart, "We know that all things work together for good to those who love God, to those who are the called according to His purpose" (Romans 8:28). What a divine purpose this is, that God set His love on me long before I came to faith and then He called me and justified me and will glorify me at last! In the meantime, the greatest good I get out of my trials is to be "conformed to the image" of Christ (Romans 8:29–30). In heaven, Jesus will be the firstborn among many brethren. He will be honored as the King, the heir and portion of all believers who are made like Him. They will find their eternal joy gathering around Him in worship.

## CONFIDENCE AND STRENGTH FOR
## THE RENEWED BATTLE

Now, this is certain: "If God is for us, who can be against us?" (Romans 8:31). God's *goodness* to me allows me to say,

> Surely goodness and mercy shall follow me
> All the days of my life.
>
> —PSALM 23:6

In His *wisdom,* God has already planned my life and He has chosen what will be best for me, though I do not always understand it initially. I can say, as David did, "The LORD will perfect that which concerns me" (Psalm 138:8). God's *power* for us upholds us, defends us, protects us, and delivers us. God's *faithfulness* is promised to us—that He will never leave us nor forsake us (Hebrews 13:5). If God's goodness, power, wisdom, and faithfulness is for us, who then can be against us? Who can overthrow us? Who can defeat God who is upholding us?

To be sure, we will have many painful experiences and pass through many trials as we progress to the maturity of complete faith. Remember though, if God did not spare His own Son who died on the cross for us, He will also freely give us all things. (See Romans 8:32.) Note that Paul says that God gives us all things "with Him." He gives us all things in fellowship with the Lord Jesus, to enjoy Him in the midst of it all. This is the best gift of all—to be called the friend of God, as Abraham was.

Our conquest is in the battle for the soul. For those who do not come to Christ, though they would sacrifice the world to have their soul delivered in the final day of judgment, it will be too late (Mark 8:36–37). The battle for faith is to be fought now, in this life, as we bow at the foot of the cross, where we find peace and rest in the Savior. He has accomplished all that we require for forgiveness and a new life—eternal life.

And the Scriptures promise that we are more than conquerors through Him who loved us (Romans 8:37). "Loved," in the past tense, shows us that it was at the cross that we were redeemed.

161

We are also reminded that He loves us now as much as He loved us then, as according to the Scriptures, "Jesus Christ is the same yesterday, today, and forever" (Hebrews 13:8).

When this divine love is your source of spiritual strength, you grow nearer to God through the fight of faith. With this spiritual vision you are set on a course of living a life that will bear blessed fruit in eternity. You learn more and more to quickly run to Jesus and rest on what He has done and not try to believe God loves you because of any "good things" you are doing.

## LOSING HEART, BUT CONQUERING AGAIN

When our faith is strong, these spiritual realities are as bright as the sun. But emotions deceive us as we experience failure, heartbreak, disappointment, betrayal, setbacks, and broken dreams. It is here that our fight of faith must be renewed each day, in each trial—in each assault of the devil.

What is it that will pick us up, revive us again, and help us regain our sight? The apostle Paul tells us it is the love of Christ—His love for us poured out freshly in us by the power of the Holy Spirit—that renews us. It is beyond our comprehension how it is possible, but in the midst of debilitating circumstances, we are made "more than conquerors through Him who loved us" (Romans 8:37). The heavenly Enabler—the Holy Spirit—spoke these words through the apostle to reinvigorate us in even our darkest hours: "Who shall separate us from the love of Christ? Shall tribulation, or distress, or persecution, or famine, or nakedness, or peril, or sword?...Yet in all these things we are more than conquerors through Him who loved us" (Romans 8:35, 37).

## PERSUADED OF GOD'S INVINCIBLE LOVE

As we follow Christ, we will be repeatedly surprised at how the devil does not give up. He is determined to separate all of us from the love of God. But it is God who has hold of us! It is the Spirit who renews our reliance on God's grip.

We are in God's hands, and His heart is determined to keep

His bride and to sustain His children. The faithful Shepherd has pledged Himself to protect His flock (Psalm 23:4). Only as we keep in mind His faithfulness and feed on it will we be able to say, as Paul does, that we are persuaded, we are convinced, we will not lose heart, we will keep believing in God's love. We will keep abiding in it. We will keep leaning on the everlasting arms. The apostle had this assurance when he declared, "*For I am persuaded* that neither death nor life, nor angels nor principalities nor powers, nor things present nor things to come, nor height nor depth, nor any other created thing, shall be able to separate us from the love of God which is in Christ Jesus our Lord" (Romans 8:38–39, emphasis added).

Love engages a person's whole being and all their resources and abilities toward the one loved. Therefore, God's love engages all that He is and has toward us. His heart and hand are for us. Therefore nothing can separate us from the love of God that we have "in Christ" (in union with Him). By the love of God we will conquer as we continue on with Him, by profiting through our trials, by enjoying greater communion with Him, and by being used of God in our trials to be a witness of His all-sufficient grace.

The love of God that sent the Son to die and the Spirit to be poured out in your heart will revive, or quicken, you again and again. God will keep manifesting His love to you by His Word and Spirit so that you learn more and more to keep God's love for you as the great motive of your life.

When you and I fail to do so, we see how foolish we have been and painfully experience the lament, "O wretched man that I am!" (Romans 7:24). In all of these trials and temptations, the Spirit of God is at work to bring us to again cry out, "Abba, Father." So, the challenge of Romans 7 and 8 is one that is lifelong, and only as we *look* to Jesus as the Author and Completer of our faith will we find the Spirit of God leading us in triumph.

## The Gem of the Ring

It has been said that if the Bible were a diamond ring, Romans 8 would be the peerless gem itself. You certainly cannot find a chapter more full of comfort and assistance. It has also been noted that this passage begins with no condemnation (v. 1), it ends with no separation (v. 39), and all things in between work together for our good (v. 28). In this manner, Romans 8 is a summary of the great promises of the Christian life: the promise of forgiveness is given at the beginning of our "chapter" or life with God; the promise of heaven awaits us at the end of our life; the promise of God's help along the way describes the blessed middle of our life! To have genuine 20/20 vision, we must look upon life from the vantage point of Romans 8, and be fully persuaded of God's love and the Spirit's heavenly help.

Chapter 16

# PREVENTING SPIRITUAL BLINDNESS: GROWING IN GRACE

I N 2 PETER 1, as we mentioned earlier, the Holy Spirit issues a call to believers to grow in the grace and knowledge of our Lord and Savior Jesus Christ. In that way, we may avoid the spiritual blindness that we are all prone to when we are not living in the glorious presence of God. Here, Peter gives a beautiful description of the outworking of grace in the details of the Christian life. It was written to help believers avoid the pitfalls of false teachers, heresies, and complacency. The parallels of these issues in our present day are impossible to ignore.

"Grace and peace be multiplied to you in the knowledge of God and of Jesus our Lord" (2 Peter 1:2). Again, this peace—this *shalom*—is "perfect well-being, all necessary good, all spiritual prosperity, and freedom from fears and agitating passions and moral conflicts" (2 Peter 1:2, AMP). The *shalom*, or spiritual prosperity, can only be realized when you have truly rested in God's redemption, rested in the arms of the Savior, and have willfully relinquished your struggle, passions, agitations, and moral conflicts. When you embrace God in the surrender of your life to Him, *shalom* received from the Spirit dispatches your spiritual blindness and gives you spiritual vision. The scales will not be removed from your eyes until you immerse yourself fully in Christ and rest in His redemption by the power of the Holy Spirit.

God's peace is our spiritual sight, which produces power to grow, or mature. We are certain to encounter difficult trials but "His divine power has given to us all things that pertain to life and godliness" (2 Peter 1:3). When we truly accept Him, He will develop our endurance, character, and hope. We must continue in communion with the Lord to keep growing and avoid backsliding. This is the cure for complacency, and it hinges on our appreciation for our Lord.

We are saved by grace. Our salvation and spiritual growth, or sight, does not depend upon good deeds. Reading the Bible or walking down the church aisle will not give us redemption or empower us for life. It is a spirit of appreciation for God, His grace, and His gift of life that motivates us to accomplish His will. *The whole purpose of our life is to appreciate God, the Creator and Savior.* Christians can never become passive and indifferent; it is imperative that we stay in the faith that is rooted in love and nourished by the filling of the Holy Spirit through the Word of God. (See Ephesians 3:17.) By the work of the Spirit, God's Word comes to us with specific and personal application.

Permeated by a knowledge of Him, through love, we then continue to focus on Christ and serve Him. Our blindness settles deeply only as we turn from God, stop appreciating Him, and cease believing His promises. Through His great promises we participate in the divine nature and sidestep the corruption of the world. This deliverance is the fruit of resting in redemption. It represents the quickening of John Wesley who became greatest in his weakness because he trusted in the Lord and saw God's promises were for him personally. The apostle Peter describes a fruitful walk in Christ, contrasting it with spiritual blindness.

> But also for this very reason, giving all diligence, add
> to your faith virtue, to virtue knowledge, to knowledge

self-control, to self-control perseverance, to perseverance godliness, to godliness brotherly kindness, and to
brotherly kindness love. For if all these things are yours
and abound, you will be neither barren nor unfruitful
in the knowledge of our Lord Jesus Christ. For he who
lacks these things is shortsighted, even to blindness, and
has forgotten that he was cleansed from his old sins.

—2 PETER 1:5–9

## MARKERS OF GROWTH AND SIGHT

Our spiritual sight is discovered, and uncovered, in that which
Peter proclaimed as Christian truth—the authority of the Scriptures, our salvation by grace, and the certainty of Christ's return.
He challenges us to grow more like Christ, to partake in the likeness of the divine nature. (See 2 Peter 1:4.) For continued growth
in Christ—spiritual sight—it means that to this faith we must add
virtue—the excellence that disallows either laziness or pretense.
And this virtue, in turn, is founded upon the true knowledge of
getting to know God better as He speaks to us through His Word.
Are we willing to heed the Word, this "light that shines in a dark
place" (2 Peter 1:19)?

Routinely, we are lured and enthralled by the distractions
and temptations of the world. Therefore, God calls us to pursue
self-control. It is possible to lose heart and grow weary in well-
doing. (See Galatians 6:9.) We may be frequently tempted to lose
heart in the constant battle with our desires. So, to self-control,
we must add perseverance. Self-control and perseverance are not
the symbols of drudgery. Rather, through these godly character
traits, the Lord revives us and renews our strength. They are the
beacons that guide us on the heavenly highway where God Himself meets with us to provide the endurance necessary for being
good soldiers of Jesus Christ. (See 2 Timothy 2.)

Perseverance is continuing to walk with God as Enoch and
Noah did. (See Genesis 5:24; 6:9.) This is where you find the
eternal God as your refuge and the everlasting arms underneath. So when you are discouraged, shudder to think of selling

the pearl of great price and, instead, pray believing that God will answer this prayer: "Will You not revive us again, That Your people may rejoice in You?" (Psalm 85:6).

If you seem to be growing cold in your relationship with God, please look to His beloved promises and believe that the Spirit will revive you and that Christ will be all the more precious as you go on your way rejoicing like the Ethiopian eunuch who had just entered his "first love." (See Acts 8.) "Let us not grow weary while doing good, for in due season we shall reap if we do not lose heart" (Galatians 6:9). This is the blessedness of perseverance!

Perseverance marks the path of growing in grace and of maturing in Christ. Maturity is the important goal of spiritual sight. It is not enough to have the seed of God planted in our hearts; it must grow and bear fruit, as seen in the pattern of the natural: "For the earth yields crops by itself: first the blade, then the head, after that the full grain in the head" (Mark 4:28). We realize that it is not our strength but His that enables us to persevere. Faith is deepened when perseverance leads us to godliness, which is our devotion in cleaving to our Lord Jesus, our heavenly Bridegroom, in all situations. Godliness, which is our obedience to God's commands, flows not out of a spirit of self-righteousness but out of a heartfelt conviction that, "We love Him because He first loved us" (1 John 4:19).

Godliness is an absolutely essential characteristic of the walk of the Christian who is in love with God. It should be manifested in everything we do. It remains a constant struggle, however, "For the flesh lusts against the Spirit, and the Spirit against the flesh; and these are contrary to one another" (Galatians 5:17). Let us not forget that godliness also concerns the determination not to lose our joy in God's holy ways. The prolific Christian author C. S. Lewis referred to this joy as the "serious business of heaven," that is, the rejoicing and exultation in the wonder of the beauty of our heavenly King.[1]

## GROWING IN DIVINE LOVE

This progression in godliness, which Peter maps out for us, is accomplished in the presence of our fellow pilgrims—our brothers and sisters in the family of God. So, we are called upon to entrench the attributes of spiritual sight in brotherly kindness. Some of our greatest blessings in this life are the Christian friends that God has given us. Paul said of the Philippians, "My beloved and longed-for brethren, my joy and crown" (Philippians 4:1).

I trust that each of us knows someone who, when they came into our lives, represented a high-water mark and a red-letter day to us. May God give us more relationships like this that we may strengthen one another as David and Jonathan did! What a joy it was for Paul and Silas to praise God together at midnight in the Philippian jail after they had been beaten. Soon they welcomed another brother into their fellowship—the jailer who came in trembling after the earthquake and asked "what must I do to be saved?" (Acts 16:30).

Christian fellowship is a blessing, but it can also be a profound challenge. In relational difficulties, the sense of betrayal is doubled when we are hurt by those who call themselves God's people. This can too easily lead to disillusionment and bitterness, and you can see the great wisdom in Peter now pressing our commitment to love as the keystone in our progression from blindness to sight.

Showing the love of God to others—charity, *agape* love—is what Jesus gives to us as the one great mandate above all others: "This is My commandment, that you love one another as I have loved you" (John 15:12). A whole book could be written regarding our need to be engulfed by, and completely resting within, God's love, so that it will pass through us and on to others. Total love comes together with total peace, and in *shalom* we become spiritually quickened with a sighted faith. When we see others from God's perspective, we understand His love for them. That makes the place of abiding in Christ our safety and absolute necessity.

Much of our spiritual blindness is both a cause of and a product of purposeful, personal deception. This deception is seen in many people we deal with in business, in government, and in the church. Anything that is intentionally unfair or unjust is deception, and it is found in many forms and expressions. Government officials can deceive by claiming they are "for the people" while, in truth, their most important considerations are getting votes and generating financial support. In the church, the drive for finances and new buildings may be more for the sake of the egos and careers than for building the kingdom of God. In such cases, spiritual growth is not developed, and may even be extinguished. All of this faulty motivation is based on selfishness, deception, and blindness.

You must take care, though, to avoid being harsh and judgmental of those who would deceive you. Remember that each of us is alike to a certain degree, with each being prone to the same failings. The easiest thing in the world to do is to criticize, and the most difficult thing is to comprehend another. It is in the latter that we find our sight. Our love of God, based in John 3:16, can prevent us from destroying ourselves with bitterness, vengefulness, self-pity, and cynicism: "For God so loved the world that He gave His only begotten Son, that whoever believes in Him should not perish but have everlasting life." Only this Calvary love will enable us to totally forgive our brother. Only in such love can we become spiritually mature and see our enemies as brothers.

You can understand why Peter sums it all up by saying, "If these things are yours and abound, you will be neither barren nor unfruitful in the knowledge of our Lord Jesus Christ" (2 Peter 1:8). Yet, the warning remains in the following verse: "He who lacks these things is short-sighted, even to blindness." We are all blind, complacent, and spiritually unsuccessful when we do not appreciate our Creator or want to be closer to Him. *God is real; shalom is real.*

Replace the shortsightedness and blindness, which looks only at this life, with spiritual sight that views eternity in the face of God and the Spirit. Peter's words call us to a growing faith that lives on the "exceedingly great and precious promises" upon which you may rest and experience the power of the Spirit in redemption. (See 2 Peter 1:4.)

## SOLDIERS OF CHRIST ARISE

Soldiers of Christ arise and put your armor on,
Strong in the strength which God supplies through His
   eternal Son,
Strong in the Lord of Hosts and in His mighty pow'r,
Who in the strength of Jesus trusts is more than con-
   queror.

Stand then in His great might with all His strength
   endued,
But take to arm you for the fight the panoply of God,
Leave no unguarded place; no weakness of the soul,
Take ev'ry virtue, ev'ry grace, and fortify the whole.

To keep your armor bright, attend with constant care,
Still walking in your Captain's sight and watching unto
   prayer,
From strength to strength go on; wrestle and fight and
   pray,
Tread all the pow'rs of darkness down and win the well-
   fought day.[2]

—CHARLES WESLEY, 1749

Chapter 17

# DIVINE DEFENSES DETERMINE SPIRITUAL VICTORY

P AUL'S LETTER TO the Ephesians provides one of the most surprising endings of any of the New Testament books. In this letter, Paul describes the Word of God as armor for spiritual warfare. One distinct aspect of our spiritual blindness is our lack of perception of the true nature of our spiritual battle and the enemy that engages us. Not understanding the satanic forces set to destroy us, we assume that people are our problem, causing us hurt and opposing our welfare. Rather, the truth is that the devil uses people to hurt and oppose us, causing us to sin the sins of unforgiveness and bitterness, among others. Our true enemy can only be seen clearly with spiritual sight, insight, and divine understanding.

> For we do not wrestle against flesh and blood, but against principalities, against powers, against the rulers of the darkness of this age, against spiritual hosts of wickedness in the heavenly places.
>
> —EPHESIANS 6:12

Just as physical armor of leather and metal equipped the ancient soldier to face his lethal foe with confidence, the divine armor of the truth of God's Word—His promises, prayer, and the other spiritual weapons depicted in Ephesians 6—equip us against the "wiles" of the *real* enemy, namely, the devil (Ephesians 6:11). These divine defenses are hidden to the natural eye. Only when we are armed with the spiritual perspective of a vibrant, abiding faith will we be prepared to resist the beguiling lures that lead us into sin. Properly defending our faith, we will not become as easily discouraged or hurt by others. Instead, we become enabled to pray that those whom we think of as enemies be delivered themselves from the snare of the devil. It then becomes possible to fulfill the biblical command: "Love your enemies, bless those who curse you, do good to those that hate you, and pray for those who spitefully use you and persecute you" (Matthew 5:44).

We are to pity those who oppose us in the work of God and intercede for them rather than to be bitter against them. There is so much assistance and protection from the Word of God that we dare not proceed without it.

## STRONG IN THE LORD

You may ask me, "How could I possibly face the devil, who is so much stronger than I am?" My answer to you from the Word of God is that "the battle is the LORD's" (1 Samuel 17:47). Paul also tells us that our source of strength must be "in the Lord" (Ephesians 6:10). And John writes, "He who is in you is greater than he who is in the world" (1 John 4:4). Satan is a creature, but God is the Creator who is Almighty and Invincible. When we recognize and acknowledge that our strength is in God, He makes us "more than conquerors through Him who loved us" (Romans 8:37). To truly live our faith, to have spiritual sight, is to be armed with the reality of our divine armor.

The devil will surely try to intimidate and dishearten you. You may be tempted to flee or give up, but God's voice comforts and emboldens, "Fear not, for I am with you" (Isaiah 41:10). Only through a personal relationship of resting in His redemption are you given the strength of the Holy Spirit to overcome.

Paul instructs us to cleave to God's Word, and then, "having done all, to stand. Stand therefore" (Ephesians 6:13–14, KJV). He also expresses this challenge to stand against the enemy in other passages (Philippians 4:1; 1 Corinthians 15:58). With resolve and determination, the Christian can hold Martin Luther's stance: "Here I stand! I can do no other! I am bound by the Word of God." [1]

Everything we need for spiritual sight and a living faith is found in the Word of God as applied to our lives by the Holy Spirit. A living relationship with our Savior, resting in His redemption, living in dependence on the power of the Holy Spirit—all of these great truths are pressed upon us in the Word of God as God's means of transforming our minds and quickening our spirits. The written Word is God's way of allowing us to know Him, worship Him, and serve Him. This is the armor that will equip your soul to fight the battle as well as to assist others in the warfare.

Note the familiar terms of protection Paul described, such as the breastplate, the shield, and the helmet, and how each piece of armor—the belt of truth, the gospel of peace, and the sword which is the Word of God—calls us to the truth. The armor of God describes the hand of God's grace, protection, and power toward us and in us—all promised in the Word. God's Word strengthens and motivates us to go forward into the battle without fear. For He will help us, deliver us, and use us to crush Satan under our feet. (See Romans 16:20.)

## THE BELT OF TRUTH

The first piece of armor provided by the Captain of our salvation is "the belt of truth." The robe or loose clothing of a soldier in the Roman era needed to be tucked in and secured by the belt that also held his sword. This "girding of the loins" speaks of reigning in a mind and heart with loose, foolish, and wayward thoughts and desires by embracing the Son of God as Lord. As a "good soldier of Jesus Christ," we march under His banner, not our own, wearing this belt of truth. (See 2 Timothy 2:3.)

Has the truth of God's Word gripped you, as a belt, so that you have been changed by its revelation of the glorious Son of God? His truth heightens your awareness of who you are, and who God is, and it clarifies the enemy of your soul.

## THE BREASTPLATE OF RIGHTEOUSNESS

Another important article of armor described for the believer is the breastplate of righteousness. A sword through the heart would be fatal, so our Captain has given us the crucial breastplate. While we cannot boast of any righteousness within ourselves, God Himself provides us with His righteousness.

We, like the prophet Isaiah, are blind to our unrighteousness until we see the King! (See Isaiah 6.) To sense God's infinite wrath against us would unnerve us, to say the least. To be truly awakened to the guilt and evil of our sin would certainly crush us, immobilize us, and frighten us. The devil adds to this prospect his shadows of despairing darkness.

However, God does not leave the Christian warrior in this dismal condition. Through our receiving Christ as Savior, He has given us His righteousness. We stand before God, cleansed from our sin, based on our acceptance of what our Savior did on the cross. When He said, "It is finished," all that was necessary to forgive and cleanse us was accomplished. (See John 19:30.) Now we are called to rest in His finished work. In that way we put on the breastplate of Christ's righteousness. In Christ, God is infinitely pleased with you. You are welcomed into His presence at all times. "Therefore, having been justified by faith, we have peace with God through our Lord Jesus Christ" (Romans 5:1). To be justified is to have the perfect righteousness of Christ credited to your account. No matter how completely you may fail and sin, the perfect obedience of Christ grants you God's pardon and acceptance.

We can forget this far too easily, becoming downcast and losing heart for the battlefield. Many of us have forgotten that He has given us the breastplate of righteousness, that we are "accepted in the Beloved" (Ephesians 1:6). We are His forgiven children and are called to believe this promise: "The blood of Jesus Christ His Son cleanses us from all sin" (1 John 1:7).

Lift up your head and honor the Redeemer who secured this pardon for you. Rejoice in His great love and sing with the saints in heaven: "Thou wast slain, and hast redeemed us to God by thy blood" (Revelation 5:9, KJV). In deep gratitude and devotion you will be encouraged to step back onto the battlefield with renewed vigor.

"*Jehovah Tsikenu!*"—"The Lord Our Righteousness"—is our battle cry. He is our strength. Our salvation is based on what He did on the cross. To Him be all the glory! Accepting this truth alone will protect our hearts from the sword of unbelief that has the thrust to destroy any man's soul. We cannot say it any better than the psalmist did: "Blessed are the people who know the joyful sound! They walk, O LORD, in the light of Your countenance. In Your name they rejoice all day long, And in Your righteousness they are exalted. For You are the glory of their strength, And in Your favor our horn is exalted" (Psalm 89:15–17). This is the voice of the believer rejoicing in the privilege of wearing the breastplate of righteousness.

## GOSPEL SHOES

When we have this joy of believing, we will also have an eagerness to share the gospel with others. This is the gospel of peace that may be likened to the shoes of a Roman foot soldier. Those shoes provided the strength and flexibility that a fighter would need to be fleet. However, perhaps even more important than the mobility provided by the shoes was the stability it gave him in battle. The Roman soldier's shoes were heavily studded with nails in the sole. This gave him the ability to hold his ground against the enemy. The believer likewise has a sure footing in the gospel. He is grounded in the "gospel of peace" where there is a wholeness, a completeness, a satisfaction that he possesses, and a peace in the fullness of God's covenant blessing—*shalom*.

"The LORD bless you and keep you; The LORD make His face shine upon you, And be gracious to you; The LORD lift up His countenance upon you, And give you peace" (Numbers 6:24–26). When you are able to see, and look into the face of God, and know deep in your soul that this great benediction is yours, then you are ready to meet God, ready to worship God, and ready to serve God. To have this benediction flood your heart daily is to be wearing the shoes of the gospel of peace. Are you prepared to run with the gospel of peace?

Pushed and harried by the enemy, we are also endowed with God's strength that enables us to remain fixed and not be moved. The strength that gospel peace gives to the believer is expressed in Psalm 62:6–7: "He only is my rock and my salvation; He is my defense; I shall not be moved. In God is my salvation and my glory; The rock of my strength, And my refuge, is in God." As the apostle says, "Having done all, to stand. Stand therefore" (Ephesians 6:13, KJV).

## THE SHIELD OF FAITH

The most versatile defensive armor of the soldier was his shield. With great quickness, he could quickly divert blows and fiery arrows from many angles. This shield, Paul says, is our faith—faith in God's Word and in the living, reigning God who spoke it and stands by it. It is in faith that we are protected by Christ—our Shield.

Spiritual blindness deadens our faith and leaves us unshielded from the enemy. However, true living faith holds up what God's Word says to divert the lies that the devil shoots into the mind. These lies are the soul-damaging and soul-destroying deceptions that come at us out of our blind spots and stir us to reject God's way—the good way, the only way—and pursue the way of self and sin. In 1 Peter 5:9, we are told to resist the devil steadfastly in the faith. And John declares, "This is the victory that has overcome the world—our faith" (1 John 5:4).

The Bible declares that God is our shield and exceedingly great reward (Genesis 15:1). And He is our very present help in time of trouble (Psalm 46:1). When I can see clearly, I am shielded from the debilitating effects of accusation and malicious criticism by believing only what God says about me. He says I am loved with an everlasting love (Jeremiah 31:3). Accusers will say that God has cast me off, but faith says He will never leave me nor forsake me (Hebrews 13:5).

Young college students are assailed these days with lies of a godless, evolving universe. But God's truth, as defended by the shield of faith says, "He [God] who made them at the beginning 'made them male and female'" (Matthew 19:4). The majesty and mystery of the DNA code in the sixty trillion cells of your body is too great to be bound by such deceit.

The devil challenges our faith, telling us that our sin is too wicked and God will not forgive it. Jesus, however, tells us, "The one who comes to Me I will by no means cast out" (John 6:37). The devil says, "Go ahead and yield to temptation; nobody will see you." Faith grabs the shield of God's truth and says, "The eyes of the LORD run to and fro throughout the whole earth, to show Himself strong on behalf of those whose heart is loyal to Him" (2 Chronicles 16:9). The devil stirs up sinful desires and passions. Abiding faith takes up the shield and quenches these flaming arrows by laying hold of God's promise that greater is He that is in you than he that is in the world (1 John 4:4). Faith declares, "If God is for us, who can be against us?" (Romans 8:31).

God says that His Word will thoroughly equip us for every good work (2 Timothy 3:17). By God's Word, embraced in faith, we will be able to quench all the fiery darts of the wicked one as we raise the shield of faith, and thereby are free to see and continue our walk beside Him.

## THE HELMET OF SALVATION

Paul tells us that the helmet of salvation represents hope (1 Thessalonians 5:8). Hope is the sure confidence and expectation promised to the believer in God's Word. It is worked in our hearts by the Holy Spirit. Many believers' heads have sustained, and survived, heavy blows because they knew that God the Father Almighty works for good in their lives. Hope, as armor, gives us the assurance that the Son of God will not fail to shepherd us through our trials. God will prevail for us, and through us, not in our own strength but that which He supplies.

The helmet of hope protects our heads from mortal wounds, and it also allows us to advance with our hands free. Rather than covering our heads with our hands in fear, we can proceed with our heads up, hands ready—courageous and confident. Our King and Captain urges us on as He speaks to us through the Word: "For I, the LORD your God, will hold your right hand, Saying to you, 'Fear not, I will help you'" (Isaiah 41:13). "Now may the God of hope fill you with all joy and peace in believing, that we may abound in hope by the power of the Holy Spirit" (Romans 15:13).

## THE SWORD OF THE SPIRIT

The one *offensive* weapon given to the Christian soldier for spiritual warfare is "the sword of the Spirit, which is the word of God" (Ephesians 6:17). We have discussed the importance of the Word of God for every aspect of our spiritual life. However, in this passage, *rhema* is the Greek for this "word" of God, brought forth in specific, direct application to the issue at hand. It carries a very personal encouragement by the Spirit for the individual receiving it. This is the powerful application of God's Word that is "sharper than any two-edged sword" (Hebrews 4:12). It is the Word of God, not just written on the page, but drawn smartly and thrust deeply into the enemy.

When the Lord Jesus was tempted by the devil, He met each approach with a specific and devastating counter: "It is written" (Matthew 4:4). Those three words are Satan's worst nightmare; using God's Word against him thwarts his attacks. We must study the Bible diligently in order to use it in this manner with God's direction.

The sword of the Spirit can also cut through the hardest layers protecting a heart that opposes God. When told that "every knee shall bow" to Christ, some people may laugh and ridicule, but when the Spirit uses the Word in their hearts it becomes different. Like Belshazzar, ancient King of Babylon, whose knees clattered against each other when he saw the handwriting on the wall, men made to hear the voice of God are humbled and brought to the end of themselves. (See Daniel 5:9.)

We thank God that the sword of the Spirit continues to work in cutting away sin in our own lives. When God quickens His Word to our hearts, our occasionally prayerless and cold spirits are pierced. Then we return to our first love for Christ, and see through the vanity of temporal things; again we hunger for the satisfaction alone that comes from being in His presence. The sword of the Spirit is mighty and we need it desperately to fight against our own sins as well as in seeking to free others from the enemy who does not easily let his captives go free.

Spiritual blindness represents our fight against God. It is the battle of "king self" to reign in ways in which we excuse ourselves, minimize our faults, rationalize our sins, blame others, and whine over our disappointments. These reactions reveal our spiritual blindness and show that we are unarmed in the great spiritual warfare against our souls. How blessed it is to know God's direction in the battle, to be equipped, courageous, and assured that those who follow King Jesus will wear the victor's wreath.

## NOT WITHOUT PRAYER

Paul knows how devastating battle is to the unwary, superficial person who remains naive concerning the great enemy of our souls. Such lack of sight and vigilance, sadly, has eternal consequences. You are in the midst of a savage fight in which God's kingdom passionately beckons you while, simultaneously, the world passionately deludes and entices you. In this spiritual war for your soul, the mental turmoil can leave you gasping for air like a drowning man, desperately looking for hope or meaning and purpose in life. Knowing this, Paul unlocks the secret strength of the believer—a life of prayer.

We are called to be "praying always with all prayer and supplication in the Spirit, being watchful to this end with all perseverance and supplication for all the saints" (Ephesians 6:18). Only by cultivating a lifestyle of prayer can we live in God's strength and be strong in the Lord and the power of His might.

You may have the full complement of armor and still be knocked about mercilessly. It is only when you become a spirited, lively, courageous, and quickened soldier that you can stay sharp while absorbing blows. Prayer innervates you, steels you, and fills your veins with fire. It channels through you the power of God's Almighty Spirit. Consider praying this powerful prayer.

> *O Spirit of God, stir up the fire that lies in the cooling embers of my first love to Jesus! Revive me, bend me, melt me, grip me—give me wings as the eagle to soar beyond the squalor of this dark world! Open my eyes to see the beauty of my Savior! O, that I might know Him in the power of His resurrection!*

The Spirit of God delights to bless true pleading and wrestling with God. Such blessing is only found through fervent prayer. Half-hearted, lazy, indifferent prayers show that we have not relinquished our independence to Him. Again we hear our Savior say, "This kind does not go out except by prayer and fasting" (Matthew 17:21). Here is the source of power and courage for the vigorous, advancing Christian warrior. Such a warrior is a humble believer who draws strength from the Spirit of God through prayer. Is this the strength of my life or of your life? If not we are both blind indeed!

So important is prayer to the believer's life, that it will be helpful to discuss another powerful prayer from the Scriptures.

## ETERNAL VISION THROUGH WORSHIP

In the profound prayer found in Ephesians 3, the apostle Paul asks that God would bless all believers with an intimate and close communion with the Savior. The apostle indicates to the believer that such a deepening fellowship with the Lord Jesus requires a genuine heart of faith (Ephesians 3:17), as well as both the power of the Spirit within us (Ephesians 3:16), and our pursuit of a greater knowledge and experience of the immeasurable love of Christ (Ephesians 3:18–19). In a state of spiritual blindness, none of us is aware of our impoverished spirit. The Holy Spirit is the one who enables us to comprehend our need to be strengthened.

Paul wrote his letter to the Ephesians from a prison cell. He reminds the Ephesians that his own imprisonment, rather than being a source of discouragement, was being used by God to glorify Himself to the churches (Ephesians 3:13). Additionally, since Paul was temporarily removed from their lives, the believers were learning to deal more directly with God themselves. Paul wanted to show them that if they learned how to walk closely with Christ, God would work through them in ways beyond what they could imagine (Ephesians 3:20–21).

As Paul calls upon God the Father (Ephesians 3:14), we are to follow his example. To do so means that we need to be confident of the love of God for us. God not only gives us His greatest gift, which is Christ Himself, but He also gives us the Holy Spirit to draw us into this divine relationship (Ephesians 3:16). Usually, however, we are so self-centered and so full of self-advantage and self-pity that we lose sight of this high calling of God for us. The Spirit of God must "strengthen our spirit in the inner man" before our greatest longing—the need to know Christ as our chief portion in life—can possibly be realized. The work of the Spirit within us must first reverse the human heart's inclination toward that which is selfish, degrading, and disinterested in God.

Altering the course of your soul flowing away from God can seem as difficult as trying to reverse the direction of the Colorado

River. However, the believer who sees the foolish propensities of his own heart gains a deeper understanding of why only "with might through His Spirit" God can turn and bend that heart. Only when you long for nearness to God above all else, will you appreciate this reality. The power of the Holy Spirit changes lives. When you fully comprehend the rich description Paul gives the Ephesians of coming to know God—when you begin to *see*—you will be astonished that you could have passed over that which is incomparable for what is clearly insignificant.

In blindness, all of us too easily forfeit glorious intimacy with God for the pursuit of the "golden calves" that appeal to the natural man. The Father's purpose in strengthening us with the Holy Spirit is that Christ may dwell in our hearts. This "dwelling" speaks of living with Him as in your own home where there is a closeness, fellowship, and intimacy of which the unbeliever knows nothing. The Son of God is so great and glorious and precious that the Bible refers to Him as the Pearl of Great Price (Matthew 13:46), the King of kings (Revelation 19:16), the "heavenly" bridegroom (Mark 2:19), and a hundred other titles as well.

To live with the Lord Jesus and share a mutual communion and joy with Him is the closest experience to heaven on this earth. This is what Paul prays for us and what we are to pursue in prayer ourselves. This pursuit is one of faith. By faith we listen to the words of Jesus and hear them spoken to our hearts according to His promise: "My sheep hear My voice, and I know them, and they follow Me" (John 10:27). By faith, we pray with a sense of beholding the face of our Savior, "looking unto Jesus" (Hebrews 12:2) and leaning upon His bosom as John did.

## RECEIVING GOD'S LOVE

You may allow yourself to fear that God will eventually be driven out of this relationship, but that is impossible because of His love for you. This is the truth in which you must allow your faith to be "rooted and grounded"—His unchanging love (Ephesians 3:17). The prophet Malachi wrote, "For I am the LORD, I do not change. Therefore you are not consumed, O sons of Jacob" (Malachi 3:6). If this text were written on your heart, you would hear it ringing in your ears and could renew your focus by saying, "My faith is planted in His love." Faith puts its roots deeply into this divine love and draws its nourishment from God's heart toward us, rather than in our weak inclination toward Him. This is the foundation you must build upon—Christ's love to you.

The only way to fathom the full depth and height and length and breadth of God's love is to see that it is the love of the cross. Why would Jesus suffer the agony, shame, pain, and death—and separation from God—on the cross to pay for your sins? Why would He love you that much? Such love, as Paul says, "surpasses knowledge" (Ephesians 3:19, NIV). Here is a paradox in which you seek to comprehend the incomprehensible. Instead, you are only able to embrace it by faith, because God has declared it in His Word. *That* is the meaning of spiritual sight.

Paul shows us the blessedness of knowing the crucified and risen Lord as Savior in Galatians 2:20: "The life which I now live in the flesh I live by faith in the Son of God, who loved me and gave Himself for me." As surprising as it may seem, Paul elevates this theme even more and prays that we may be filled with all the fullness of God. God is infinite, transcendent, and sovereign. How can I be filled with all of this fullness? It is clear that I must be filled with His love—love from Him, love to Him, and love to others. This fullness of God's love is the power that can change each of us beyond what we can imagine, ask, or think (Ephesians 3:20). Great is the love that filled the heart of Christ to come to earth and endure the wickedness of humanity. In love, He persevered in His pity and compassion and purpose for us until He gave Himself on the cross and rose again.

Now He pours out this same indescribable love into your heart (Romans 5:5). In that love you will be strengthened by His Spirit in the inner man, Christ will dwell in your heart, and you will be filled with all the fullness of God. This power of God's love alone can change you from bitter to sweet. It can change hearts of stone to hearts of flesh, and change wills from cold and lukewarm to a burning fire that cannot be quenched. This is the power of the Spirit. This is the fullness of God's love channeled through you.

It is helpful to see the practical application that Paul draws from his prayer for the Ephesians. The apostle summons us to walk worthy of our calling. According to Paul, we do this by a gentle, longsuffering, forbearing, loving spirit toward one another. (See Ephesians 4:1–3.) When we live close to the Son of God, we will know how to forgive others and understand their faults without becoming cynical, like the older brother in the story of the prodigal son.

It is spiritual blindness to have no view or interest in these great realities. Spiritual blindness will leave us to wander, hurting others and ourselves. How blessed, instead, to have spiritual sight through God's Spirit working within us, quickening us, filling us, and focusing us on the glory of Christ. This is the refreshment for our soul as it is drawn into the ecstasy of communion with heaven's King and the Friend of sinners.

## Chapter 18

# A Divine Paradox:
# God's Ways vs. Man's Ways

T HE BIBLE CONTAINS many paradoxes. A paradox presents a puzzle without solution to the human mind. However, scriptural paradox is a way of *imparting truth* that is grounded in revealed principles that seem contradictory. Let me explain.

Paradoxical language is beyond the terms of human logic and ordinary thinking. It emphasizes a discontinuity: the difference between God and man, God's sight and man's sight. Only by those liberated from the limitations of human knowledge can the utter majesty, beauty, and fullness of God's "otherness," sovereignty, and purpose be genuinely glimpsed. Man cannot reach knowledge of God through his own wisdom, theology, philosophy, or science. Without the truth of the Bible, which includes paradox, our understanding of God is based on mere human theories. To understand the Bible, faith must precede reason. Therefore, a great church father declared:

"*Credo ut Intelligam.*" (I believe in order to understand.)[1]
—AUGUSTINE

Faith is believing what we know to be true. Reason is the handmaid of faith. Otherwise stated, through faith we receive divine inspiration that we are then able to confirm with our minds. And sometimes, according to Scriptures, we have to believe what we cannot confirm through reasoning: "...faith is...the evidence of things not seen" (Hebrews 11:1).

Faith embraces God as the Creator, and science—the physical, biological, and cosmological details—confirms our faith in God's creation. Such details suggest a transcendent intellect and the intelligent design of a universe of irreducible complexity, rather than the empty, random universe of naturalistic Darwinian theories. The infinite reality of God is not attainable by human experience and mental frameworks alone. Paradox is the scriptural way of distinguishing God's sight—spiritual sight—from our blindness. What initially appears to the human eye as nonsense becomes, through the paradoxes of Scripture, understanding and sight as we embrace God's point of view, in faith.

## WHY PARADOX?

For as the heavens are higher than the earth,
So are My ways higher than your ways,
And My thoughts than your thoughts.

—ISAIAH 55:9

John Wesley believed that since God is rational, human reason and experience are our tools for discerning the Word. However, as a teacher he strived not only to enlighten the reason of the person listening, but to summon them to spiritual quickening.[2] For Wesley, the Bible was God's unique revelation to us, and as such it could only be spiritually understood as God Himself revealed it by His Spirit.

A simple fact: *faith is not reason.* Faith is beyond, even above, reason; faith is founded in principles of revelation; faith makes sense, though these foundational principles are not what human reason would have devised. To see God's face, to hear His truth, requires a faith that *embraces* God's revelation, though it may seem paradoxical to the mind. The living dynamic of faith—submission to God's Word and the death of self—is not rational. Faith is what we know to be true, based solely on the fact that God said it. God must remain transcendent to man and his rational mind.

Consider how God is revealed to us in Scripture as a single, divine unity that exists in the form of three distinct Persons: the Father, the Son, and the Holy Spirit. Our human logic is power-less to penetrate the truth of the Trinity, and yet we must accept it because the Word is infallible truth. This is how God has cho-sen to reveal Himself to us. He remains distinct and omniscient as He appears to us in a manner that the overwrought spin-cycle of human reasoning alone cannot apprehend. God's Word pres-ents paradox to us to reveal Himself in *His* words to the believer. We must, then, relinquish our ego to the Holy Spirit and approach God's Word and revelation to us with humility. With complete abandonment of our own understanding, God provides us with His wisdom and spiritual sight. And, of course, we must remember that "without faith it is impossible to please Him" (Hebrews 11:6).

Paradox in the Scriptures demonstrates how God is transcen-dent, that is, infinitely greater than our minds, and how we may come to Him by faith *alone*. God is eternal and infinite, while we are mortal and finite. God alone sees reality and purpose as a whole and all at once. If we can see reality at all, it is in bits and pieces, locked within the period of our brief experience. The fam-ily dog may well recognize its master as a friend and provider, but it certainly has no perception of the spiritual cascades deep in the heart of that master. Likewise, is it not prideful to presume we can understand God through the filter of our own senses and understanding?

We are necessarily limited, but it is to our detriment that we choose to be evasive before God's truth. Man is sinful and runs from God and His truth. Human reasoning is most commonly employed as rationalization and self-justification. We might hear the truth revealed in the Scripture, but we normally seek to hide from it, as Adam did in the garden after sinning. God reveals

Himself to us as He chooses. Through biblical paradoxes, understanding and spiritual sight become more acute for those with a childlike faith that embraces God's revelation so given.

## WHAT PARADOX?

Through His Word, God has presented us with many profound paradoxes about His nature, our nature, and the nature of our faith in Him.

### His nature

As we have mentioned, God is revealed to us as a Trinity: one Being in three Persons. Jesus came and walked among us as *man and God—divine being*. The Scriptures declare: "But when the fullness of the time had come, God sent forth His Son, born of a woman" (Galatians 4:4). Jesus' disciples acknowledged this fact: "Then those who were in the boat came and worshiped Him, saying, 'Truly You are the Son of God'" (Matthew 14:33). And Jesus testified to the fact of His divine Sonship: "All things have been delivered to Me by My Father, and no one knows who the Son is except the Father, and who the Father is except the Son, and the one to whom the Son wills to reveal Him" (Luke 10:22). The apostle Paul declared: "No one can say that Jesus is Lord except by the Holy Spirit" (1 Corinthians 12:3).

Through Christ, the eternal, *infinite* God enters the world and is revealed to *finite* man. In response, we can only echo the words of the psalmist: "Great is our Lord, and mighty in power; His understanding is infinite" (Psalm 147:5). And we bow before God who declared, "'I am the Alpha and the Omega, the Beginning and the End,' says the Lord, 'who is and who was and who is to come, the Almighty'" (Revelation 1:8).

### Our nature

Humans are born physically alive, though spiritually dead. Paradoxically *it's in dying that we live*. By dying to the self, we are reborn and live in God. Then, we say with the apostle Paul, "I have been crucified with Christ; it is no longer I who live, but Christ lives in me; and the life which I now live in the flesh I live by faith in the Son of God, who loved me and gave Himself for me" (Galatians 2:20). When we lose our lower life to find Him, we find our higher life. Conversely, if we keep our life to ourselves, we will lose it (Matthew 10:39). This is a divine paradox.

Another paradox is found in the reality that when we acknowledge our weakness, cast off our pride, and abandon ourselves to the Lord, we are made strong in Christ. Paul declared: "Therefore I take pleasure in infirmities, in reproaches, in needs, in persecutions, in distresses, for Christ's sake. *For when I am weak, then I am strong*" (2 Corinthians 12:10, emphasis added). Chuck Colson, a former Nixon aide who went to prison for his involvement in Watergate, is a perfect example of this weakness-to-strength paradox. Colson gave up the desire to cling to the great power and strength to which he was accustomed and surrendered to Jesus in a beautiful way. As he abandoned himself to his Savior, he discovered destiny and became the founder of a powerful ministry called Prison Fellowship.[3] So, in a period of great embarrassment and disgrace, falling from strength to weakness, brought down from the political stratosphere to imprisonment, Colson became strong in God's kingdom.

"Blessed are you who weep now, For you shall laugh" (Luke 6:21). The doorway to joy is through mourning. This seems counterintuitive to our logical minds—it is a paradox. In God's mind, however, returning to Him in the mourning of repentance brings us into the light of forgiveness and knowing Him. And there we experience inestimable joy.

"Therefore we do not lose heart. Even though our outward man is perishing, yet the inward man is being renewed day by day" (2 Corinthians 4:16). Our biological, bodies are in inevitable decay. We will die, yet, "Most assuredly, I say to you, he who believes in Me has everlasting life" (John 6:47). The temporal body that we occupy while we inhabit this earth must eventually give way to a greater reality—eternal life. "For as in Adam all die, even so in Christ all shall be made alive" (1 Corinthians 15:22). Through God's grace we are invited to enter His presence and enjoy eternal life with Him. While we continue our labors in life and continue our inevitable slide toward death, God comes to us and reveals Himself. There, in a faith fully lived, our spirits can be refreshed and rejuvenated day by day.

**Nature of faith**

In giving, we receive. "There is one who scatters, yet increases more; And there is one who withholds more than is right, But it leads to poverty. The generous soul will be made rich, And he who waters will also be watered himself" (Proverbs 11:24–25). This seems to be the opposite of what we know as "human nature."

Those of us who seek to be superior to our brothers and sisters will end up being inferior. "But many who are first will be last, and the last first" (Matthew 19:30). "But whoever desires to become great among you shall be your servant. And whoever of you desires to be first shall be slave of all" (Mark 10:43–44). Christ Himself, on earth, showed this to us: "For even the Son of Man did not come to be served, but to serve, and to give His life a ransom for many" (Mark 10:45).

Consider Lazarus and the rich man in Luke 16:20–31. The man clothed in purple during life was denied entrance to heaven while the man who had dogs licking his sores in his miserable, mortal existence was taken straight to paradise into the bosom of Abraham. The rich man's lack of compassion through his pride had determined his fate. In humility, Lazarus had depended on God for his redemption.

The same holds true of the tax collector and the Pharisee in Luke 18 as we have mentioned. The Pharisee elevated himself in the pride of his own works and observation of religious laws and was brought low. The tax collector, conversely, humbled himself before God and was elevated above the Pharisee to the place of pardon and acceptance before God.

Men reward works; God rules by grace. "But to him who does not work but believes on Him who justifies the ungodly, his faith is accounted for righteousness" (Romans 4:5). Men reward those who work for them; you and I expect such reward. However, God gives grace to those who cast themselves upon Him in repentance and faith in Christ's work on the cross. "Even the righteousness of God, through faith in Jesus Christ, to all and on all who believe. For there is no difference; for all have sinned and fall short of the glory of God, being justified freely by His grace through redemption that is in Jesus Christ" (Romans 3:22–24).

Just as works are not our ticket into God's presence, so too, trying to figure out God's methods in human terms is no path to faith. Faith is confidently standing on what God has said; that is the only way we can know God. God reveals Himself to sinful man and only the "Word made flesh" (see John 1:14)—Jesus Christ—can bridge the gap between them. Humanity understands only incompletely; God sees all, for all time and eternity. Scriptural paradoxes are the wisdom of God coming to us by grace that we might gain spiritual sight through faith in God alone.

## PARADOX

God, to us is paradox,
Making man from only dust,
Forming stars we'll never see,
Setting rules—obey we must.

Cleansing sins with staining blood,
Calling forth what is not now,
Asking trust in things unseen,
Melting hearts—we know not how.

Calling faith a substance known,
Healing what cannot be cured,
Choosing wayward souls to love,
Using what His Son endured.

Blessing those who have been cursed,
Taking time for you and me,
Loosing us who have been bound,
Planning our eternity.

—RALPH E. MCINTOSH

# PART IV:

# UNDERSTANDING THE NATURE
# OF SPIRITUAL VISION

I N THE FOLLOWING chapters, we will explore in more depth the
wonderful provision and promises the believer experiences
in receiving true spiritual vision. Though not without pain, the
life of a mature believer who sees more and more as God sees
becomes fruitful, full of trust, and fulfilled through walking in
divine destiny.

As we explore the value of suffering in the light of God's Word,
you will discover the benefits of allowing God to work in your
life, even in difficult circumstances. And as we review the grid
of T.R.U.S.T., you will recognize places of maturing love in your
life and become aware of areas that need to change. The deeper
truths of prayer, praise, and worship will help you to see those
changes effected in your life, so that you will be able to walk in
the fullness of divine destiny that God has ordained for you.

Chapter 19

# THE VALUE OF SUFFERING

YOU ARE HUMAN and you surely suffer. But do you understand your suffering? Do I understand my own? *Can* suffering be understood by us at all? Is it possible to learn, or even be enriched, by pain and trouble? Can we draw nearer to our Creator and Savior through suffering? As we have discussed, Jesus indicates to us that suffering is a kind of "pruning" that will lead to more abundant spiritual fruitfulness. (See John 15.)

Some people trip and fall upon themselves. Many others absorb the kicks, the slings, and the arrows of their fellow man. You already know what it means to be crushed by the many weights of living. Some, like Jacob, wrestle mightily and then walk away from their trial with a noticeable permanent limp. That limp is the outward sign that they have been hurt and are humbled inside. To walk with a limp, whatever its cause, is to be continuously humbled. One is humbled in suffering only if one can *see* from God's perspective.

A limp is a symbol of our shared, inherent human weakness and inability to carry the weight of existence alone. It is a "symptom" constantly reminding us of the distance we have fallen from God. It is a metaphor of our need to be forgiven and sanctified. It becomes a sign of one's understanding of total dependence upon our Lord who is the Star illuminating our path.

"Therefore humble yourselves under the mighty hand of God, that He may exalt you in due time" (1 Peter 5:6). The familiar maxim "no pain, no gain" is as true of our spiritual life as it is of our sporting life. Jamie Buckingham was humbled by the pain of his sin when, as a very young minister, he plummeted from a first-class act to a man without a job, respect, or fellowship. As a result, he learned that we can only become strong after we have been made weak. Jamie, like all of us, had trusted in his own intelligence and his abilities as an entrepreneur to achieve what he wanted and what he felt his church needed. He trusted in himself. It was only after he had suffered that he learned to depend fully upon God. Then he found himself and his destiny—*in* God alone. Jamie Buckingham needed to be "crippled" to become strong; he learned to walk with a limp. It was his firm conviction that you cannot trust anyone that does not limp. One who does not limp, who does not exhibit a wounding, may not have withstood sufficient misery to have become completely prostrate before the Creator in humility—to have been brought under the mighty hand of God through suffering.

In the biblical account of the life of Joseph, we see incredible suffering. He had endured unimaginable suffering of body, mind, and spirit at the hands of his brothers. However, after he had been made ruler in Egypt and was reconciled to his brothers, Joseph told them, "As for you, you meant evil against me; but God meant it for good, in order to bring it about as it is this day, to save many people alive" (Genesis 50:20). Joseph had embraced his "limp" as the sovereign will of God and forgave his brothers, *seeing* from God's perspective.

Suffering, trial, and affliction are difficult for us to accept, or even comprehend—certainly they are nearly impossible to *appreciate*. Suffering appears as evil for a spiritually blind person. The person with spiritual sight, however, can see suffering as meant for good by God. Suffering has purpose. Suffering brings us closer to God as we learn to live our faith. I have observed five major aspects of our suffering and its meaning for our soul.

## Suffering Is Common to All People

When a jet airliner drops too abruptly from the clouds and burns in a corn field, prematurely ending the strivings of many hearts, the suffering of those trapped in its seats is common to each one aboard. In the cabin, the righteous die holding hands with the unrighteous. Believers and unbelievers weep the same hard tears under the choking terror. Each mind, whether godly or worldly, is as uncomprehending and exhausted as the other before the door of death.

We are united in our suffering. Because of sin, it is a common, universal experience in God's created world, and therefore it is as significant as the labor of childbirth. Paul used that analogy for suffering: "For we know that the whole creation groans and labors with birth pangs together until now" (Romans 8:22). Just as the pain of childbirth results in the joy of new life, the very creation awaits the joy of its re-creation.

Not only is suffering common to all of us—mortal inhabitants of this earth—but it is communal, a *shared* attribute of our existence. You and I are called to exercise compassion toward each other in our suffering as willfully as the good Samaritan of Jesus' parable did. (See Luke 10.) As believers, we share a mutual sympathy with fellow believers. In suffering, we recognize our membership in the body of Christ as believers. With that we are reminded of our responsibilities to each other. Our own suffering increases our capacity for empathy. In my own suffering—when I can see that you also are afflicted—I learn to fulfill Christ's most fundamental desire for us: that we love our neighbor as we love ourselves.

## SUFFERING SERVES TO CORRECT US

It is God's idea that we should attain our spiritual growth through adversity. In God's eyes we are wayward and wanton, like disobedient children. Every one of us needs instruction, direction, and discipline: "For whom the LORD loves He chastens, And scourges every son whom He receives" (Hebrews 12:6). God hates sin; yet we sin. A requirement of life in God is that we walk according to the Spirit so that we might be transformed into creatures of light and sight.

Our suffering is a means to a glorious, God-centered end, rather than a dismal, world-centered end in itself. "For God did not send His Son into the world to condemn the world, but that the world through Him might be saved" (John 3:17). We must be broken first to be free to see His purpose and willingly obey.

## SUFFERING IS CONSTRUCTIVE

The process of tempering steel is perhaps the most appropriate metaphor for the role of suffering in the development of our spiritual sight. Tempering utilizes the stress of extreme heat alternated with cooling to produce a metal of a strength and suppleness that would never occur naturally. Testing the limits of the elements improves the object. Without the pain, there will be no awareness, no need for dependence, and we will remain in darkness; we will not seek our Lord.

"And not only that, but we also glory in tribulations, knowing that tribulation produces perseverance; and perseverance, character; and character, hope" (Romans 5:3–4). This process of tempering a human heart by the grace of the Holy Spirit endows all the attributes that God needs in one of His stewards, soldiers, or saints. Hope also blossoms in the hearts of the believers who understand their limping and do not lapse into the snare of self-pity.

## SUFFERING GLORIFIES GOD

When Jesus cured a man of his blindness, the townsfolk who observed the miracle were divided between themselves. Distrusting Jesus, the leaders discounted the miracle and cast the blind man out. Jesus sought the newly sighted man, *as He does you*, and inquired, "'Do you believe in the Son of God?'" The answer was resounding: "'Lord, I believe!' And he worshiped Him" (John 9:35, 38). Through his suffering, the man had come to know God's grace and healing. Then, despite his newfound stature as a social outcast, an uncomfortable position to say the least, the man with new eyes and a new spirit was brimming with praise and rejoicing. He had *really* gone from blindness to sight and from darkness to light—both physically and spiritually. In the blind man's adversity, God was glorified. God's greatest glory is found in our weakness.

## SUFFERING IS A COSMIC REALITY

Suffering has a reason for existing in our experience of life and our relationship with God. When we suffer there are only two possible reasons under the sun that it is so: it is God's sovereign will for us that we endure the pain for a higher calling, or we have fallen and our own failings have brought calamity to our own doorstep. In the latter case, our pain must bring us to seek God's grace. In the former we are brought into the light of His majesty and dominion over all as our almighty, all-wise Father.

There are many wonderful purposes of grace that God will fulfill in our lives through our trials. He will even overrule the consequences of our own faults to deepen our repentance and draw us closer to Him again—to make us more like the Lord Jesus. The surprising and disappointing circumstances that come our way in God's will are designed to teach us many things, to make us more useful servants, and to strengthen the power of an eternal perspective in our daily lives. God stirs up our faith to interweave these heavenly influences into our souls and to beautify our lives. Suffering is organic, a natural aspect of a spiritual organism's life. In each instance of suffering, we can be brought to the presence of God, either with a repentant heart in supplication or with a grateful heart of praise.

Unfortunately, suffering may cause you to seek an escape into sin and darkness, away from God's assistance and light. One theologian states this reality succinctly.

> Real life is harsh... The temptation to escape from it by flight is stronger the more sensitive we are... The land of dreams is close at hand, so that one can escape into it at any moment, far from these painful realities... [1]
>
> —PAUL TOURNIER

Many escape the harshness of life by running into self-pity, into themselves and each other, into alcohol, drugs, sex, eating, or even shopping. The avenues of escape are as varied and numerous as the sufferings that inspire their necessity. Sandy LeSourd has written a frank account of her retreat from God into obsessive-compulsive dissolution in *The Compulsive Woman*.[2] In her suffering and her desire to be whole in Christ, she frequently called out to God while she continued to depend upon herself. She continued to find a means of escape that caused her even more pain. It was after she truly saw her powerlessness in the face of suffering and finally relinquished her self-will that she was able to enjoy the unction of the Holy Spirit, to meet God, and move back from a dysfunctional life to one of fulfillment and happiness in Him. Her spirit of desire for her Lord, in her suffering, finally led her to Him. Now, Sandy LeSourd understands limping and the grace of God for living her faith.

Suffering is universal, inescapable, shared, cosmic, necessary, and edifying. We suffer when we trust in ourselves. We suffer when we disobey. Still, even in *righteous* ways, we suffer *with* Him, and *in* Him—growing and fulfilling His ultimate purpose in us. Suffering is not an obstruction to spiritual vision; it is a means of enhancing it.

## A Breakthrough Prayer for Those Who Want to Trust God Fully[3]

*Lord God, almighty Father, I trust in You. You are my rock, my fortress, my deliverer, my God, and my strength. I choose to trust in You—with all my heart—instead of leaning unto my own understanding. In all my ways, I will acknowledge You, and I know that You will direct my paths. Thank You for this truth, Father.*

*Your Word, O God, gives me the faith to trust You. Your Word, O God, is forever settled in heaven. You watch over Your Word to perform it. Your Word never returns unto You void. It always accomplishes Your purposes.*

*I commit my way to You, Lord God. Because I have put my trust in You, I will not fear what others can do to me. I will call upon You, and I know You will hear me.*

*You are my trust, almighty God. You are my hope. I look unto You continually. I have chosen to trust You, and I will remember Your name, Lord God. You are Jehovah Jireh, my Provider. You are Jehovah Shalom, my peace.*

*My joy increases in direct proportion to my ability to trust You, Father. Let me ever shout for joy because I trust in You. Thank You for the happiness that comes to me as I learn to walk in trust.*

Chapter 20

# REVIEWING THE
# GRID OF LIVING FAITH:
# T.R.U.S.T.

I FIRST MENTIONED THE T.R.U.S.T grid in my introduction as an organizing concept for embracing spiritual sight. I would now like to share how it is vital for you to exercise the element that each letter represents in helping you progress to true faith and spiritual sight.

One aspect of spiritual blindness is found in our belief that God simply exists "somewhere above." However, His immanence is seen in His design of the human body, its mechanics and its mechanisms, which should cause us all to appreciate and worship Him. Unfortunately, we live with a dysfunctional unction. That is, we cannot relate to God, or each other, in a meaningful way, and we live without peace until we humble ourselves and trust God fully. Scripture describes the remedy for our dysfunction.

> Trust in the LORD with all your heart, And lean not on your own understanding; In all your ways acknowledge Him, And He shall direct your paths.
> —PROVERBS 3:5–6

If we trust God fully, we will find the perfect peace and joy that will prevent our self-destruction. Our whole task in life is to trust Him with the whole mind, heart, and spirit. The Huguenots, devout French Protestants of the sixteenth century, believed that we must carry God's Word within—enlivened by the Holy Spirit—to experience such trust. As the prophet, Habakkuk, says, we must learn to trust God *regardless* of what happens.

> Though the fig tree may not blossom, Nor fruit be on the vines; Though the labor of the olive may fail, And the fields yield no food; Though the flock may be cut off from the fold, And there be no herd in the stalls—Yet will I rejoice in the LORD, I will joy in the God of my salvation. The LORD God is my strength; He will make my feet like deer's feet, And He will make me walk on my high hills.
> —HABAKKUK 3:17–19

A superficial faith, not based on Scripture, fails to acknowledge God in moments of need. We must learn to see spiritually by choosing to walk in the Lord's design rather than our own. *This* walk of trust is what it means to be a Christian. In true faith we trust God, while in the conventional sight of the mind, we lack such trust and are blind.

## T.R.U.S.T.

The letters, T.R.U.S.T., are simply a handy mnemonic device to remind us of the fundamental aspects of a spiritual life that progresses from insincerity or distraction to the full flower and richness of life in Christ. Each letter represents an aspect of our *trust* in the Lord and our faith in Him as follows:

**T**hank God,
**R**ejoice in Him,
**U**nderstand His Word,
**S**ing out to Him, and exhibit
**T**houghtfulness of others.

To develop spiritual sight, to genuinely make a step past the ways of the world, and to seek the triune God in faith, we must learn to trust God. Our American dollar bill states, "In God We Trust"—but *do* you? Real trust in the Creator ought to spread throughout your work, sports, leisure, home-life, friends, and social activities. This trust needs to be *complete* in your desire and effort to be closer to Jesus, even during your struggle with the influences of the world and human existence. You can refer to this grid of T.R.U.S.T. as a basis upon which you can build and grow into the kind of faith that my friend Solomon understands. (See Introduction.)

To come to God fully, we must be willing to humbly surrender our lives to Him and to *rest* in His love and power. Such trust needs to be developed and sought—and it is in that development that a true life of faith, of daily communion with the Lord, progresses to completion.

Let's discuss each of the vital elements represented in this acronym, T.R.U.S.T., which will help you to remember these important concepts for growing into full faith.

**T: Thank God**

"Offer to God thanksgiving, And pay your vows to the Most High" (Psalm 50:14). God is the Most High, Director and Designer of the universe above and the human heart within. He created you with a body so complex that our human science can neither fully explain nor copy it.

Our lack of gratitude and appreciation for the Lord's handiwork and gifts is our deepest—and saddest—shortcoming before our God. Life is so beautiful, so profound, and so beyond our attempts to understand its mysteries. By being alive we are the beneficiaries of God's immeasurable goodness. As believers we know the depth of His love, grace, mercy, and salvation.

Scripture teaches us how to know God: "Therefore humble yourselves under the mighty hand of God, that He may exalt you in due time" (1 Peter 5:6). You and I must genuinely humble ourselves, recognizing and acknowledging God's sovereignty, before we can come to Him with a truly thankful heart. It is only as we express that appreciation and thankfulness that we may begin to see.

All that life is to us—our bodies, loved ones, daily bread, experiences (good and bad), the weather, a joke, a smile, a pet—everything springs from God. The meaning of my life is to appreciate Him, and worship Him for all of it. Refusal to do so is not mere oversight; it is sin. "In everything give thanks; for this is the will of God in Christ Jesus for you" (1 Thessalonians 5:18).

When we genuinely humble ourselves to acknowledge God as the origin of our blessings and to offer pure thanks to Him, we enter a new world of peace and complete sufficiency. No longer hounded by worry, nor preyed upon by wrong desires, we find the Savior's face coming into sharper focus, and the meaning of our presence here among others becomes more apparent. "Whatever you do in word or deed, do all in the name of the Lord Jesus, giving thanks to God the Father through Him" (Colossians 3:17).

Appreciation within a thankful heart is the first building block in the foundation of a living faith. Things may not always, if ever, work out the way I would like, but I have to know that they happen for God's reasons, according to His Word. "And we know that all things work together for good to those who love God, to those who are the called according to His purpose" (Romans 8:28).

God has two purposes for our experiences. The first is for our good. That means they teach us, humble us, make us better servants, prepare us to help others, and bring us back to His path. God's second purpose, in any circumstance, is for His own glory. We must see that in our weakness God is glorified, and thank Him for His presence, mercy, and love.

### R: Rejoice in Him

"Rejoice always, pray without ceasing" (1 Thessalonians 5:16–17). Joy in the Lord, through communion in prayer, is another foundation stone of a faith lived as we progress from mere external practice into a deeper relationship with God. His gracious delight in us as believers is the cause of our rejoicing in Him. (See Psalm 149:4.) Even through what seems to us to be adversity in life, the larger truth of our salvation and eternity in Christ is the ultimate source of our joy.

A wonderful source of rejoicing and blessing can be found in the psalms. Listen to the psalmist as he extols the Lord:

> Bless the LORD, O my soul; And all that is within me, bless His holy name! Bless the LORD, O my soul, And forget not all His benefits: Who forgives all your iniquities, Who heals all your diseases, Who redeems your life from destruction, Who crowns you with loving-kindness and tender mercies, Who satisfies your mouth with good things, So that your youth is renewed like the eagle's.
>
> —PSALM 103:1–5

To rejoice is to feel great delight and to express that feeling, even with abandon. As I have indicated in my book, *Believe and Rejoice*, we experience this celebration of wonder only when we have submitted to God's authority and have been released from the darkness of our own egos and independence. There, in our relinquished heart, is the place that joy in God springs up. The psalmist knew that the source of his joy was in God alone: "You will show me the path of life; In Your presence is fullness of joy; At Your right hand are pleasures forevermore" (Psalm 16:11).

However, even the heart submitted in dependence on God is still exposed to temptation, worldly problems, a return to a shallow faith, sin, and an ongoing desire to reassert independence, as we have discussed. Staying surrendered to God is a continuous struggle, and so our ability to rejoice in the Lord ebbs and flows with our distance from, and proximity to, Him. Separation from God means sadness; being intertwined with Him means rejoicing. God is present with us in everything— that is why we can rejoice in Him always. He will never leave us nor forsake us.

## U: Understanding God

> My son, if you receive my words, And treasure my commands within you, So that you incline your ear to wisdom, And apply your heart to understanding; Yes, if you cry out for discernment, And lift up your voice for understanding, If you seek her as silver, And search for her as for hidden treasures; Then you will understand the fear of the LORD, And find the knowledge of God.
>
> —PROVERBS 2:1–5

The Lord wants to enlighten and enlarge you with discernment, wisdom, and understanding. This aspect of the grid is as active as the others insofar as you must *seek* understanding in the same way in which you might search for material riches buried in the woods. God's Word is eternal, unchanging, and relevant for the duration of your life. "All Scripture is given by inspiration of God, and is profitable for doctrine, for reproof, for correction, for instruction in righteousness" (2 Timothy 3:16).

Understanding God through His Word is central and primary to our spiritual sight. "The entrance of Your words gives light; It gives understanding to the simple" (Psalm 119:130). God speaks to us and imparts understanding through *logos* and *rhema* words, Greek terms for "word" with differing emphases. The Gospel of John tells us *Who* the Word of God is: "In the beginning was the Word, and the Word was with God, and the Word was God...And the Word became flesh and dwelt among us" (John 1:1, 14).

The wisdom of God is proclaimed to all humankind in the *logos* of His eternal truths. These are found in His Word and fleshed out in the life and teachings of our Savior Jesus. God also speaks to us by *rhema*—a word that has a special, personal significance to the one receiving it, as we mentioned. The Holy Spirit imparts a *rhema* to you for a personal application and for personal attainment of spiritual sight.

"Every word of God is pure; He is a shield to those who put their trust in Him" (Proverbs 30:5). Our sight develops with our deepening trust in the Lord and our understanding of His Word, both universal and personal, and we are transformed. "A man's wisdom makes his face shine, And the sternness of his face is changed" (Ecclesiastes 8:1).

### S: Singing out to God

To see spiritually, to draw ever closer to His presence, we need to sing and cry out to Him. Raising our voices heavenward in praise, when we are exhilarated and when we are desperate and in need, is another necessary aspect of the grid that reinforces the path of our pilgrimage to a living faith. We are all His creatures and we need our Creator. God wants us to depend upon Him. The Scriptures teach that He is our provision for life: "For the Lamb who is in the midst of the throne will shepherd them and lead them to living fountains of water. And God will wipe away every tear from their eyes" (Revelation 7:17). What He begins now, He will continue in eternity.

Walking closer to Christ's side, I learn to sing God's name in worship, giving thanks for my life, its various experiences, my blessings, and my redemption in Him. We all must cry out in intercession for those who are suffering. We must humbly ask Him to take our hand in our moments of darkness and tribulation and to give us wisdom. And we must sing to Him in thanksgiving for His wonderful blessings. Again the psalms are filled with songs of praise that we can use as a source for our praise.

> Sing praises to God, sing praises! Sing praises to our King, sing praises! For God is the King of all the earth; Sing praises with understanding.
>
> —Psalm 47:6–7

God's voice reaches to you through His Word and the inspiration of the Holy Spirit. As you grow toward Him, you will learn to use your voice to return to God in communion.

### T: Thoughtfulness of others

Jesus said, "A new commandment I give to you, that you love

one another; as I have loved you" (John 13:34). The world understands this love to be the underlying idea of Christianity. Even for nonbelievers, Christ's image—His birth and life among us—is symbolized by love for one another. In fact, the call to live out our faith in love to others is the primary, overriding principle of Christ's message. It is essential to spiritual sight. Throughout the Scriptures, love has been given preeminence, as when the apostle Paul declared, "And now abide faith, hope, love, these three; but the greatest of these is love" (1 Corinthians 13:13).

Again, Paul confirms the importance of love: "For in Christ Jesus neither circumcision nor uncircumcision avails anything, but faith working through love" (Galatians 5:6). Practicing faith, doing works, making sacrifices—these aspects of life *must* all be focused through a lens of love; only that way is faith really lived and really meaningful to God. Again, Paul makes love paramount: "And though I bestow all my goods to feed the poor, and though I give my body to be burned, but have not love, it profits me nothing" (1 Corinthians 13:3).

Psychologists indicate that an important element in maintaining control when a person feels himself "going over the edge" is immersion in some kind of service to others. A thoughtful care of one's neighbor is a continuous aspect of living our faith in God. It was the basic principle of Jesus' teaching when He was here, and it remains essential to the Christian walk. It is in loving one another that we can try to emulate Christ. It is in the selfless, loving service of others that we can come to genuine spiritual sight.

## ABANDONMENT

There will be occasions when I find myself pitching back and forth on the continuum of progression into vital faith. The same is for you. That is, despite our best intentions, we move between distraction and selfishness on one hand, and prostrating ourselves before the Lord on the other. A living faith is not something we can accomplish by ourselves even when we know that we are hiding from God. We must *trust* and *abandon*.

There will also be times when we are despondent, disappointed, ill, crushed, or struggling in life. It is in these extraordinarily taxing times that the seemingly impossible also becomes the most necessary—we must trust God. And the T.R.U.S.T. grid is your touchstone to remind you of that reality.

We will never be able to see which way to proceed or how to endure unless we learn how to live near to the Lord. God, the Creator, is most glorified when we, the creation, need Him and submit to Him with humility. If we fall into a spirit of self-dependence, or collapse into any kind of spiritual cataract, we will wander in unprofitable paths until God restores us. However, when we live the grid of T.R.U.S.T., lay our wills at the feet of our divine Deliverer, forget about ourselves, and keep our eyes on every pilgrim's goal—the Celestial City—we will continue to enjoy the light of God's countenance! We will have found His arms, His way, and His vision. Our spiritual sight will be restored.

## BE THOU MY VISION

Be Thou my vision, O Lord of my heart;
Naught be all else to me, save that Thou art.
Thou my best thought by day or by night,
Waking or sleeping, Thy presence my light.

Be Thou my wisdom, and Thou my true word;
I ever with Thee and Thou with me, Lord;
Thou my great Father, I Thy true son;
Thou in me dwelling, and I with Thee one.

Be Thou my battleshield, sword for my fight;
Be Thou my dignity, Thou my delight;
Thou my soul's shelter, Thou my high tow'r;
Raise Thou me heav'n-ward, O Pow'r of my pow'r.

Riches I heed not, nor man's empty praise,
Thou mine inheritance, now and always:

Thou and Thou only, first in my heart,
High King of heaven, my treasure Thou art.

High King of heaven, my victory won,
May I reach heaven's joys, O bright heav'n's Sun!
Heart of my own heart, whatever befall,
Still be my vision, O Ruler of all.

We see through a glass darkly but then face to face.[1]

—ANCIENT IRISH POEM

Chapter 21

# Intimate Relationship in Prayer, Praise, and Worship

This psalm of David exemplifies the true spirit of prayer, praise, and worship.

> O God, You are my God;
> Early will I seek You;
> My soul thirsts for You;
> My flesh longs for You
> In a dry and thirsty land
> Where there is no water.

—Psalm 63:1

King David had a craving, a hunger, a homesick longing for God. This insatiable desire is the true spirit at the heart of all spiritual worship. Worship, praise, and prayer are the foundation of our walk with God.

Worship is a response to the Person of God, a blending of man's spirit with God's Spirit. Worship is an interaction of wills and emotions in which we give ourselves to God in complete abandon to His love. Praise is an expression of our hearts uplifted, raised heavenward to the Creator, in adoration and thanksgiving. Prayer is our dialogue with the Lord in which listening is as important as talking. Worship, praise, and prayer are the paths along which we connect with our Lord and Creator. If we are blind, however, we do not find these paths nor touch our Savior.

Responding to God in worship, being involved with *who God is*, is inclusive of many activities: confession of sin, preaching, and praise and prayer as well. Praise and prayer are necessary aspects of our spiritual life, which are integral to worship. Worship is the attitude and expression of a spirit in the presence of its Maker and Master. In worship, we speak to God about Himself. Prayer, the communication, prepares the heart and mind for worship. In prayer, we seek to pour ourselves out to God with *our* needs, *our* desires, and *our* feelings. Praise, the effervescence of affection, allows enthusiastic release into worship.

It appears that, as Oswald Chambers claims, much of the church has suffered a theft: a fear and resistance toward praise have removed joyful praise from a central position in the church program. Likewise, we frequently get so involved in thinking about the performance of worship of those around us that we are incapable of genuine worship. As for prayer, too often this can become an unfeeling way of speaking *at* God rather than engaging in true exchange *with* Him. None of the paths to greater unity with Him are, or ought to be, unthinking routines of religious performance or, as many view them, merely duties. Praise is effusive; it is the joy of the heart percolating up out of voice and body. Should you have to think about being joyful? Worship is not work, it is enjoying our God. What kind of relationship do you have with a lover if you see interacting with that person to be a chore?

## PRAYER

The basis of prayer is not human earnestness, not human need, not the human will; it is redemption, and its living

center is a personal Holy Spirit. Prayer on any other basis
is stupid.[1]

—OSWALD CHAMBERS

My book, *The Prayerful Spirit*,[2] discusses prayer in more
depth, but for our purposes here, let's consider these important
ideas regarding prayer.

## Redemption

Redemption, not our needs nor human effort, but resting
in His redemption accomplished on the cross and the personal work of the Holy Spirit in our hearts, is the foundation
of our prayer. Any other basis is biblically unsupported and,
as Chambers indicates, becomes senseless. Not only does worship involve prayer but, says author Judson Cornwall, "Worship
without prayer is like daytime without light, a school without
music, or an automobile without fuel."[3] He also indicates that,
in fact, prayer cannot be separated from worship. "Prayer is the
entrance to our worship, the energy of our worship, the expression of our worship, and the enhancer of our worship. Prayer
establishes worship, embraces worship, enlarges worship, and
enlightens our worship."[4] Prayer, then, is essential to the Christian walk and to spiritual sight.

Prayer is not merely a religious activity conducted at church,
before meals, and at bedtime. According to 1 Thessalonians 5:17,
we need to "pray without ceasing." Though that is not a physical
possibility, it *is* possible to maintain a prayerful spirit as we walk
through life. Paul was talking about maintaining a continuous
fellowship with God as much as possible within the distracting
details of daily living. First and foremost, prayer is a relationship—an intimate communion with our glorious Savior.

Prayer is, or should be, a two-way conversation. When we find
ourselves simply practicing a religious faith without passion for
God, we may see prayer as merely a petition to God *for* something
rather than an element of, and preface to, worship and praise.
Prayer is not simply a way to *get* things *from* God, it is a way to get
to *know* God. As Chambers points out, the biblical idea of prayer

is that "God's holiness, purpose and wise order may be brought about." It is the nourishment of a true life of faith. "Prayer ... develops the life of God in us."[5]

### Need

Improving our spiritual sight depends upon our progression in faith to get closer to God, become more like Him, and relinquish selfishness. In selfishness we are led to believe that God exists to answer our prayers when, really, it is through prayer that we come to see His face and understand His will more clearly.

Prayer is as much proclamation as petition. Rather than declaring wants and needs, we proclaim God's Word, thereby pleading His will. This faith-filled proclamation calls on God to fulfill His promises and to meet our needs. This understanding of prayer describes a relationship that precedes problems. If we are blinded by our needs, however, we try to make prayer a submission of our petitions rather than a viable, vibrant relationship. In fact, as Bible teacher Henry Blackaby states, "You can't even think a prayer that comes close to what God wants to give you."[6] Only His Spirit knows what He wants for us, and the basis of real prayer becomes God's promises.

When we are blind, self-sufficient, and complacent, we do not want God because we feel that we do not need Him. However, when we are in distress, we often find ourselves calling on Him in desperation. If we compare our relationship with God to a human relationship, it would be equivalent to a child's view of his or her parents. A child's thinking is not rational or mature; it may even be manipulative. Though believers know their responsibility to pray, how many have the passion for an ongoing conversation with Jesus?

### Intercession

Prayer as petition engages God to action. Your supplication and intercession are petitions to God on the behalf of others. And in our compassionate petitioning, it is apparent that prayer changes us, and then God helps us to change things. We begin to be different; we begin to see that God also changes others. God in His providence can change the entire landscape of our circumstances overnight.

## Communion and communication

God speaks to us through prayer. Prayer is much more than talking to God. It is also approaching God with an attentive heart and listening for His response. It is Blackaby who observes, "In fact, what God says in prayer is far more important than what you say."[7] Prayer is how we adjust to God's will revealed by the Holy Spirit. Prayer is also thanksgiving and praise. It is our spirit blending with God's Spirit.

Many Christians associate costs in time, concentration, and exertion with their prayer. Judson Cornwall goes so far as to say that the responsibility that many practicing believers attach to prayer can invoke a sense of guilt greater than that which the word *sin* does. If prayer is not our passion, Satan is gaining a victory. It is redemption—resting in His finished work on the cross—that is the basis of our prayer, making relating to our Lord our greatest joy. (See John 19:30.)

Again, *redemption, not need, is the basis of our prayer.* Jesus introduced the prayer referred to as the Lord's Prayer, teaching that "your Father knows the things you have need of before you ask Him. In this manner, therefore, pray..." (Matthew 6:8–9). Only if you are truly in love with the Lord, can you see God's promises. If you are not complacent about your relationship with the Creator, you will really commune with Him in prayer.

Since such communion involves adoration and submission in solitude before the throne of God, frequently the most appropriate posture in prayer is to lie flat upon your face. Prayer requires a quiet place and quiet time in which you can speak with God. In that quiet place and time, complete prostration on the ground may often be the most honest physical position for the activity. Even more important than your physical position, however, is that your soul is prostrate before Him. In that inner posture of reverence, you might even be physically taking a quiet prayer walk in solitude with God.

## PRAISE

"I will bless the LORD at all times; His praise shall continually be in my mouth" (Psalm 34:1). Praise glorifies God. In your search for Him, God reveals Himself, and you are allowed to know Him more intimately by His initiative. With this intimacy, this very personal relationship, you will wish to express your gratitude and give voice to exultation and ecstasy. Praise is demonstrative. The thanksgiving of praise is open and active. It is an inborn instinct of the creation toward its Creator: "Let everything that has breath praise the LORD. Praise the LORD!" (Psalm 150:6). Praise is adoration of God: "Enter into His gates with thanksgiving, And into His courts with praise" (Psalm 100:4). Still, praise is not mindless celebration.

Job continued to praise God even in the midst of his many weighty trials while his wife scolded him for his apparent naiveté in the face of life's realities. Job asked her, "Shall we indeed accept good from God, and shall we not accept adversity?" (Job 2:10). When we have wrongly felt forsaken of God, we are incapable of worshipful praise to Him. Yet our praise is not dependent upon our blessings; rather, it is dependent on the eyes through which we see God and His gift of life, our spiritual perspective. Therefore, praise comes forth out of a proper attitude. It is appreciation for the Lord and Creator of everything, our trials as well as our blessings.

God is sovereign. Praise is the only appropriate response before His glory and majesty. There is joy in the recognition of God and praise is the exultation. As pastor and author Jack Taylor indicates, praise is the hallelujah of redemption, complete retribution, confirmation of God's reign, and the consummation of our relationship with Him.[8] We worship God *with* praise. Such worship, through praise, often honors God by acknowledging His names revealed in Scripture.

At different times we will be led to call God by different names and in doing so come to a better understanding of who He is, thank Him for His different attributes, and approach Him more intimately. For example, *Elohim* is the mighty Creator, the God who designed our DNA and sixty trillion cells. *Jehovah Elohim* reveals Himself to us as the sovereign Lord God, and our God of Glory is called *El Hakabodh*. If we can see, we know that we have much to be thankful for in this life, and we will want to praise *Jehovah Jireh*, the Lord the Provider. *Jehovah Mekaddishkhem* is our sanctifier; *Jehovah Uzzi* is our strength; *Jehovah Maginnenu* is our defense.

Like Job, you will run into difficulties in life. And like Job, you must recognize God for His mercy and continue to praise Him. In these rough times, you may turn your praise toward *Jehovah Mephalti*, our Deliverer; *Jehovah Makkeh*, the Lord that Smiteth; and *Jehovah Rophe*, our Healer.

When we look for our Lord and seek Him in a continuous living faith, we find the names that submit us to Him and enjoy the rest found only in Him. *Jehovah Roi* is the Lord my Shepherd. We experience calm in *Jehovah Shalom*, the Lord of Peace. In seeking Him and striving to swing from the cares and diversions of the world that dilute faith to the richness of complete devotion, we gratefully acknowledge *Jehovah Ori*, the Lord my Light.

## WORSHIP

> ...the twenty-four elders fall down before Him who sits on the throne and worship Him who lives forever and ever, and cast their crowns before the throne, saying: "You are worthy, O Lord, To receive glory and honor and power; For You created all things, And by Your will they exist and were created."
>
> —REVELATION 4:10–11

Even the heavenly crowns bestowed upon the elders in heaven are left at God's feet. Worship is *all* about God. Only a truly spiritually sighted believer will be willing to submit entirely. Judson Cornwall has described it like this: "Worship consists of the finding of my own life and the yielding of it totally to God for the fulfillment of His purpose. Worship is discovering God's law, answering that law with life, and walking in the way of His

217

appointing. It is allowing our Creator to direct every facet of our lives to the fulfillment of His purposes... it is the worship of a life submitted to God's law and will that makes the worship of our lips and emotions acceptable before the throne of God."[9]

### Submission

You were created for God, not for yourself or the world. Rick Warren writes concerning submission: "It's not about you. The purpose of your life is far greater than your own personal fulfillment, your peace of mind, or even your happiness."[10] It is about God and His purposes. To experience true worship, your heart must be centered on Christ. The more diverted you are from Him, the weaker is your worship. It is important that worship be addressed directly to Him. "Therefore God also has highly exalted Him and given Him the name which is above every name, that at the name of Jesus every knee should bow, of those in heaven, and those on earth, and of those under the earth, and that every tongue should confess that Jesus Christ is Lord, to the glory of God the Father" (Philippians 2:9–11).

We are redeemed by Christ's blood, and our worship flows from this relationship to our Savior. As Cornwall indicates, redemption is not only the basis of worship, but its theme and song as well.[11] As the Holy Spirit leads us into worship, we must acknowledge Christ's worthiness. Responding completely to the Person of Christ is worship.

### Celebration

In heaven, worshipers venerate God and enjoy Him. Part of trusting completely in, and relinquishing to, our Lord and Redeemer is learning to rest and relax in His presence. When we are relaxed in God, our worship is not hampered by solemnity. Neither is it the worship itself that we enjoy—we worship God. We learn that He is enjoying us as well. Frequently, our feelings of guilt may lead us to draw back from God. When that is the case, we must flee to this text: "But if we walk in the light as He is in the light, we have fellowship with one another, and the blood of Jesus Christ His Son cleanses us from all sin" (1 John 1:7).

## Fulfillment

By the worship of God, the human soul finds fulfillment. Jesus taught His disciples how to pray in His model prayer, which we call the Lord's Prayer. He admonished them not to pray in vain like the heathen with their repetitions of words: "For your Father knows the things you have need of before you ask Him" (Matthew 6:8). Worship involves the whole man—mind, body, spirit—which includes needs and desires. In worship, need is satisfied through the soul's nourishment in Christ.

## Redemption

> Let the redeemed of the Lord say so, Whom He has redeemed from the hand of the enemy.
>
> —Psalm 107:2

It is when we come to the end of ourselves that we give ourselves to petition and intercession—prayer. When we have been restored, however, and can see the truth of our redemption, we are freed to worship Him. Through a daily application of the Word to our lives, God cleanses us from the ways of the world and leads us to the one who died and rose again for us. There we witness what Jesus accomplished on the cross. His sacrifice for us allows us to enter His presence in worship.

## Spiritual sight

Worship is not a learned response. It is an existential mandate inside the creature toward the Creator. When you worship, you humbly come before the throne of God in abandonment to Him, releasing your ego and seeking His face. But what of pride? Pride prevents us from entering a proper posture before God. If attention is focused upon ourselves, we are not free to relax and enter His presence. In our worship, praise, and prayer, we must always observe God's worthiness and humbly place ourselves below, prostrating ourselves spiritually, if not physically as well. In worship, praise, and prayer, we enter into His presence to love and be loved. We are blind until we relinquish ourselves to that and to

Him. Essential to all is that we "enter the Holiest by the blood of Jesus" (Hebrews 10:19).

In worship, we are no longer the subject—God is—and we are able, then, to pour forth our love and gratitude. Worship is active. In worship, we are doing things that allow us to enter God's heavenly courts. According to Judson Cornwall, "The very foundation of worship is an element supplied outside the experience of man. It is an intervention of God that returns to man his rightful position before God, for true worship demands being in God's presence. We may praise from afar, but we worship only before the Throne of God."[12]

## Breathe On Me Breath of God

Breathe on me, Breath of God, fill me with life anew,
That I may love what thou dost love, and do what Thou
  wouldst do.

Breathe on me, Breath of God, until my heart is pure,
Until my will is one with Thine to do and to endure.

Breathe on me, Breath of God, till I am wholly Thine,
Until this earthly part of me glows with Thy fire divine.

Breathe on me, Breath of God, so shall I never die,
But live with thee the perfect life of Thine eternity.[13]

—Edwin Hatch, 1878

## Chapter 22

# THE DYNAMIC OF LIVING FAITH: THE UNCTION FUNCTION

*U* NCTION—DERIVED FROM the Latin verb meaning "to anoint with oil"—is a necessary element of all believers' spiritual sight. It is the powerful anointing in our lives by God, through the Holy Spirit, that allows us to see Him. The function of unction is to allow the relationship with God described in Ephesians 3:16–19.

> ...strengthened with might through His Spirit in the inner man, that Christ may dwell in your hearts through faith; that you, being rooted and grounded in love, may be able to comprehend with all the saints what is the width and length and depth and height—to know the love of Christ which passes knowledge; that you may be filled with all the fullness of God.

Jesus is the Christ, the Messiah. *Messiah* is Hebrew for "the anointed one" and *Christ* is the Greek word for "anointed." Jesus the Christ, the Messiah, was anointed and appointed as Prophet,

Priest, and King. He has come to bind up the brokenhearted and to heal them—to set the prisoner free (Luke 4:18). John the Baptist said of Jesus, "For He whom God has sent speaks the words of God, for God does not give the Spirit by measure. The Father loves the Son, and has given all things into His hand" (John 3:34–35). Jesus has the Spirit without measure and the believer, by union with Christ and by the indwelling of the Spirit, receives a divine anointing. (See 2 Corinthians 1:21–22.) The Scriptures declare, "But you have an anointing from the Holy One, and you know all things" (1 John 2:20).

## A BIBLICAL CONTRAST

The importance of unction is illustrated in the Old Testament story of King Saul, the first king of Israel, and contrasted later in the life of King David, which we have previously discussed. Saul was a popular man, whom God told Samuel to anoint as king of Israel in response to the request of the people to have a king like other nations.

> Now the LORD had told Samuel in his ear the day before Saul came, saying, "Tomorrow about this time I will send you a man from the land of Benjamin, and you shall anoint him commander over My people Israel…So when Samuel saw Saul, the LORD said to him, 'There he is, the man of whom I spoke to you. This one shall reign over My people'…Then Samuel took a flask of oil and poured it on his head, and kissed him and said: 'Is it not because the LORD has anointed you commander over His inheritance?'"
>
> —1 SAMUEL 9: 15, 17; 10:1

Saul stood, literally, head and shoulders above his subjects and carried himself with the confidence of a natural leader. Yet Saul, in his egoism, though anointed by God, chose to put himself above obedience to God's Word. Believing more in his independence and ability to control and conquer by his own means than in the unction of God, Saul closed his ears to God. He became stone deaf to the Spirit and failed miserably as king, almost destroying his nation.

In his sermons, R. T. Kendall has referred to Saul as "yesterday's man." Yesterday's man is naturally at odds with "tomorrow's man." After Saul's failure, when God declared he had torn the kingdom from him, David was the man of tomorrow, the leader of the future. God led Samuel to anoint David to be the next king. In contrast to Saul, David, a physically unimpressive youth, had something far more important and potent than his outward appearance or even his appointment as the new king. During the years that Saul continued to sit upon Israel's throne, David walked before God in obedience to the divine unction he had received. David had learned to walk with God, even as a shepherd boy, and to honor Him in his heart.

> He [God] also chose David His servant, And took him from the sheepfolds; From following the ewes that had young He brought him, To shepherd Jacob His people, And Israel His inheritance. So he shepherded them according to the integrity of his heart, And guided them by the skillfulness of his hands.
>
> —PSALM 78:70–72

David not only had the unction of the Spirit, he was guided by obedience to the Word of God. He knew the joy of living in God's presence and worshiping Him. During the interim years, when King Saul called David to the palace to serve him, Saul felt threatened by David and became jealous of him. King Saul sensed that David possessed a divine unction that he did not have. In fact, after his great rebellion and failure, the Scriptures declare of King Saul: "But the Spirit of the LORD departed from Saul, and a distressing spirit from the LORD troubled him" (1 Samuel 16:14). It was the worship of David on a stringed instrument that actually soothed the torment of King Saul. Nevertheless, Saul eventually determined to kill David. However, David was a man after God's own heart, and his unction allowed him to be victorious in the face of years of torment at the hands of King Saul. And eventually, after being crowned king over all of Israel, David was able to lead his people according to God's will rather than by his own resolve and imperfect wisdom, as Saul had done.

## THE PURPOSE OF UNCTION

The Holy Spirit has a purpose to fulfill in each of our lives as much as He had in the destiny of Israel and its leaders. However, many of us remain blind to this purpose and never reach the intended summit of fully living our faith in God. The presence of the Holy Spirit within us is the pure source of our unction. The Holy Spirit within us sensitizes our heart and leads us into the light. Scriptures teach that "ye have an unction from the Holy One" (1 John 2:20, KJV). The Holy Spirit's work in our lives is a heavenly unction, an anointing, that transforms us and satisfies us. It is our part to choose to obey and yield to the work of the Spirit in our lives.

The Holy Spirit leads us in a closer walk with God. He brings the reality of Jesus' presence into our lives so that we know the Savior personally, deeply, and with satisfaction. Prayer is stirred up within and there is a new hunger for God's Word. Without the sound basis of the Word, however, we self-destruct. When we yield to a true spirit of praise and worship from our hearts, we begin to change. More willing to submit and surrender, we are blessed with a more trusting spirit through our trials. He quickens us to fully believe that the promises of God are true for each of us individually. We also acquire a more teachable spirit that releases us from stubbornness. In our transformation, our desire to serve others grows and begins to bear tangible fruit. It is very important that we surrender to the power of the Holy Spirit working in us—this unction function. If we do not submit, surrender, grow, and seek, we will suffer an *unction malfunction*.

When we yield to the work of the Holy Spirit to work in us, we begin to *see spiritually*. Unction means "being anointed."

Many, even earnest believers, find the strength of God's unction difficult to maintain. It may be most difficult for pastors whose task is to lead the flock, the body of Christ, made up of many different minds, perspectives, and backgrounds. It is a very difficult task to refrain from giving in to opinions and "natural" desires of people, which can divert focus to human accomplishment and blind one to the divine purposes of the Holy Spirit.

## THE EFFECTIVENESS OF UNCTION

The effectiveness of the unction function depends upon believers working quietly with God's Spirit. We are often too busy with our own endeavors but—as Mary understood even while her sister Martha fussed—our hearts remain empty until they are filled with God's presence, sitting at the feet of Jesus. The fruit of a life filled with the Spirit is evident.

> But the fruit of the Spirit is love, joy, peace, longsuffering, kindness, goodness, faithfulness, gentleness, self-control.
>
> —GALATIANS 5:22–23

Our lives reflect the fruits of where we spend our "sitting" time. The fruit of the flesh can only produce lust, envy, or bitterness—familiar obstructions to our sight. Often, we are sidetracked and pursue the things that prevent the Word of God from bearing fruit in our lives. (See Mark 4:19.) Yet, the believer, by union with Christ and by the indwelling of the Spirit, can have an effective unction that produces a fruitful life, revealing the character of Christ, *despite* the influence of our indwelling sin principle. God's Spirit working in us produces love when it is hard to be loving, joy when we are disappointed, and peace in times of duress.

You may also expect to become more long-suffering, kind, and gentle, even when tired, angered, or hurt. You will understand God's goodness and faithfulness in the face of betrayal and mistreatment. You can develop self-control when tested and stressed. This is the function of unction. Divine anointing of the Holy

Spirit enables you to worship, to praise, and to have a submissive heart to God's sovereignty—to say "Thy will be done" regardless of our present circumstances.

As believers, we cannot rise to the summit where we experience God's fullness until we shed the *supplemental* in favor of the *fundamental*. This means that, like a person climbing a mountain laden with nice things that are not central to the task of scaling the height, we need to drop the camera, the binoculars, or the book and depend upon only the most fundamental equipment for the climb—the ropes and crampons.

Charles Carrin, a wonderful conference speaker, has employed a lovely little metaphor for this priority of the fundamental in his sermons. He describes our spirit as that which resembles the leaves of autumn. At the end of summer, the energy-producing season, the trees curtail production of the green chlorophyll that makes the leaves green. As the chlorophyll levels decrease, other pigments—pigments that were *always there* but masked by the green—are released. The yellow of carotene begins to shine and the red color of anthocyanins ignites the surface of the leaf. Our autumn leaves display the magnificent colors that were present in them all summer long.

However, these fundamental "fall" colors had been overpowered by the supplemental concerns of the green chlorophyll. Likewise, in the human soul, the workings of the outer man cover up and hide the beauty of the inner man. God resolves this dilemma, giving us a yearning heart in pursuit of God by the anointing of the Holy Spirit. And as we yield to the unction of the Spirit within, the beautiful colors of the character of Christ transcend the power of the "chlorophyll". The fundamental is liberated from the supplemental, and everything else pales in the divine beauty of the "colorful pigments"—the effectiveness of the unction of Christ's life revealed.

Enjoying communion with Christ and receiving anointing by the Holy Spirit requires us to drop the useless baggage of pride and ego that we are trying to haul up the mountain. The power and beauty of the unction function is experienced by us when we, like the elders before the throne, fall on our faces before God and cast our crowns before Him. (See Revelation 4:10.) There is a continuous struggle within us, as we have discussed, between self and true spirituality. The Scriptures describe this struggle: "For the flesh lusts against the Spirit, and the Spirit against the flesh; and these are contrary to one another, so that you do not do the things that you wish...And those who are Christ's have crucified the flesh with its passions and desires. *If we live in the Spirit, let us also walk in the Spirit*" (Galatians 5:17, 24–25, emphasis added).

We must be continually vigilant to surrender to the divine unction within, learning to walk in the Spirit, obeying His direction, if we are to be victorious over the "flesh" and its desires. We cannot expect to enjoy spiritual sight and live a life of full faith if we settle for mere ceremonies and religiosity rather than vital relationship with God. Jesus warned us of this sightless condition: "These people draw near to Me with their mouth, And honor Me with their lips, But their heart is far from Me. And in vain they worship Me, Teaching as doctrines the commandments of men" (Matthew 15:8–9).

In our conversion, we realize that we only come to trust God when we have nothing else in which to trust. In Christian experience, we find that God progressively removes our false trust in other things to teach us to trust Him more completely. An authentic unction function can be attained only in humble surrender and abandonment to the Savior. The Scriptures teach clearly that God resists the proud and gives grace to the humble. Stubborn, self-willed, and self-assured people will remain confused and spiritually blind until broken and left with a limp. When we rest in Christ's redemption, the Spirit of God is sent into our hearts and lives to fulfill the unction function. (See Romans 3:24.) Only then are the chains of bondage broken, and we are delivered from our blindness.

Only by walking in the Spirit can we have an effective unction function. We are spiritually blind when we give importance to works or behavior rather than seeking the Spirit of God. As we have discussed, life represents a continuum that stretches from spiritual blindness on the left to a vital and living faith on the right. It could also be considered a continuum between the supplemental and the fundamental. The action of the Word and Spirit upon your heart is the fundamental aspect of your divine life and spiritual sight. How you express that life depends upon your gifts and circumstances. To welcome the Holy Spirit into our hearts—to yield to the unction function—makes us sound and complete. It means receiving our *sight*.

## EARTH DESPICABLE—HEAVEN DESIRABLE

In hope to sing without a sob
The anthem ever new,
I gladly bid the dusty globe,
And vain delights, Adieu.[1]

—RALPH ERSKINE

# PART V:

# YOUR SPIRITUAL SIGHT DETERMINES YOUR ETERNITY

I T IS POSSIBLE for us to learn much about God and to experience Him and yet have our sight remain dim by spiritual limi-
tation. The apostle Paul referred to those limitations.

> Love never fails. But whether there are prophecies, they
> will fail; whether there are tongues, they will cease;
> whether there is knowledge, it will vanish away. For we
> know in part and we prophesy in part. But when that
> which is perfect has come, then that which is in part will
> be done away. When I was a child, I spoke as a child,
> I understood as a child, I thought as a child; but when
> I became a man, I put away childish things. *For now we
> see in a mirror, dimly, but then face to face. Now I know in
> part, but then I shall know just as I also am known.*
> —1 CORINTHIANS 13:8–12, EMPHASIS ADDED

First, the apostle Paul likens our ability to understand to a
child's ability or, rather, *inability* to understand. We know so little

of just how God moves in mysterious ways. Only in eternity will God, His knowledge of us, and what He has done in our life, be fully revealed. At that point we will become aware how much more we could have trusted Him and why we should have worried less and prayed more.

Second, even when reaching the mature vital faith like that of my friend Solomon (see Introduction), the Scriptures liken our sight to the poor quality of reflection particular to the piece of polished metal used as a mirror in Paul's day. As far to the right of our continuum as we can possibly go in this life—living our faith fully in obedience to the Spirit of God within—we are still only beginning our eternal relationship with God. Heaven alone offers perfection. Our paltry knowledge—our ability to understand and perceive spiritually—is imperfect and limited. We see through a glass only dimly, though our hope is that the heavenly fullness is yet to come. We cannot now see the beauty of heaven, but under the perfect reign of God's love in eternity, we will finally see the blessed life that God has appointed for us with clarity.

Today, we are like those in Isaiah's day who were tossed about and not comforted (Isaiah 54: 11). But when that which is perfect has come in eternity we will see even more fully the "beauty for ashes, The oil of joy for mourning, The garment of praise for the spirit of heaviness" (Isaiah 61:3). On that day we will know the love of God in full measure. More than anything else, we will see Him as He *is*, as though face to face. We will be overwhelmed by the infinite majesty of God. We will know the kiss of the Father for His prodigal sons and daughters. The seemingly impenetrable paradoxes and perplexities of fractured and shattered lives will ultimately be resolved. We will see and experience life and love from God's perspective.

However, the contrast between what you know now—that which you can presently see—and what you *will* know in eternity does *not* mean that you are incapable in this moment of seeking the Lord or the fullness of an abiding walk with Him. God's Word is an accurate and faithful revelation of Himself to the believer, and our knowledge of God today *does* correspond to that reality.

Receiving the truth of God that only the blood of Christ can save us, and only the Holy Spirit can give us new birth, we begin to see that the promises of God are true; God does indeed work all things together for good for those who love Him (Romans 8:28).

In heaven, our knowledge will be mature, unclouded, and complete. With veils finally lifted we will feel the nearness of God and see that above all—above knowledge, hope, and even faith—is love. Unlike our present episodes of weakness and weariness in praise and prayer, at the consummation of the marriage union with Him, our experience and knowledge of the Lord will fill eternity with Hosannas, Hallelujahs, and Amens!

As we conclude these last two chapters, we will consider the vital concepts of learning to walk in faith in light of the "hiddenness" of God, and the wonder of walking in divine destiny—forever.

Chapter 23

# WE SEE THROUGH A GLASS DARKLY

PAUL MINISTERED TO the Gentiles as he preached the *unsearchable* riches of Christ. From the apostle's teaching, we can conclude that although I can know something of His blessings, the mystery of the true spiritual depth of the Creator of the universe cannot be fully fathomed.

> To me, who am less than the least of all the saints, this grace was given, that I should preach among the Gentiles the unsearchable riches of Christ, and to make all see what is the fellowship of the mystery, which from the beginning of the ages has been hidden in God who created all things through Jesus Christ; to the intent that now the manifold wisdom of God might be made known...
>
> —EPHESIANS 3:8–10

## GOD'S HIDDENNESS

To some extent, even as we walk by faith with God on this earth, He remains hidden to our eyes and understanding. We will see "through a glass darkly" until we meet Him face to face. God's nature is revealed to the searching believers who are inspired by His hiddenness to seek Him with their whole heart. Our purpose and meaning in life, walking with Him and progressing toward an authentic faith, is to continually seek God and acknowledge Him as He is revealed to us in His truths. It must be our desire to seek increasing intimacy with Him as He beckons from that hiddenness.

In his *Pensees*, Blaise Pascal, the seventeenth-century scientist, philosopher, and Christian, wrote about light and sight. He put his finger on God's hiddenness to our conventional wisdom and comprehension, and its purpose.

For it is certain that those who have the living faith in their hearts see at once that all existence is none other than the work of the God whom they adore. But for those in whom this light is extinguished, and in whom we purpose to rekindle it, persons destitute of faith and grace, who, seeking with all their light whatever they see in nature that can bring them to this knowledge, find only obscurity and darkness; to tell them that they will see God openly, to give them, as a complete proof of this great and important matter, the course of the moon and planets...is to give them ground for believing that the proofs of our religion are very weak.

It is not after this manner that Scripture speaks, which has a better knowledge of the things that are of God. It says, on the contrary, that *God is a hidden God, and that since the corruption of nature, He has left men in darkness from which they can escape only through Jesus Christ, without whom all communion with God is cut off.*

This is what Scripture points out to us, when it says in so many places that those who seek God find Him.

It is not of that light, "like the noonday sun", that this is said...the evidence of God must not be of this nature. (emphasis added)[1]

You and I need the godly vision that the Holy Spirit inspires through the Word as we heed the instruction: "Let this mind be in you which was also in Christ Jesus" (Philippians 2:5). Without the vision of God—which is in union with Him, incorporation into Him—we die: "Where there is no vision, the people perish" (Proverbs 29:18, KJV).

Many people look for the easy road into heaven, but the secret to victory in our pursuit is in continuing to seek to know God in His Word through the Spirit of God. In his book, *Experiencing God*, Henry Blackaby writes that we experience God and understand His nature in *knowing and doing His will*.[2] We cannot *find* God's will, however, apart from His Word. He *reveals* Himself to us and brings us into a relationship of love, when we seek His name and presence. This is the hiddenness of God: our imperfect sight demands that we seek Him out and abandon ourselves to the Word and to the Spirit, submitting ourselves to God's will.

Perhaps you worship God in "spirit and in truth." However, you are blind if you think that everything is *either* Word *or* Holy Spirit. It is the working together of both the Spirit and the truth of the Word that gives us abundant life and eternal life. We must receive the life of the Spirit: "The Spirit of truth, whom the world cannot receive, because it neither sees Him nor knows Him; but you know Him, for He dwells with you and will be in you" (John 14:17). God reveals Himself to us by His Spirit.

As we have discussed, we cannot find understanding by the strength of our own minds, but only by asking the Holy Spirit to illumine us will we be able to comprehend what God is saying to us in His Word. "However, when He, the Spirit of truth, has come, He will guide you into all truth" (John 16:13). *This* is what we call spiritual sight, because "the natural man does not receive the things of the Spirit of God, for they are foolishness to him;

nor can he know them, because they are spiritually discerned" (1 Corinthians 2:14).

The great teacher John Wesley began to really *see*, and progressed to a full, living faith when he acknowledged the *Spirit* in the Scripture. Simply put, to find spiritual sight means overcoming in the constant battle between practicing faith incompletely, or insincerely, or distractedly, and *acknowledging* the Lord as He reveals Himself through the Spirit and the Word, and *abandoning* ourselves to Him.

## KNOWLEDGE

After you first come to the Lord, the progression of faith and your closeness to Him originate in the changes in your understanding, your values, and motivations to act. Immediately after salvation, you are summoned to present your body as a living sacrifice to the Lord, with your soul's desire for God encompassing your mind, will, and emotions. (See Romans 12:1.) As we have discussed, the battlefield of the soul remains, however. Intimacy with God depends *so* much upon, not only our salvation, but also our willingness to seek the blessing of unction. The wisdom with which it endows us, as well as a functioning pattern—such as the T.R.U.S.T. grid—can guide and discipline our motivations and imaginations until they are transformed into the image of Christ.

Many obstructions to our sight prevent Christ's unfettered inhabitation of our spirit. The dark glass of human existence obscures the teachings of the Holy Spirit. Nevertheless the desire for growth in faith is testimony to a change in motivation, values, ideals, actions, and habits. Imaginations determine such values and motivations, as Jesus discussed, beginning with the beatitudes. The distinction between the outward displays and actions and the inner landscape starts in the attributes that the Scriptures teach are most important.

> . . . that He would grant you, according to the riches of His
> glory, to be strengthened with might through His Spirit
> in the inner man, that Christ may dwell in your hearts

> through faith; that you, being rooted and grounded in love, may be able to comprehend with all the saints what is the width and length and depth and height—to know the love of Christ which passes knowledge; that you may be filled with all the fullness of God.
>
> —EPHESIANS 3:16–19

There, between the inner man and the outer, is the expression of the Christian walk, living faith, and spiritual sight. Strengthened by the Spirit, indwelt by Christ through faith and grounded in love, we are able to comprehend God's vital love. Complete comprehension of this love is beyond the possible faculties of human sight. Though the depth, meaning, and necessity of the Father's love may still be partially obscured from our hearts now, *without* it we are like cymbals: noisy and lacking the substance that makes the music of life. (See 1 Corinthians 13.)

The inner spirit is altered as we come to know God in faith. Then it is strengthened with might through *His* Spirit. In this place with God, only the inner man—the believer's innermost being—rather than the outer man of the world, possesses peace, freedom, and spiritual sight. Someone has said that in our relationship with Christ, He is either "Lord of *all*, or He is not Lord *at all.*" To recognize this reality, to acknowledge God as He reveals Himself, is how we move along the continuum toward our living faith and spiritual sight.

What strikes me most obviously is the face of God in the biological, scientific creation of life. It is amazing that people can be intelligent, knowledgeable, and have a scientific wonder about the world, yet still remain unaware of God's genius in His design and rendering of our universe and everything in it. It seems odd that humanity mostly satisfies itself by peering at the surface of mysteries rather than diving into their depths.

Do you thoughtfully consider the miracle of the massively complex DNA that directs your development and function? In my book, *Darwinism Under the Microscope*, I examine the impossibility of a worldview founded in the tenets of evolution amid the obvious evidence of a glorious Creator.[3] The blindness that prevents many people from seeing that truth is obviously a willful desire *not* to acknowledge God and His providence. Humans are naturally selfish beings; we desire to do "our own thing," our way, to serve our own ends. We often—or always, for some of us—refuse to surrender ourselves to God's words, ways, and will. Again, Pascal had something to say about this tendency.

> What completes our incapability of knowing things is the fact that they are simple and that we are composed of two opposite natures, different in kind, soul, and body. For it is impossible that our rational part should be other than spiritual; and if anyone maintains that we are simply corporeal, this would far more exclude us from the knowledge of things, there being nothing so inconceivable as to say that matter knows itself...So, if we are simply material, we can know nothing at all; and if we are composed of mind and matter, we cannot know perfectly things which are simple, whether spiritual or corporeal. Hence it comes that almost all philosophers have confused ideas of things, and speak of material things in spiritual terms, and of spiritual things in material terms...[4]

We board planes, cars, and elevators and trust them. Why is it so easy to trust ourselves and our machines while we do not trust in God? It is not in *knowing,* but rather in faith, that we grow from trust in ourselves to trust in the Lord. Such a leap requires a *metanoia*[5]—a transformation of thought; we must affirm that we know little, next to nothing really, and that we need the Holy Spirit to endow us with insight, wisdom, knowledge, and discernment. Otherwise, we are blind to the degree that we are limited within our own minds. Such a *metanoia* is impossible for the natural man.

Transformation comes from the Spirit of God living within us, working in us, and providing there, complete satisfaction and peace—*shalom.* The hidden face of God, working in the hidden part of man—the spirit—can deliver us from the destructive power of the flesh and make us successful in our journey toward a complete faith. The world will see the divine unction working in us and desire to know our Lord as well. And we will be satisfied that we are learning to walk in divine destiny, as God promised.

## WE SHALL SEE HIS LOVELY FACE

We shall see His lovely face some bright, golden
  morning,
When the clouds have rifted, and the shades have
  flown;
Sorrow will be turned to joy, heartaches gone forever;
No more night, only light, When we see His Face.[6]
                        —NORMAN J. CLAYTON

Chapter 24

# LIVING YOUR
# DIVINE DESTINY—FOREVER

THE GREAT KING Solomon made a request of God that pleased Him very much. Rather than asking for riches or power, the wise king besought God for divinely inspired wisdom—for spiritual sight. As king of all Israel, he asked humbly, "Therefore give to Your servant an understanding heart to judge Your people, that I may discern between good and evil" (1 Kings 3:9). Each one of us is in the position to make that godly petition. The New Testament confirms God's response: "If any of you lacks wisdom, let him ask of God, who gives to all liberally and without reproach, and it will be given to him" (James 1:5).

Too often, however, the requests of natural man, in contrast to King Solomon's righteous desire, are driven by emotion, intellect, passion, and carnal desire. This is the blindness of the natural man. The fact is that our focus will remain on temporal, corruptible life, and our *blindness will persist* until we decide to gaze on God and to worship Him in the beauty of holiness.

As we have discussed, the Scriptures teach that the natural man cannot comprehend or receive things from God's Spirit because those things are *only* spiritually discerned. (See 1 Corinthians 2:14.) For such a man, these things of God's Spirit are nonsense. We must acknowledge and accept the Spirit of God in our hearts in order to be free to receive the same wisdom for which the mighty King Solomon prayed.

The world's wisdom and its ideas of man's independence and preeminence under the sun are "vanity" and without meaning, according to the Scriptures. (See Ecclesiastes 1–2.) "And again, 'The LORD knows the thoughts of the wise, that they are futile'" (1 Corinthians 3:20). It is in understanding and *accepting* this truth that we move toward spiritual sight. Your sight now as a believer, and your enjoyment of eternity later, requires the inward obedience that you can exercise only by abandoning yourself to the Spirit of God and embracing His sovereignty, declaring, "God rules all and I delight in it."

## DIVINE *KOINONIA*

As we ask the Lord for unction, which is the understanding we receive from the anointing of God, we will receive direction that will allow us to work to the best of our abilities in service to Him (1 John 2:20). Receiving His anointing allows us to *live* our faith. It is that divine anointing of appreciating God's ultimate sovereignty that is the cure for our blindness. It teaches us how to deal with independence and the materialism of a world that touts diversions and Darwinism. This anointing allows us to relinquish our life entirely to His eternal will, and it provides the peace to walk in *koinonia*—the Greek word for "fellowship" and sharing with our Lord.[1] The presence of the Holy Spirit in our lives is light, allowing sight; the absence of the Holy Spirit is darkness, veiling our eyes.

The anointing of universal sovereignty brings the believer into a living faith; it inspires real anticipation and passion that human emotions alone cannot generate; it bathes us in joy, peace, and healing. The anointing of universal sovereignty is another way of saying *"Believe and Rejoice!"*[2]

That anointing, which is the Holy Spirit's presence in us, calls us to specific tasks and empowers us to accomplish those assignments in God's name. Through that anointing, we learn to walk in the divine destiny for which we were born. We observe the divine anointing in the lives of biblical heroes who lived by faith—Joseph, Daniel, and Moses. Through the anointing of the Holy Spirit and the empowering nature of the Word of God, they lived by the power of God's sovereignty and made it manifest to others. It is this individual, anointed purpose of life that makes our lives more meaningful, productive, and passionate in the present and holds as well, a beautiful, eternal significance. Our labor is not in vain but is meaningful, now and forever. To fulfill that divine purpose we must seek the Lord's will in everything we do.

## PURPOSE

In his book, *The Purpose Driven Life*, Rick Warren has discussed the importance and impact of an anointed purpose for our lives.

> The purpose of your life is far greater than your own personal fulfillment, your peace of mind, or even your happiness. It's far greater than your family, your career, or even your wildest dreams and ambitions. If you want to know why you were placed on this planet, you must begin with God. You were born by His purpose and for His purpose.[3]

In this understanding that your existence is not accidental, Darwinist theories are thoroughly refuted. As Warren further points out, the opportunity that each of our purposes present us—the opportunity to serve God and our fellow human—is for this lifetime *and beyond*. "The counsel of the LORD stands forever" (Psalm 33:11). We must remain aware that our time here is very brief indeed and that the real meaning of our existence lies in the eternal. That is why it is so important that we not become absorbed by temporal pursuits. Malcolm Muggeridge observed, "The only ultimate disaster that can befall us, I have come to realize, is to feel ourselves at home here on earth."[4]

At the seventy-fifth anniversary of the Wilmer Ophthalmologic Institute at Johns Hopkins Hospital in April, 2000, I sat at the head table with various well-known speakers and dignitaries. I noticed, however, that the interest of the guests was more drawn to the presence of a black man, whom I did not recognize. I learned that he was the blind pop singer, Stevie Wonder.

Stevie proceeded to play the piano and then began to speak to the guests. He related the story of how, when he was very young, his mother, distraught over his blindness, cried, prayed, and took him to healing services. At age five, he consoled her with these words: "Mama, please stop crying. I know I'm blind and poor, but I'm meant for something greater than sight. Mama, I have the ability to make people happy, and I'm happy. Maybe I can be a vision to peoples' hearts. Please stop worrying."

The Holy Spirit can show us *our* purpose as we abide in God's grace and redemption, and we can live in faith, hope, joy, and most of all, love. We don't need physical eyes for this purpose; it represents our *spiritual sight*. For all believers, we share the wonderful purpose Peter described: "That you may proclaim the praises of Him who called you out of darkness into His marvelous light" (1 Peter 2:9). Jesus first taught His disciples that truth, declaring, "You are the light of the world...Let your light so shine before men, that they may see your good works and glorify your Father in heaven" (Matthew 5:14, 16).

## ETERNAL REWARDS

A book by Bruce Wilkinson, *A Life God Rewards: Why Everything You Do Today Matters Forever*, contributes to the idea that our task in life and our attitudes through it are significant, meaningful, and carry eternal implications for which we are individually responsible.[5] Everything we do in this life will be judged by the Lord when we stand before Him in glory. He not only enables us to live faithfully for Him here on earth, but He will reward us in heaven for doing so. His Word clearly outlines the direction that brings blessing and reward: "You have made known to me the path of life; you will fill me with joy in your presence, with eternal pleasures at your right hand" (Psalm 16:11, NIV). Spiritual blindness prevents us from perceiving what the Holy Spirit reveals when we prayerfully search the Scriptures for understanding of His desires for us.

Those who have rejected the Lord during their lifetime will receive eternal judgment accordingly. Others, who have received Jesus as their Lord and Savior, will also be judged for every thought, word, and deed. They will be evaluated for their service and stewardship in every area of life and receive a corresponding reward. In the New Testament, Paul understood this future assessment and made pleas for the church to hold an eternal perspective:

> ...we do not look at the things which are seen, but at the things which are not seen. For the things which are seen are temporary, but the things which are not seen are eternal.
>
> —2 CORINTHIANS 4:18

Believers with spiritual blind spots missed Paul's challenge then, and many of us do today. We will be measured by how we acted and performed while living, and we will receive the appropriate reward. God's eternal reward system is truly generous. (See Matthew 11:21–22; 23:14; Revelation 20:11, 15; John 5:22; 2 Corinthians 5:10; Matthew 16:27; Luke 6:23.) Spiritual sight for the believer is an abiding desire to live today with God's eternal values in view. Such a purpose-driven life is our present reward until we meet Him face to face.

It is here and now—*today*—where you develop your fulfillment in eternity. This is accomplished by the faithful surrendering of the body, soul, and spirit to God: "Be faithful until death, and I will give you the crown of life" (Revelation 2:10). In much the same way that a trained musician can glean more from a concert than the untrained listener—*though the music has beauty for all listeners*—your faith in, love for, and stewardship to God *in this life* is rewarded with a deeper capacity to understand and enjoy Him now and forever.

## FAITH AND SIGHT

A living faith of true intimacy with God graces the believer with joyfulness, contentment, freedom from fears and excess, help in moments of hardship, anticipation of eternity, and peace that passes all understanding. There is a paradox involved in spiritual sight owing to the realization that the rewards for faith and service may not always be apparent *to the natural eye.* However, our spiritual sight reveals something else: faith determines our destiny.

Wilkinson concludes, "Our eternal destination is the consequence of what we believe on earth."[6] For example, the Scriptures teach, "Believe on the Lord Jesus Christ, and you will be saved" (Acts 16:31). And Wilkinson observes, "Our eternal compensation is the consequence of how we behave on earth."[7] In the Lord's parable, that reward is clear: "His lord said to him, 'Well done, good and faithful servant; you have been faithful over a few things, I will make you ruler over many things. Enter into the joy of your lord'" (Matthew 25:23).

Those who give and serve are truly free. Your reward for faith, faithfulness, and love is the capability for greater works to God's glory—the privilege of serving others more—and a greater opportunity to serve in heaven when the day comes. Scripture clearly promises your personal destiny fulfilled in Christ.

> For we are His workmanship, created in Christ Jesus for good works, which God prepared beforehand that we should walk in them.
>
> —EPHESIANS 2:10

You were created *to do something*—individually created for a time such as this. Your purpose, in God's plan, is the most important aspect of your life now and in the future. But it can only be realized by walking in faith: "Now faith is the substance of things hoped for, the evidence of things not seen" (Hebrews 11:1). It is your salvation in Jesus, sensitivity to the Holy Spirit, and *abiding faith* in God that open your eyes to the truth. It is God's truth of seeking intimacy with the Lord and submitting yourself unreservedly at His feet—loving and serving in His name—which is your meaning, purpose, and desire. It is when God reveals His glory and truth to you that you truly *see*. God has a glorious purpose for you. Have you embraced it?

# CONCLUSION

I CONCLUDE THIS BOOK the same way I began it, by repeating the formula our friends at International Cooperating Ministries: "Jesus plus anything equals nothing; Jesus plus nothing equals *everything*." There is nothing you can accomplish on your own. There is nothing outside of Jesus. When you are distracted by life, perhaps wayward, buried in formal structures, or lost in your own selfish concerns, *you cannot be free, and you cannot see.* The idea that any of us can add anything to our lives besides Jesus is wrong. When we try to add anything to Jesus, it becomes nothing. As we read in Romans, when we have Jesus alone, we have everything, "being justified freely by His grace through the redemption that is in Christ Jesus" (Romans 3:24). Focus is necessary for functional vision, and likewise, spiritual sight requires that we center our focus on God. We need to realize that all we need is Jesus—and Jesus alone!

We must look at God's grace in Christ's dying for us and understand that it is not our works, but His sacrifice on the cross, and the outpouring of the Holy Spirit into our lives, that has changed everything. Even a focus on "goodness" is off target. We do not want to become so involved in our work for Jesus that we forget to love Him. He must be our priority and the subject of our focus. When we seek a relationship with Jesus and receive His peace—*shalom*—by the Holy Spirit, our values, ideals, and motives all change in that direction.

The Holy Spirit allows us to be transformed and come into this peace of God—and it comes so easily and quietly, as a dove. Here is the blissful presence of the Lord—a humble consciousness of confidence in Him that is not present when we are not in a place of complete, replete faith. Similar to chasing a dove away, it is possible to *quench* or *grieve* the Spirit. When we willfully choose to sin, we are grieving the Holy Spirit. To refuse the leading of the Holy Spirit in our lives is to quench the work of God's Spirit. On the contrary, the fruit of the Spirit is the result of our abiding with spiritual sight. (See Galatians 5:22.) We must seek the fruit of the Spirit for the full enjoyment of faith, but it becomes *even greater* after we have sought "just Jesus" and His grace. Rather than striving for God's *presents*, we seek His *presence*.

## CHOOSING BLINDNESS

Consider a powerful observation made by Malcolm Muggeridge: "There's no such thing as darkness; only a failure to see."[1] Our refusal to acknowledge God, the Creator, is the cataract that clouds the lens of our understanding and blinds us to the truth of God. In this state of independence and distance we cannot fully live the life of worship and proximity to Him that God greatly rewards. Our lack of surrender to the Creator of the universe will keep our eyes veiled and prevent us from progressing to the living faith that provides peace and perfect satisfaction.

Do not forget that even the earnest believer, who wants greater intimacy with God, can find his sight dimmed by choosing to be absorbed by the distractions of life. Our spiritual blindness, the blindness that causes us to turn our hearts and minds from God, originates in the misdirected focus of selfishness—*our lack of appreciation for Him.* As we have discussed, spiritual blindness is our state when we are not in a right relationship with our Creator. It is a lack of communion with God that results in such blindness. The absence of communion intimates faulty commitment, faulty love, and faulty understanding of the mind of God, His purpose, and who we are in Christ. Our blindness is the lack of an abiding, vibrant faith. We cannot be in complete communion with Him until we are reconciled to God, according to the apostle Paul.

> Now all things are of God, who has reconciled us to Himself through Jesus Christ, and has given us the ministry of reconciliation, that is, that God was in Christ reconciling the world to Himself...
> —2 CORINTHIANS 5:18–19

God wishes to draw each one of us into a relationship with Him that is real, personal, intimate, and loving. According to Henry Blackaby, it is "probably the most important aspect of knowing and doing the will of God. If our love relationship with God is not right, nothing else will be right."[2]

## CHOOSING SIGHT

Living faith is spiritual sight; it is faith at work and, like a diamond, spiritual sight is multifaceted, reflecting the light of heaven. God is Spirit, and you will not see spiritually —*see as He sees*—until you surrender to the work of His Spirit within you. His Spirit opens eyes and directs focus.

Our sight is adjusted and, in that adjusting, our relationship to God, to the body of Christ, and to the nonbeliever is transformed. Our entire method of living changes when we have God's eternal view and we learn to live a life according to His eternal purpose. The transition from dark to light begins with acknowledgment and abandonment. We must acknowledge the Creator's existence and His sovereignty over every star, banana tree, barn cat, and human heart. We must acknowledge our position as fallen and lost without God, and pray for the Holy Spirit to direct us toward

Him in humility. We have to acknowledge who we are in Him, which is the beginning of our walk in faith, and then surrender ourselves to Him. Until we have abandoned our egos, independence, and self-serving inclinations at His feet, we have nothing and we remain blind.

The transition to a living faith is found in understanding and acknowledging justification: we are justified before God—instantly, when we believe—by Christ's work on the cross. Then, sanctification is the power of the Holy Spirit working in our lives to release us from bondage and change our lives. When we embrace God, seek the Holy Spirit, and abandon ourselves, we come to know Him personally and His grace becomes more and more a part of us. Then, in unification, change becomes corporate as well as individual—within one person and the church. We are one body in Jesus Christ and are called to work together through the power of the Holy Spirit. The Holy Spirit must work within us; without the Holy Spirit there is no life in Christ and no vision.

## ABIDING LOVE

When I broke my leg years ago, my life was radically changed. The physical pain was accompanied with the greater pain of having to give up competitive athletics. However, I thought about it and told myself, "Hey, you live in your head, not your body—*be thankful!*" So I immersed myself in a computer for fun and profit, and took up painting as well. Without a thankful heart, the transition after bitter disappointment would have been impossible.

God has a plan for you, and it may be very different from what you think you want. Trust in Him, surrender to His will, and always be thankful. This attitude will extend beyond what you want and past what you can see.

We have a natural, deep longing for joy, which is not equivalent or identical to happiness; joy is much more profound. C. S. Lewis called this joy *sensucht*, which describes "the imagination in its purest state." For him, this joy meant a longing that was really a lifelong nostalgia to be united with the Absolute Truth, which lies outside of ourselves—that is, with God, our Creator.[3] The diverted and distracted—anyone on the left of our continuum who is not living a full faith—is seeking earthly happiness rather than this joy. That is spiritual blindness.

Spiritual sight is found in the joy that finds Jesus a great treasure, in knowing that our sins are forgiven and in believing the Word of God "in much affliction" (1 Thessalonians 1:6). Rejoice and be thankful, because you are loved! "As the Father loved Me, I also have loved you; abide in My love" (John 15:9). Realize that He is sovereign and remains with us now and forever.

Spiritual sight is found in communion with the Lord, walking with Him in faith, and living in Him. The secret to living in Him, as we discussed, is in abiding. Perhaps the following acronym will help describe the power of living a life of abiding:

**A**nointed
**B**lessed
**I**ndwelt
**D**elivered
**E**mpowered

This abiding life is anointed by Christ, the Anointed One, in whose presence we choose to live. In this abiding, we find the desire to live faithfully in the stewardship of His gift of life.

## GODLY APPRECIATION

I cannot overemphasize the importance of one's appreciation of God. Your lack of it, my lack of it, is the sin that indicates blindness. When we become aware of the Creator and can look in the mirror every morning and marvel at the miracle of our being, humbled before Him, we will be filled with thanksgiving, rejoicing, and peace. As the Scripture teaches,

> …be filled with the Spirit, speaking to one another in psalms and hymns and spiritual songs, singing and making melody in your heart to the Lord, giving thanks

always for all things to God the Father in the name of
our Lord Jesus Christ.

—EPHESIANS 5:18-20

The thankful spirit underlies faith, love, and complete abandonment to God and His will. A spirit of unwavering appreciation is the key to spiritual sight. We are appreciative when we see
His intelligence and wisdom in our design. We are appreciative
when we realize that God is with us and within us, now and forever, according to His present and eternal purpose. Joy and peace
come from the Holy Spirit assuring us of God's love and salvation.
Such thanksgiving, joy, and peace are the blessed effects of insight
and spiritual sight, because we are seeing things as the really are,
rather than as the world sees them.

There is no way for you to draw closer to the Lord in living
faith until you consider the miracle of your existence and thank
God for it. Please consider honestly, and with wonder, the fact
that nine months before you were born, "you" consisted of thirty
million bits of information stored in the DNA of a single, microscopic fertilized egg, called a zygote. That information was used to
determine your growth, size, shape, skin color, the many aspects
of your personality, and much of how you live. It also determined
your present ability to heal. It was all designed before you were
born—before time itself. Imagine that!

I have discussed this divine phenomenon at length in my
book, *God's Prescription for Healing*, and I encourage you to read
it.[4] Why do you and I refuse to live in constant wonder of the
beauty of life and the intelligent Designer behind it? How can we
*not* live in appreciation for the Creator of all that we are?

## A FINAL EXHORTATION

God created us, He has saved us, and He is our future grace. We
must live in a state of unbroken, joyful thanksgiving to Him. We
need a grid for our thoughts, perceptions, and *focus*. The truths
of the T.R.U.S.T. grid can provide that direction. It must never be
forgotten that the mindset we establish before the Lord will set

the direction of our mind-set for eternity. This should put our focus strictly on God's glory, God's will, and His eternity while it diminishes our spiritual obstructions of living entirely for the present. It will assist us in our trials. It will make stewardship more prominent in our life. Scripture clearly teaches the rewards for stewardship.

> Do not be deceived: God cannot be mocked. A man reaps what he sows. The one who sows to please his sinful nature, from that nature will reap destruction; the one who sows to please the Spirit, from the Spirit will reap eternal life.
>
> —GALATIANS 6:7–8, NIV

This is the stewardship of the mind. As a man thinks, that is what he becomes before God—for eternity. We live with the concerns of this world, but, as John Piper says, "God is most glorified when we are most satisfied in Him."[5]

When you finally come to embrace the Lord's promises and rest in His redemption, you are forgiven and have a welcome acceptance in heaven as His own child. This transformation, this change of focus, this "pilgrim's progress," is a genuine emergence from the dark world into the light of God's kingdom. You are responsible for the mind-set that will either keep you in darkness or introduce you to the light dispensed by the Holy Spirit. You must challenge yourself to seek the Holy Spirit's entrance into your heart, to anoint the Word of God in you, and to direct your mind.

Simply stated, you must appreciate—then you will see.

# NOTES

The poems of Ralph and Susan McIntosh are used with the permission of the authors. You can contact their international prayer and teaching ministry, the ACTS Foundation, at P.O. Box 1013, Solvang, CA 93464, or www.actsfoundation.org

## PREFACE

1. Oliver Sacks, "Greetings From the Island of Stability", *The New York Times*, Feb. 8, 2004, p.15.

### Introduction

1. International Cooperating Ministries (ICM), 606 Aberdeen Rd., Hampton, VA: Web: www.icmmbc.org.

2. Michael Molinos, *The Spiritual Guide* (Auburn, ME: The SeedSowers Christian Books Publishing House, 1982), 107.

3. This is my version of a similar outline found in Bill Gothard, *The Power for True Success* (Oak Brook, IL: Institute in Basic Life Principles, 2001), 22–28.

4. The Cyber Hymnal, www.cyberhymnal.org/htm/t/wtpwidon.htm (accessed July 8, 2004).

## PART I: PROGRESSIONS TO LIVING FAITH

1. Michael Molinos, *The Spiritual Guide* (Auburn, ME: The SeedSowers Christian Books Publishing House, 1982).

2. John Bunyan, *Pilgrim's Progress*. Text is in public domain, found on internet at www.ccel.org/b/bunyan/progress/title.html - 2k.

3. Jeanne Guyon, *Song of the Bride* (New Kensington, PA: Whitaker House, 1997), 11–12.

4. *The Hymnal for Worship and Celebration*, Tom Fettke, ed. (Waco, TX: Word Music, 1986).

## Chapter 1
### Surrender to God—Not Trusting Self

1. Owen Milton, *Christian Missionaries* (Bridgend, G.B.: Evangelical Press of Wales, 1995), 44.

2. Ibid., 48–50.

## Chapter 2
### Internal Relationship—Not External Rituals

1. Nigel Clifford, *Christian Preachers* (Bridgend, G.B.: Evangelical Press of Wales, 1994), 148–158.

2. Arthur T. Pierson, *George Mueller of Bristol*, found at www.whatsaiththescripture.com/Voice/George.Mueller .of.Bristol/George.Mueller.Bristol.1.html (accessed July 2, 2004).

## Chapter 3
### Eternal Priorities—Not Temporal Pursuits

1. Nigel Clifford, *Christian Preachers* (Bridgend, G.B.: Evangelical Press of Wales, 1994), 302.

2. Ibid., 297.

## Chapter 4
### Living Faith of the Spirit—Not Rational Faith of the Mind

1. Owen Milton, *Christian Missionaries* (Bridgend, G.B.: Evangelical Press of Wales, 1995), 76.

2. Ibid., 74.

3. Carl Jung quoted at Christian Sarraf "Quotefolio," 1999, www.musicfolio.com/quotes/religion.htm (accessed April 25, 2004).

4. Henry Scougal, *The Life of God in the Soul of Man* (Ross-shire, G.B.: Christian Focus Publications, 2002).

5. *Logos*, #3056, in James Strong, *Strong's Exhaustive Concordance* (Grand Rapids, MI: Baker Book House, 1989), 45.

6. *Rhema*, #4487, in James Strong, *Strong's Exhaustive Concordance* (Grand Rapids, MI: Baker Book House, 1989), 63.

## Chapter 5
### God's Security—Not Personal Insecurity

1. Nigel Clifford, *Christian Preachers* (Bridgend, G.B.: Evangelical Press of Wales, 1994), 20–22.

2. St. Augustine, *The Confessions of St. Augustine,* Book 8, Ch. 12, quoted in Nigel Clifford, *Christian Preachers* (Bridgend, G.B.: Evangelical Press of Wales, 1994), 23.

## Chapter 8
### Insightful Gratitude—Not Blindness of Ingratitude

1. For a more complete discussion of the human body and its marvelous design see: Richard A. Swenson, *More Than Meets the Eye* (Colorado Springs, CO: Navpress, 2000).

2. Tom Fettke, ed., *The Hymnal for Worship and Celebration,* (Waco, TX: Word Music, 1986), 325.

## PART II: UNDERSTANDING THE NATURE OF SPIRITUAL BLINDNESS

1. Mark Delahanty, "Space science section: Dark Matter," *Astronomy Today,* 2004, http://www.astronomytoday.com /cosmology/darkmatter.html (accessed July 14, 2004).

## Chapter 10
### Spiritual Cataracts Obstructing Sight

1. R.T. Kendall, *Total Forgiveness* (London, G.B.: Hodder & Stoughton, 2001).

2. Paul Tournier, *The Meaning of Persons* (Cutchogue, NY: Buccaneer Books, 1957), 13.

3. Richard J. Foster, *Money, Sex & Power* (San Francisco, CA: Harper & Row, 1985), 91.

4. Ibid., 121.

5. James P. Gills, *Rx For Worry: A Thankful Heart* (Lake Mary, FL: Creation House Press, 2002).

6. John Piper, *Desiring God: Meditations of a Christian Hedonist* (Sisters, OR: Multnomah Publishers, 1996), 50.

7. "The Cyber Hymnal," June 2004 www.cyberhymnal.org

/htm/w/t/wtpwidon.htm (accessed July 12, 2004).

**Chapter 11**
**Battlefield: Motivations and Imaginations**
1. James P. Gills, *Imaginations: More Than You Think* (Lake Mary, FL: Creation House Press, 2004).
2. Joyce Meyer, *Battlefield of the Mind* (Tulsa, OK: Harrison House, 1995).
3. Michael Molinos, *The Spiritual Guide* (Auburn, ME: The SeedSowers Christian Books Publishing House, 1982), 78.
4. Ibid., 76.

## PART III: BIBLICAL INSIGHT INTO SPIRITUAL BLINDNESS

**Chapter 13**
**Repentance: Remedy for Spiritual Blindness**
1. John Newton, "Amazing Grace," found in *Hymns of the Spirit*, Conner B. Hall, ed. (Cleveland, TN: Pathway Press, 1969), 186.
2. John Newton, "In Evil Long I Took Delight (I Saw One Hanging On a Tree)" found at http://www.ccel.org/n/newton /olneyhymns/olneyhymns/h2_57.htm (accessed June 10, 2004).

**Chapter 14**
**Receiving Spiritual Sight: Abiding in Christ**
1. Arthur T. Pierson, *George Mueller of Bristol*, found at www.whatsaiththescripture.com/Voice/George.Mueller .of.Bristol/George.Mueller.Bristol.1.html.
2. *The Hymnal for Worship and Celebration*, Tom Fettke, ed. (Waco, TX: Word Music, 1986), 383.

**Chapter 16**
**Growing in Grace to Prevent Blindness**
1. C. S. Lewis, *The Business of Heaven*, found on the internet at www.deaconsil.com/catalog/product 932.html – 3k.
2. Charles Wesley, "Soldiers of Christ Arise," *The Hymnal for Worship and Celebration*, Tom Fettke, ed. (Waco, TX: Word Music, 1986), 478.

**Chapter 17**
**Divine Defenses Determine Spiritual Victory**
 1. Roland H. Bainton, *Here I Stand: A Life of Martin Luther,* (New American Library for Abingdon Press, 1978).

PART IV: UNDERSTANDING THE NATURE
OF SPIRITUAL VISION

**Chapter 18**
**A Divine Pardox: God's Ways vs. Man's Ways**
 1. Quoted at Paul Carr, "Science and Religion Quotes," March 2004, found at www.paul.carr2.home.comcast.net/SRQUOTES. htm (accessed July 22, 2004).
 2. Nigel Clifford, *Christian Preachers* (Bridgend, G.B.: Evangelical Press of Wales, 1994), 148–158.
 3. Information regarding this wonderful ministry can be found at www.pfm.org.

**Chapter 19**
**The Value of Suffering**
 1. Paul Tournier, *The Meaning of Persons* (Cutchogue, NY: Buccaneer Books, 1957), 152.
 2. Sandra LeSourd, *The Compulsive Woman* (Lake Mary, FL: Strang Communications Co., 2002).
 3. Clift Richards, *Breakthrough Prayers for Women* (Phoenix, AZ: Victory House Publishers, 2000).

**Chapter 20**
**T.R.U.S.T.: The Foundation Grid for a Living Faith**
 1. Found in *The Hymnal for Worship and Celebration*, Tom Fettke, ed. (Waco, TX: Word Music, 1986), 382.

**Chapter 21**
**Intimate Relationship in Prayer, Praise, and Worship**
 1. Oswald Chambers, *If You Will Ask* (Grand Rapids, MI: Discovery House Publishers, 1989), 32.
 2. James P. Gills, *The Prayerful Spirit* (Lake Mary, FL: Creation House Press, 2003).

3. Judson Cornwall, *Elements of Worship* (South Plainfield, NJ: Bridge Publishing, 1985), 99.

4. Ibid.

5. Oswald Chambers, *If You Will Ask* (Grand Rapids, MI: Discovery House Publishers, 1989), 10.

6. Henry T. Blackaby, Claude V. King. *Experiencing God* (New York, NY: Walker & Co., 1999), 263–264.

7. Ibid., 256.

8. Jack R. Taylor, *The Hallelujah Factor* (Nashville, TN: Broadman Press, 1983), 48–55.

9. Judson Cornwall, *Elements of Worship* (South Plainfield, NJ: Bridge Publishing, 1985), 72.

10. Rick Warren, *The Purpose Driven Life* (Grand Rapids, MI: Zondervan, 2002 ), 17.

11. Judson Cornwall, *Elements of Worship* (South Plainfield, NJ: Bridge Publishing, 1985), 199.

12. Ibid., 23.

13. *The Hymnal for Worship and Celebration*, Tom Fettke, ed. (Waco, TX: Word Music, 1986), 259.

**Chapter 22**
**The Dynamic of Living Faith: The Unction Function**

1. This is the final stanza of a somewhat lengthier poem, quoted at "Fire and Ice: Puritan and Reformed Writings," found at www.puritansermons.com/erskine/erskin14.htm (accessed July 15, 2004).

## Section V: Your Sight Is Your Eternity

**Chapter 23**
**We See Through a Glass Darkly**

1. Blaise Pascal, *Pensees, Sec. II, The Misery of Man Without God*, quoted at "The Christian Classics Ethereal Library," 2004, found at www.ccel.org/p/pascal/pensees/ (accessed July 22, 2004).

2. Henry T. Blackaby, Claude V. King. *Experiencing God* (New York, NY: Walker & Co., 1999).

3. James P. Gills, Tom Woodward, *Darwinism Under the*

*Microscope* (Lake Mary, FL: Charisma House, 2002).

4. Blaise Pascal, *Pensees, Sec. II, The Misery of Man Without God*, quoted at "The Christian Classics Ethereal Library," 2004, found at www.ccel.org/p/pascal/pensees/ (accessed July 22, 2004).

5. *Metanoia*, #3341, in James Strong, *Strong's Exhaustive Concordance* (Grand Rapids, MI: Baker Book House, 1989), 47.

6. *The Hymnal for Worship and Celebration*, Tom Fettke, ed. (Waco, TX: Word Music, 1986), 545.

## Chapter 24
## Living Your Divine Destiny—Forever

1. *Koinonia*, #2842, in James Strong, *Strong's Exhaustive Concordance* (Grand Rapids, MI: Baker Book House, 1989), 42.

2. James P. Gills, *Believe and Rejoice!* (Lake Mary, FL: Creation House Press, 2004).

3. Rick Warren, *The Purpose Driven Life* (Grand Rapids, MI: Zondervan, 2002 ), 17.

4. "World of Quotes," 2003, found at www.worldofquotes. com/author/Malcolm-Muggeridge/1/ (accessed Aug., 2003).

5. Bruce Wilkinson, *A Life God Rewards: Why Everything You Do Today Matters Forever* (Sisters, OR: Multnomah Publishers, 2002).

6. Ibid., 25.

7. Ibid., 25.

## Conclusion

1. Malcolm Muggeridge quoted at "World of Quotes," 2003, found at www.worldofquotes.com/author/Malcolm-Muggeridge/1/ (accessed Aug., 2003).

2. Henry T. Blackaby, Claude V. King. *Experiencing God* (New York, NY: Walker & Co., 1999), 69–70.

3. C. S. Lewis, *Surprised by Joy* (London: Harcourt Brace Jovanovich, 1955).

4. James P. Gills, *God's Prescription for Healing* (Lake Mary, FL: Siloam, 2004).

5. John Piper, *Desiring God: Meditations of a Christian Hedonist* (Sisters, OR: Multnomah Publishers, 1996), 50.

# BIBLIOGRAPHY

Bartlett, John, ed. *Familiar Quotations*. Boston, MA: Little, Brown and Company, 1980.

Blackaby, Henry T. *Created to Be God's Friend*. Nashville, TN: Thomas Nelson Publishers, 1999.

Blackaby, Henry T., Claude V. King. *Experiencing God*. New York, NY: Walker & Co., 1999.

Blackaby, Henry T., Claude V. King. *Fresh Encounter*. Nashville, TN: Broadman & Holman Publishers, 1996.

Chafer, Lewis Sperry. *He That Is Spiritual*. Grand Rapids, MI: Zondervan Publishing House, 1967.

Chambers, Oswald. *If You Will Ask*. Grand Rapids, MI: Discovery House Publishers, 1989.

Chambers, Oswald. *My Utmost for His Highest*. Grand Rapids, MI: Discovery House Publishers, 1992.

Clifford, Nigel. *Christian Preachers*. Bridgend, G.B.: Evangelical Press of Wales, 1994.

Cornwall, Judson. *Elements of Worship*. South Plainfield, NJ: Bridge Publishing, 1985.

Fettke, Tom, ed. *The Hymnal for Worship and Celebration*. Waco, TX: Word Music, 1986.

Foster, Richard J. *Money, Sex & Power*. San Francisco, CA: Harper & Row, 1985.

Gills, James P. *Believe and Rejoice!* Lake Mary, FL: Creation House Press, 2004.

Gills, James P. *God's Prescription for Healing*. Lake Mary, FL: Siloam, 2004.

Gills, James P. *Imaginations: More Than You Think*. Lake Mary, FL: Creation House Press, 2004.

Gills, James P. *Rx for Worry: A Thankful Heart*. Lake Mary, FL: Creation House Press, 2002.

Gills, James P. *The Prayerful Spirit*. Lake Mary, FL: Creation House Press, 2003.

Gills, James P., Tom Woodward. *Darwinism Under the Microscope*. Lake Mary, FL: Charisma House, 2002.

Gothard, Bill. *The Power for True Success*. Oak Brook, IL: Institute in Basic Life Principles, 2001.

Guyon, Jeanne. *Song of the Bride*. New Kensington, PA: Whitaker House, 1997.

Guyon, Jeanne. *The Way Out*. Beaumont, TX: The SeedSowers, 1985.

Hall, Conner B., ed., *Hymns of the Spirit*. Cleveland, TN: Pathway Press, 1969.

Jeremiah, David. *Knowing God by Name*. San Diego, CA: Turning Point Ministries.

Kendall, R. T. *A Vision of Jesus*. Ross-shire, G.B.: Christian Focus Publications, 1999.

Kendall, R. T. *Total Forgiveness*. London, G.B.: Hodder & Stoughton, 2001.

LeSourd, Sandra. *The Compulsive Woman*. Lake Mary, FL: Strang Communications Co., 2002.

Lewis, C. S. *The Four Loves*. San Diego, CA: Harvest Book, Harcourt Brace & Co., 1988.

Lewis, C. S. *Mere Christianity*. New York, NY: Simon and Shuster, 1980.

Lewis, C. S. *Surprised by Joy*. London: Harcourt Brace Jovanovich, 1955.

Manley, Don. *Wisdom The Principal Thing*. Enumclaw, WA: WinePress Publishing, 2002.

Meyer, Joyce. *Battlefield of the Mind*. Tulsa, OK: Harrison House, 1995.

Milton, Owen. *Christian Missionaries*. Bridgend, G.B.: Evangelical Press of Wales, 1995.

Molinos, Michael. *The Spiritual Guide*. Auburn, ME: The SeedSowers Christian Books Publishing House, 1982.

Newbold, Charles E. *His Presence in the Midst of You*. Monterey, TN: Ingathering Press, 1998.

Newbold, Charles E. *The Crucified Ones*. Monterey, TN: Ingathering Press, 1990.

Packer, J.J. *Keep in Step With The Spirit*. Old Tappan, NJ: Fleming H. Revell Company, 1984.

Piper, John. *Desiring God: Meditations of a Christian Hedonist*. Sisters, OR: Multnomah Publishers, 1996.

Piper, John. *Future Grace*. Sisters, OR: Multnomah Press, 1995.

Piper, John. *God's Passion for His Glory*. Wheaton, IL: Crossway Books, 1998.

Piper, John. *Seeing and Savoring Jesus Christ*. Wheaton, IL: Crossway Books, 2001.

Piper, John. *The Passion of Jesus Christ*. Wheaton, IL: Crossway Books, 2004.

Richards, Clift. *Breakthrough Prayers for Women*. Phoenix, AZ: Victory House Publishers, 2000.

Rosser, Dois I. *The God Who Hung on the Cross*. Grand Rapids, MI: Zondervan, 2003.

Scougal, Henry. *The Life of God in the Soul of Man*. Ross-shire, G.B.: Christian Focus Publications, 2002.

Stowell, Joseph M. *Eternity*. Chicago, IL: Moody Press, 1995.

Strong, James. *Strong's Exhaustive Concordance*. Grand Rapids, MI: Baker Book House, 1989.

Swenson, Richard A. *More Than Meets the Eye*. Colorado Springs, CO: Navpress, 2000.

Taylor, Jack R. *The Hallelujah Factor*. Nashville, TN: Broadman Press, 1983.

Tournier, Paul. *The Meaning of Persons*. Cutchogue, NY: Buccaneer Books, 1957.

Tozer, A.W., Gerald B. Smith, ed. *Men Who Met God*. Camp Hill, PA: Christian Publications, 1986.

Warren, Rick. *The Purpose Driven Life*. Grand Rapids, MI: Zondervan, 2002.

Wilkinson, Bruce. *A Life God Rewards*. Sisters, OR: Multnomah Publishers, 2002.

Zacharias, Ravi. *Recapture the Wonder*. Nashville, TN: Integrity Publishers, 2003.

# ABOUT THE AUTHOR

James P. Gills, M.D., received his medical degree from Duke University Medical Center in 1959. He served his ophthalmology residency at Wilmer Ophthalmological Institute of Johns Hopkins University from 1962–1965. Dr. Gills founded the St. Luke's Cataract and Laser Institute in Tarpon Springs, Florida, and has performed more cataract and lens implant surgeries than any other eye surgeon in the world. Since establishing his Florida practice in 1968, he has been firmly committed to embracing new technology and perfecting the latest cataract surgery techniques. In 1974, he became the first eye surgeon in the U.S. to dedicate his practice to cataract treatment through the use of intraocular lenses. Dr. Gills has been recognized in Florida and throughout the world for his professional accomplishments and personal commitment to helping others. He has been recognized by the readers of *Cataract & Refractive Surgery Today* as one of the top 50 cataract and refractive opinion leaders.

As a world-renowned ophthalmologist, Dr. Gills has received innumerable medical and educational awards. In 2005, he was especially honored to receive the Duke Medical Alumni Association's Humanitarian Award. In 2007, he was blessed with a particularly treasured double honor. Dr. Gills was elected to the Johns Hopkins Society of Scholars and was also selected to receive the Distinguished Medical Alumnus Award, the highest honor bestowed by Johns Hopkins School of Medicine. Dr. Gills thereby became the first physician in the country to receive high honors twice in two weeks from the prestigious Johns Hopkins University in Baltimore.

In the years 1994 through 2004, Dr. Gills was listed in *The Best Doctors in America*. As a clinical professor of ophthalmology at the University of South Florida, he was named one of the best

Ophthalmologists in America in 1996 by ophthalmic academic leaders nationwide. He has served on the Board of Directors of the American College of Eye Surgeons, the Board of Visitors at Duke University Medical Center, and the Advisory Board of Wilmer Ophthalmological Institute at Johns Hopkins University. Listed in Marquis' *Who's Who in America*, Dr. Gills was Entrepreneur of the Year 1990 for the State of Florida, received the Tampa Bay Business Hall of Fame Award in 1993, and was given the Tampa Bay Ethics Award from the University of Tampa in 1995. In 1996, he was awarded the prestigious Innovators Award by his colleagues in the American Society of Cataract and Refractive Surgeons. In 2000, he was named Philanthropist of the Year by the National Society of Fundraising Executives, was presented with the Florida Enterprise Medal by the Merchants Association of Florida, was named Humanitarian of the Year by the Golda Meir/Kent Jewish Center in Clearwater, and was honored as Free Enterpriser of the Year by the Florida Council on Economic Education. In 2001, The Salvation Army presented Dr. Gills their prestigious "Others Award" in honor of his lifelong commitment to service and caring.

Virginia Polytechnic Institute, Dr. Gills' alma mater, presented their University Distinguished Achievement Award to him in 2003. In that same year, Dr. Gills was appointed by Governor Jeb Bush to the Board of Directors of the Florida Sports Foundation. In 2004, Dr. Gills was invited to join the prestigious Florida Council of 100, an advisory committee reporting directly to the governor on various aspects of Florida's public policy affecting the quality of life and the economic well-being of all Floridians.

While Dr. Gills has many accomplishments and varied interests, his primary focus is to restore physical vision to patients and to bring spiritual enlightenment through his life. Guided by his strong and enduring faith in Jesus Christ, he seeks to encourage and comfort the patients who come to St. Luke's and to share his faith whenever possible. It was through sharing his insights with patients that he initially began writing on Christian topics. An avid student of the Bible for many years, he now has authored nineteen books on Christian living, with over nine million copies in print. With the exception of the Bible, Dr. Gills' books are the most widely requested books in the U.S. prison system. They have been supplied to over two thousand prisons and jails, including every death row facility in the nation. In addition, Dr. Gills has published more than 195 medical articles and has authored or coauthored ten medical reference textbooks. Six of those books were bestsellers at the American Academy of Ophthalmology annual meetings.

As an ultra-distance athlete, Dr. Gills participated in forty-six marathons, including eighteen Boston marathons and fourteen 100-mile mountain runs. In addition, he completed five Ironman Triathlons in Hawaii and a total of six Double Ironman Triathlons, each within the thirty-six hour maximum time frame. Dr. Gills has served on the National Board of Directors of the Fellowship of Christian Athletes and, in 1991, was the first recipient of their Tom Landry Award. A passionate athlete, surgeon, and scientist, Dr. Gills is also a member of the Explorers Club, a prestigious, multi-disciplinary society dedicated to advancing field research, scientific exploration, and the ideal that it is vital to preserve the instinct to explore.

Married in 1962, Dr. Gills and his wife, Heather, have raised two children, Shea and Pit. Shea Gills Grundy, a former attorney and now full-time mom, is a graduate of Vanderbilt University and Emory Law School. She and her husband, Shane Grundy, M.D., have four children: twins Maggie and Braddock, Jimmy, and Lily Grace. The Gills' son, J. Pit Gills, M.D., ophthalmologist, received his medical degree from Duke University Medical Center and, in 2001, joined the St. Luke's practice. "Dr. Pit" and his wife, Joy, have three children: Pitzer, Parker, and Stokes.

# THE WRITINGS OF JAMES P. GILLS, M.D.

A BIBLICAL ECONOMICS MANIFESTO (WITH RON H. NASH, PH.D.)
The best understanding of economics aligns with what the Bible teaches on the subject.
ISBN: 978-0-88419-871-0
E-book ISBN: 978-1-59979-925-4

BELIEVE AND REJOICE: CHANGED BY FAITH, FILLED WITH JOY
Observe how faith in God can let us see His heart of joy
ISBN: 978-1-59979-169-2
E-book ISBN: 978-1-61638-727-3

COME UNTO ME: GOD'S CALL TO INTIMACY
Inspired by Dr. Gills' trip to Mt. Sinai, this book explores God's eternal desire for mankind to know Him intimately.
ISBN: 978-1-59185-214-8
E-book ISBN: 978-1-61638-728-0

DARWINISM UNDER THE MICROSCOPE: HOW RECENT SCIENTIFIC
  EVIDENCE POINTS TO DIVINE DESIGN
  (WITH TOM WOODWARD, PH.D.)
Behold the wonder of it all! The facts glorify our Intelligent Creator!
ISBN: 978-0-88419-925-0
E-book ISBN: 978-1-59979-882-0

THE DYNAMICS OF WORSHIP
Designed to rekindle a passionate love for God, this book gives the *who, what, where, when, why,* and *how* of worship.
ISBN: 978-1-59185-657-3
E-book ISBN: 978-1-61638-725-9

EXCEEDING GRATITUDE FOR THE CREATOR'S PLAN: DISCOVER THE
  LIFE-CHANGING DYNAMIC OF APPRECIATION
Standing in awe of the creation and being secure in the knowledge of our heavenly hope, the thankful believer abounds in appreciation for the Creator's wondrous plan.
ISBN: 978-1-59979-155-5
E-book ISBN: 978-1-61638-729-7

GOD'S PRESCRIPTION FOR HEALING: FIVE DIVINE GIFTS OF HEALING
Explore the wonders of healing by design, now and forevermore.
ISBN: 978-1-59185-286-5
E-book ISBN: 978-1-61638-730-3

IMAGINATIONS: MORE THAN YOU THINK
Focusing our thoughts will help us grow closer to God.
ISBN: 978-1-59185-609-2
E-book ISBN: 978-1-59979-883-7

LOVE: FULFILLING THE ULTIMATE QUEST
Enjoy a quick refresher course on the meaning and method of God's great gift.
ISBN: 978-1-59979-235-4
E-book ISBN: 978-1-61638-731-7

OVERCOMING SPIRITUAL BLINDNESS
Jesus + anything = nothing. Jesus + nothing = everything. Here is a book that will
help you recognize the many facets of spiritual blindness as you seek to fulfill the
Lord's plan for your life.
ISBN: 978-1-59185-607-8
E-book ISBN: 978-1-59979-884-4

RESTING IN HIS REDEMPTION
We were created for communion with God. Discover how to rest in His redemp-
tion and enjoy a life of divine peace.
ISBN: 978-1-61638-349-7
E-book ISBN: 978-1-61638-425-8

RX FOR WORRY: A THANKFUL HEART
Trust your future to the God who is in eternal control.
ISBN: 978-1-59979-090-9
E-book ISBN: 978-1-55979-926-1

THE PRAYERFUL SPIRIT: PASSION FOR GOD, COMPASSION FOR PEOPLE
Dr. Gills tells how prayer has changed his life as well as the lives of patients and
other doctors. It will change your life also!
ISBN: 978-1-59185-215-5
E-book ISBN: 978-1-61638-732-7

THE UNSEEN ESSENTIAL: A STORY FOR OUR TROUBLED TIMES...
    PART ONE
This compelling, contemporary novel portrays one man's transformation through
the power of God's love.
ISBN: 978-1-59185-810-2
E-book ISBN: 978-1-59979-513-3

TENDER JOURNEY: A STORY FOR OUR TROUBLED TIMES...
    PART TWO
Be enriched by the popular sequel to *The Unseen Essential.*
ISBN: 978-1-59185-809-6
E-book ISBN: 978-1-59979-509-6

# DID YOU ENJOY THIS BOOK?

We at Love Press would be pleased to hear from you if ***Overcoming Spiritual Blindness*** has had an effect in your life or the lives of your loved ones.

Send your letters to:

Love Press
P.O. Box 1608
Tarpon Springs, FL 34688-1608